*The*Alaska Cruise Companion

A MILE BY MILE GUIDE

Princess Gulf of Alaska Cruise
Southbound Edition

*The*Alaska Cruise Companion

A MILE BY MILE
GUIDE

BY JOE UPTON

Coastal Publishing
Bainbridge Island • Seattle

The maps in this book are not to be used for navigation.

1998 Edition

Coastal Publishing
Editorial office: 15166 Skogen Lane, Bainbridge Island, Wa. 98110
Business office: 5305 Shilshole Ave. NW, Seattle, WA, 98107

Editing by Glenn Hartmann and Joe Upton
Illustrations by Russ Burtner and Christine Cox
Maps by Joe Upton
Design by Martha Brouwer

Photographs by Joe Upton unless noted with the following abbreviations:
AMNH - American Museum of Natural History, New York
BCARS - British Columbia Archives and Records Service.
BCRM- British Columbia Royal Museum.
MOHAI - Museum of History and Industry, Seattle.
SFM - San Francisco Maritime Museum.
THS - Tongass Historical Society, Ketchikan, Alaska.
UAF - University of Alaska, Fairbanks
UW - University of Washington Special Collections.
WAT - Whatcom County (WA) Museum of History and Art

ISBN 0-9645682-2-5

For
Mary Lou, Matthew,
and Katherine Anne,
mariners all.

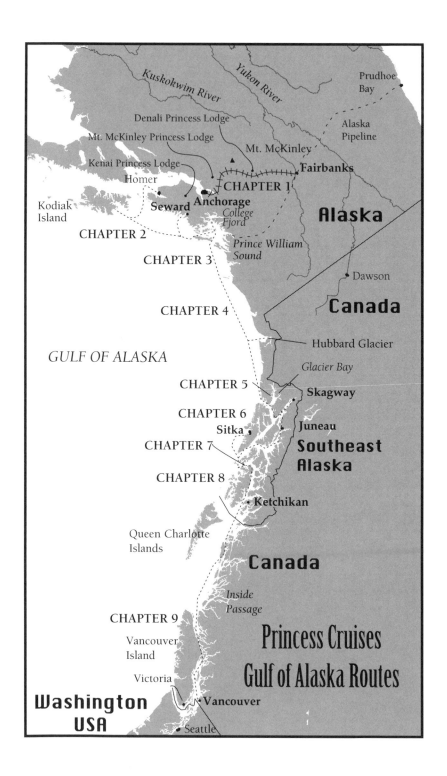

Kuskokwim River

Yukon River

Prudhoe Bay

Denali Princess Lodge

Alaska Pipeline

Mt. McKinley Princess Lodge

Mt. McKinley

Kenai Princess Lodge

Fairbanks

Homer

CHAPTER 1

Kodiak Island

Seward

Anchorage

College Fjord

Alaska

CHAPTER 2

CHAPTER 3

Prince William Sound

Dawson

CHAPTER 4

Canada

GULF OF ALASKA

Hubbard Glacier

Glacier Bay

CHAPTER 5

Skagway

CHAPTER 6

Sitka

Juneau

CHAPTER 7

Southeast Alaska

CHAPTER 8

Ketchikan

Queen Charlotte Islands

Canada

Inside Passage

CHAPTER 9

Princess Cruises Gulf of Alaska Routes

Vancouver Island

Victoria

Washington USA

Vancouver

Seattle

Contents

Frederick Sound, Alaska, 1975

To the Princess Traveler

On a June night in 1965, I felt a hand on my shoulder in the darkened fo'c's'le of the *Sidney*, a 90' fish buying boat I'd just gotten my first Alaska job on. I was 19.

"C'mon up, kid," Mickey, the 70 year old mate rasped, nodding up at the pilot-house stairs, "you gotta' see this."

He was right. We were laying almost motionless in a little bight in a steep and forested shore. Ahead of us in the thin light I could make out a torrent of water, like rapids in a river, pouring out of a gap in the trees.

"W-w-we're going in there...?" I stammered, awed at the sight, inexperienced, and totally new to the Inside Passage.

"It used to be really bad" came the soft voiced answer, "That's Seymour Narrows. There was a rock right in the middle. They blew it the hell out of there."

Two days later we arrived at our cannery in a remote fishing village, to join a large fleet of workboats. It was Alaska in capital letters - we saw icebergs, eagles and whales. And everywhere we traveled, old Mickey had a story - about the steamer that stranded there in 1920, how the passengers just waited on shore for the next boat and kept going. About the square rigged ships that used to sail up from San Francisco to the canneries. About the northern fisheries and working in the pack ice. Tales rom his life as a trapper, a fisherman, a mail boat skipper. The old gentleman took me under his wing, teaching me about the lore and legends of The North.

That long season in The North and that kindly old Alaskan instilled in me a life-long interest in northern places and history, especially the inland waterways that form the Inside Passage and Southeast Alaska.

Eventually I bought a used 32 footer, began fishing salmon, along the sheltered waterways of Southeast Alaska. In the cove where British Explorer George Vancouver and his men found desperately needed shelter in 1793, my wife and I built a cabin and a float. Nearby was a tiny, roadless, fishing settlement.

Our store and post office each floated on a log raft in the harbor, our vehicles were our outboard boats. It was a unique community, where a person could make a living fishing with an open skiff, get a piece of waterfront land with little money, and build a home with local lumber. Our store was also a floating bar, which eliminated the nasty problem of necogiating that steep walkway down to your boat at low tide. The drinks were whiskey and water, whiskey and coke, and whiskey and Tang.

The people of the community welcomed new blood, showing us the best fishing places, helping us build our home. Just two hundred yards from our house the humpback whales hung out all summer, and at night, if it was still, we could hear them breathing as they surfaced.

Mickey and me, aboard the Sidney, *1965.*

In the spring we fished the windy outside coast. In the summer, nearby Sumner Strait. In the fall we traveled north to the natural wind tunnel called Lynn Canal, for the ten dollar a fish chum salmon. And in the long, kerosene lantern- lit winters, there was time for visiting.

And during these last three decades, in a hundred little coves up and down the coast, from the very edge of the Arctic down to Puget Sound and Seattle, when the storms came, we anchored up in our little boats, waiting for the wind to stop.

Sometimes it blew for days, and while we waited, the stories came out. The experiences of my friends, and those before them, an oral history of the coast. And in my travels I would seek out the little visited communities, the out of the way places.

I was an amateur photographer, and a bit of a writer. 'Write a book,' my friends said, 'tell our story.' One book became another, and another after that.

When I first started fishing, cruise ships were few and small. Then more ships began traveling the coast, and I designed a series of illustrated maps to better share with these new visitors the drama and beauty of The North.

During the last year Princess Cruises and I have worked together to develop a unique program that allows you to share some of the very powerful experiences many including myself, have had in The North, as well as learn something of its culture and history.

The key to our program is my book and map. We've called Seattle mile zero, so that every place along the cruise route has a number. I've worked with the Captain and his officers so that your ship's position can be easily found and referenced to the numbers in the book. Also your vessel's daily newspaper will have references to the mile number of your position and specific pages in the book.

For myself, the books and maps are a way to share with you a sense of the mystery and the power of this place that has become such a big part of my life.

So, come, take this journey through this land that remains much as it was when the first explorers passed through.

Launch Foxy *in Puget Sound, Washington, about 1920. By picking their route and weather carefully, skippers of such small craft could travel to Alaska via the Inside Passage.*

The Inside Passage

To a mariner, "inside" means "protected," and when the Pleistocene glaciers scoured out the fjords and canyons of the northwest coast a million years ago, they created "protected" waters and a boater's paradise.

Behind the eight large islands between Cape Flattery, Washington, and Cape Spencer, Alaska, is a roughly northwest-southeast route that has become known as the Inside Passage. Stretching for a thousand miles from Seattle, Washington, to Skagway, Alaska, it allows small and large craft alike to travel in protection and comfort.

The Inside Passage was explored, charted, and named in the 1790s by a British Navy captain, George Vancouver, who sought a sea route from west to east.

In some places, vessels have a choice of routes. For the purposes of this book, the "Inside Passage" means the traditional route laid out for small and medium-size craft in the *Hansen Handbook* now out of print but once an essential navigational guide for mariners before the days of modern electronics.

MOHAI, Pemco, Webster, Stevens 83.10.7573.1

The Tides

A channel marker in Wrangell Narrows at Petersburg. Here savvy mariners tie up their boats before they put their engines into neutral. At times the current past the docks can run at four knots (about four and a half miles an hour) which is faster than you can walk.

In few waterways of the world does the tide so influence mariners as it does along the northwest coast. From the tipsy sailor who exits a tavern, only to face the 45-degree ramp down to his boat, to the skipper of a 6,000-horsepower tug who steams to the side of Johnstone Strait when the current is against him, the mariner here must always consider the tide.

In the Kvichak River of western Alaska, propellers of boats at anchor are turned by the tide. In Sergius Narrows, near Sitka, Coast Guard buoys disappear underwater, pulled down by the current when the tide is running.

In some constricted passages, the tide rushes with a force like rapids in a river. In Seymour Narrows and Yuculta Rapids, British Columbia, safe passage is possible only briefly each day: at slack water, the top or the bottom of the tide.

Tides are caused by the moon's gravity (and to a lesser extent the sun's) pulling the earth's oceans into bulges on either side that attempt to follow the moon. Because the moon takes one day plus 50 minutes to orbit the earth, each tide is 50 minutes later than the day before.

Tides on this coast have a great range of rise and fall, from 10 feet in Seattle to 18 feet in Ketchikan, Alaska. At certain times of the year, the alignment of moon, sun, and planets create tides higher and lower.

The Arrival of Vancouver

"April 29, 1792. At four o'clock [A.M.] a sail was discovered to the westward standing in shore. This was a very great novelty, not having seen any vessel but our consort, during the last eight months. She soon hoisted American colors and fired a gun to leeward." —Captain George Vancouver, *A Voyage of Discovery to the North Pacific Ocean and Round the World.*

This was a singular day for the British captain and his two ships and crews. They had sailed from England 15 months earlier to seek the Northwest Passage from the Pacific Ocean to the Atlantic. Vancouver had his doubts. Captain Cook hadn't found it and Vancouver was with him. For 6,000 miles, almost to the southern tip of Chile, the Pacific coast was a wall, with no interior straits and few good harbors.

The American vessel [Captain Robert Gray, a Boston fur trader, in the *Columbia*] assured them the strait existed; it was a few miles to the north. Around noon on the 29th the rain and the mists parted and Vancouver saw it: the Strait! 10 miles wide, 500 feet deep, it led east between high, snowy mountains. He thought it was the Northwest Passage.

At that time, Philadelphia and Boston had cobblestone streets and daily newspapers, yet the known world ended west of the Missouri River; beyond that was marked "unknown" on the maps. Another 13 years would pass before Lewis and Clark would uncover the vastness and the beauty of the American west.

A week after entering the strait that turned out to be *not* the Northwest Passage, the Vancouver party turned south and entered a waterway Vancouver named for one of his lieutenants, Peter Puget. Vancouver was stunned by what he saw.

"I could not possibly believe that any uncultivated country had ever been discovered exhibiting so rich a picture... To describe the beauties of this region, will, on some future occasion, be a very grateful task to the pen of a skillful panegyrist. The serenity of the climate, the innumerable pleasing landscapes, and the abundant fertility that unassisted nature puts forth, require only to be enriched by the industry of man with villages, mansions, cottages, and other buildings, to render it the most lovely country that can be imagined; whilst the labor of the inhabitants would be amply rewarded, in the bounties which nature seems ready to bestow on cultivation." — George Vancouver, *A Voyage of Discovery.*

In order not to miss the entrance to the Northwest Passage, Vancouver followed the mainland north, exploring, charting, but always following the shore. When he arrived in Puget Sound and saw the myriad channels leading off in all directions, it was obvious to him that the task was too difficult for the cumbersome ships *Discovery* and *Chatham.* The solution lay in small boats, his 20-foot cutters, rigged to row and sail. The big boats would anchor and the small boats would set out, sometimes with Vancouver and sometimes without, charting the vast land they had discovered.

A Few Traveling Companions:
Your Author And His Various Boats

Like most fishermen, many boats carried me through northern waters. On some I was the owner, on some the crew. Some were large, steel, and very able, like the 104' steel crabber *Flood Tide*. Others, were old, wood, and downright unsafe, like the 28' *Denise* on the right

No season was without its drama, adventure, or danger, be it the frustrations of a broken engine far from any port, or a genuine life or death struggle against the dreaded buildup of ice in a storm at sea.

In the fall of 1997, I traveled North on the brand new *Dawn Princess*. We had a remarkable trip with glassy sunny weather, northern lights, whales, bears, and dramatic calving glaciers.

Here and there around this book, I've put in journal entries from all those seasons as well as the *Dawn Princess* cruise.

The ill fated Denise *and I, at Kingston, Puget Sound, WA, 1970. The engine blew up and the boat caught fire; I had to shelve my Alaska plans for that season.*

The Maggie Murphy Boys

Would you go to Alaska in this rig? These men did.

For many young people, growing up on Puget Sound and hearing the stories of Alaska and the North from those who had been there, the itch to follow was strong. In the 1930s two teenagers, John Joseph Ryan and Ed Braddock, salvaged a derelict 26-footer from the mud flats at Tacoma, rebuilt it as best they could (thanks to the unknowing help of a nearby lumber mill), and set out up the Inside Passage. They had barely reached Seattle when one of the flaws of their vessel revealed itself.

"First of all, the pilothouse proved to be utterly uninhabitable. It had about two inches less headroom than was needed to permit either of us to stand erect while steering; the engine was right underfoot, belching fumes and heat that rose up to smother the helmsman; furthermore, there was no danger that either fumes or heat would escape because the windows had been nailed and puttied in place, sealing the pilothouse as tight as a mummy's crypt." —John Joseph Ryan, *The Maggie Murphy*

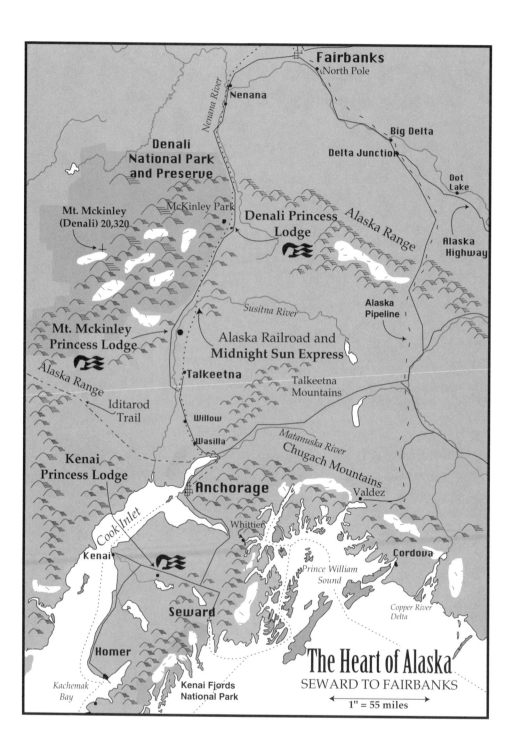

Fairbanks
North Pole
Nenana
Nenana River
Big Delta
Delta Junction
Denali National Park and Preserve
Dot Lake
McKinley Park
Mt. Mckinley (Denali) 20,320
Denali Princess Lodge
Alaska Range
Alaska Highway
Alaska Pipeline
Susitna River
Mt. Mckinley Princess Lodge
Alaska Railroad and Midnight Sun Express
Alaska Range
Talkeetna
Talkeetna Mountains
Iditarod Trail
Willow
Wasilla
Matanuska River
Chugach Mountains
Kenai Princess Lodge
Anchorage
Valdez
Cook Inlet
Whittier
Kenai
Cordova
Prince William Sound
Copper River Delta
Seward
Homer
Kachemak Bay
Kenai Fjords National Park

The Heart of Alaska
SEWARD TO FAIRBANKS
1" = 55 miles

CHAPTER 1

The Heart of Alaska

FAIRBANKS TO SEWARD

"Thirty below zero this morning. Frost has crept through the walls and caused the bedclothes to stick to the wall on that side and it is mortal agony to crawl out of the warm nest in the center of the bed when daddy called."

— Margaret Murie, *Two in The Far North*

Fairbanks

Of course it was gold that started Fairbanks, part of the great fever of exploration that swept the state, beginning in the 1890's. A passing trader on a riverboat came along just when prospectors hit a little paydirt near here, unloaded his trade goods and the town was born.

But, oh, what a bitterly cold, northern frontier outpost town it was in those early days, before the planes and the radio and the telephone came to break the cold and the isolation.

Winter in Fairbanks lasts from October to April. Before the modern conveniences like plumbing, electricity and oil heat, these long dark months were an unrelenting challenge for residents, especially for women, perhaps raising families with their men away - on the trail, trapping, or in the mines

. Margaret Murie, who came to Fairbanks in 1911 when she was nine, grew up with a keen memory of the routines and community activities that made life manageable for the women of Fairbanks:

Take the time to read the bronze plaques beneath the Pioneer's Memorial in downtown Fairbanks. It's a moving tribute to the courage and perseverence of the early settlers.

Twilight at noon, Fairbanks, December 21, 1905. Winters here are long, cold, and dark.

"A regular routine, a definate project for each day, a regular program with other people – all that helps. It is all part of the bulwark the women built, consciously or unconsciously, against the isolation, the wilderness, the cold, the difficulties of housekeeping..."

— Margaret Murie, *Two in The Far North*

For much of this century, the nearby Tanana river was the only highway, and the nearest town was ten days away by river boat. Between freeze-up in the fall and ice out in the spring, there was only the weekly horse-drawn mail sleigh that traveled a difficult trail through the mountains and over the frozen rivers to Valdez.

Ice out was a big event - notices were posted around town to keep resident's informed: "Ice moved at Fort Gibbon this morning at 8 a.m.", for the first steamer of the season meant fresh vegetables, followed shortly therafter by the 'slaughterhouse boat' with its pens of cows, sheep, pigs, geese, and chickens, brought up from Seattle.

In a town of log homes that heated with wood, fire was always a worry. A big steam pump at the Northern Commercial Company power plant was always ready to pump river water from under the river ice to fight fires. On at least one occasion, when the wood fired boilers couldn't keep up with the demands of a big fire, the cry went out to 'Bring the bacon' - case after case of oily bacon was brought from the warehouse, thrown into the boilers, the steam pressure rose, the water flowed once more and the fire was contained.

Many early area residents were involved in small gold mining operations such as this one with a rocker box located near a stream.

Today Fairbanks is the most northerly city in North America. There are many of the conveniences found elsewhere, but the long winters are still bitter, bitter cold, with all its unique problems like having your car go bumpity bump in the mornings because of the frozen flat place in the tires from sitting on the street all night long.

Hydraulic mining consisted of diverting creeks and small rivers to provide the power to wash promising ore bodies into sluice systems to extract the gold.

UW 17946

Dredge No. 3 working away on a Yukon Tributary, in 1913. Such machines worked Alaskan rivers until the 1960's.

UW 17945

From Gold Rush to Oil Rush

There's a lot of gold still left in Alaska, but today's miners have to follow rules that were totally unknown just thirty years ago. The gold dredge above, for example, did a great job of extracting gold dust from river bottoms, leaving still visible hedgerows of tailings. Can you imagine trying to get a permit for something like that today?

Oil and gas are today's gold in the North, and generally speaking, the companies involved have worked hard to ensure that their operations are compatible with the new environmental awareness.

UW 16854

Moose

Building the 810 mile Trans Alaska Pipeline was probably the engineering challenge of the decade. Ways had to be devised to build in permafrost like these finned heat transfer units on top of support posts. Also notice the moose passing underneath.

New Alaska Pioneer, 1974. The tens of thousands of people that came to Alaska during the Oil Rush years transformed the state in many ways.

Native land claims had to be resolved before the pipeline received all the necessary permits.

The Oil Rush

Every Thursday in Seattle in the winter of 1974-5, there was a curious sight at the Alaska Ferry Terminal at Pier 48. (Before it moved to Bellingham in 1985, the Alaska ferry left each week from downtown Seattle.) Dozens of old beat-up cars pulling trailers, or pick-up trucks with campers on the back, full of whole families and their possessions were lined up, waiting to get on the Alaska-bound ferry. One wondered how many had those $1200-a-week jobs already lined up, or where those who didn't might end up.

It was no less than another Gold Rush, though with substantially less hardship and a lot more winners.

For Alaska and its citizens, the Oil Rush brought a sea change. The state's budget rose to unprecedented levels, affording programs found in few other states. But to many Alaskans it brought too many people, and too many new rules on what a person could or could not do on public land.

Before the Oil Rush, Federal land managers would sometimes turn a blind eye on squatters or trespassers, as long as they kept a low profile. But the state's new prominence brought many people north that found land or rents too expensive, and naturally wanted to simply set up camp on a piece of that vast land. What had worked for a

Left: The Riverboat Discovery III is one of the most popular excursions in Alaska (See following pages) Below: Panning gold at the El Dorado Mine is part of the Fairbanks City of Gold tour and you get to keep what you pan!

few didn't for many, and agencies had to crack down.

Oil and natural gas development continue to generate controversy. Currently the hot button topic is the Arctic National Wildlife Refuge, a vast area to the east of Prudhoe Bay, which is thought to contain significant oil and gas reserves. However, it also is the range for wildlife species that would be disturbed by development activities.

The competing interests of those who wish to develop the wilderness and those who wish to preserve it will always be part of Alaska politics.

Fairbanks Excursions
Tours include:

Fairbanks City of Gold Tour - 3.5 hours.
Palace Theatre & Saloon - 1.25 hours.
Riverboat Discovery Cruise - 4 hours.
The Malemute Saloon 1.25 hour
The Northern Lights Experience - 45 min.
See your Princess representative for more detailed information.

Riverboat Discovery III Scrapbook

We stop at an Athabascan native village for craft and culture presentations. Note very large cabbages in garden.

A native Alaskan demonstrates the elaborate beadwork and hide clothing.

We pull up to the shore next to 3 time Ididarod race winner Susan Butcher's house and kennel to get a look at her new puppies.

One of Captain Binkley's friends is happy to show us some bushplane acrobatics.

Chena River homestead.

A floating fishwheel on the Tanana River. Behind is a smoker and a traditional cache, for storing food out of the reach of predators.

The *Discovery III* is a diesel powered sternwheeler, similar to the steam powered craft that were the lifeblood of the river country of interior Alaska for almost a hundred years. The vessel is operated by the Binkley family, the third generation of this family to be involved in Alaska paddlewheelers.

Much of the north is covered by tundra. Wide areas are sometimes covered with tussocks, little round elevated bits of soil and vegetation, particularly difficult to travel over.

The Far North

North of Fairbanks, the roads, for the most part, disappear: first to gravel, then dirt tracks, then simply stop.

The taiga and tundra that covers the vast Yukon basin rises into the Brooks Range, falls away again to become the lonely north slope.

Beyond is only the bleak and desolate Arctic coast, active for a few brillant months in summer with spectacular whale and bird life.

But frozen, seemingly abandoned in winter, stretching seamlessly from the shore to the very pole itself.

Olaus and Margaret Murie - Olaus Murie came to Alaska in 1921 as field biologist for the U.S. Fish & Wildlife Service. Over the next several decades he and his wife Margaret traveled through much of the far North, banding birds, exploring animal habitat, making records and writing journals that were to become classics of Alaska literature. Making friends like Supreme Court Justice and Mrs. William Douglas and bringing them to Alaska, Murie eventually became head of The Wilderness Society. The Muries and others were instrumental in creating much of the vast parkland, monuments, and refuges that today ensure the integrity of Alaska's ecosystems. Margaret Murie's book, *Two in The Far North*, published by Alaska Northwest Books, selections of which follow, gives a wonderful account of their travels together.

On the Trail - The Muries' many dogsled trips give a real flavor of those winter days when dogs and sleds were the only way to get around The North:

"It was... dark when we labored up the last steep pitch to the mail cabin. Twenty four miles from Alatna, dogs pulling and puffing, we pushing and puffing; and when we were within a few yards of the cabin, my legs seemed to go out from under me and I crawled the rest of the way and through the square door hole and collapsed on a straw-strewn bunk. Olaus, who is never 'all gone,' put up the dogs, brought in our beds and grub and started a fire."

Many of Olaus Murie's early trips throughout Alaska were to determine the range and habits of the caribou.

Dangers – dog sled travelers were pretty much on their own, dependent on their skill and knowledge in a harsh environment. They also depended on the skills of their dogs. A well trained dog team would keep its driver away from some of the unique hazards of the trail, like overflows. These were created when river ice reached the river bed causing what water was still liquid to come to the surface of the ice.

"...the overflow is more deadly because it is accompanied by cold weather, and only those who have experienced it can appreciate the horror of a plunge into ice water in forty-below weather. This is another reason for the waterproof match safes and the candle stubs or can of Sterno which Olaus and other mushers carry in the big front pockets of their parkas."

On Northern Rivers – on a goose banding trip to the Old Crow River, the motor of their boat broke, and Margaret watched, day after day, from the confines of a 4'x4' mosquito net with their 6 month old son, as Olaus and Jesse, his native assistant, pulled and poled their boat upstream:

"By leaning forward and putting my eyes close to the netting I could catch glimpses of the outside world. It remained unvaried for five weeks: Jesse's booted legs, the tip of the red painted bow, a green blur of grass and willows on the shore, maybe a bit of sky. Sometimes I caught a view of Olaus, trudging along on shore, the line over his shoulder. He was 'pulling her by the whiskers,' as the trappers say. Jess, experienced with the pike pole, leaned his weight on every stroke, in a steady rhythm all day long."

The Mosquitoes of the Old Crow country were legendary. Mealtimes were a particular challenge:

"Some days we merely went ashore with the tin grub box and ate a bowl of stewed fruit or tomatoes with pilot biscuits or cold sourdough pancakes, and a bit of cheese. Bowl in hand, you loosened the string of the head net, poked the spoonful of food into your mouth and quickly let the net down again. It was the same with all the bites."

Inupiat
Glimpses of An Eskimo Past

Scattered along the northern and western coasts are the Eskimo communities. Traditionally dependent on seals, whales, and caribou, this was a culture in which winter was another word for hunger. Today's Eskimos are more apt to live in prefab houses delivered by the annual barge, and depend on seasonal construction or oil related work.

UW Thwaites 0134-493

Above: a shaman in a mask and carved hands tries to exorcise evil spirits from a sick child. Shamans were unable to cure the deseases like smallpox brought by the white explorers and lost much face in their villages.

Below : A umiak or traditional native craft made with sealskins stretched over a driftwood frame. In these craft Eskimos sometimes traveled long distances along the northern Alaska coast.

UW Nowell W5

UW 17963

Ivory carver and wife, in tent at Nome, circa 1910. Many Eskimos from King Island would travel to Nome each summer to carve and sell ivory to visitors. The long white object is a walrus tusk decorated as a cribbage board.

UW 17964

Eskimo group with fish drying on racks, near Cape Prince of Wales, circa 1915.

Shopping, Eskimo style, circa 1910. This group is aboard one of the several trading schooners that traveled northern waters each year to trade food stuffs, rifles, etc. for ivory and furs.

UW 17962

Alaska Cruise Companion 25

In the stillness of a September morning, Princess Ultra Dome cars wait for their northbound travelers.

This route is one of the most scenic in North America.

The Alaska Railroad

This railroad is sort of a 'You can't get there from here' line - it just runs from Seward to Fairbanks via Anchorage, with a spur to Whitter. The engines and cars all came by barge, from 'outside'; there's no connection to any Canadian railroad, no way to get to the rest of the USA by rail - there's just too much rugged territory in between. It was begun in 1915, and finished after much difficulty in 1923.

Until just 15 years ago, when the George Parks Highway north to Fairbanks was completed, the train was the only transportation there was for the folks along much of the Anchorage - Fairbanks corridor.

Whistle stops were an everyday part of train life as the 'local' trains dropped homesteaders off with their bags and boxes of groceries and supplies, often at trail heads where horses or four wheel drive vehicles waited to take them down some lonely dirt track to a remote home. Since the road was completed, the railway is strictly freight for seven months out of the year.

But every spring the passenger specials begin, with the domed cars that make it one of the most scenic rail rides in North America. Each day there is a northbound and a southbound passenger run. In most places the track is only lane, so one train must pull over onto a siding and let

the other go past.

These trains generally have three different kinds of domed cars. The Alaska Railroad domed cars are essentially the Vistadome cars still seen on some routes through the US west today - only part of the car has a dome, and passengers either pay extra or rotate through the domed section. Another tour operator has rail cars with the dome running the full length, but with less glass and fewer amenities than Princess's Ultra Dome cars. The Princess cars also offer a rear open air viewing and photo platform, gift shop, and excellent dining.

The first series of Ultra Dome cars were used originally by the Southern Pacific RR, on their San Francisco - San Jose run, then rebuilt in Tillamook, Oregon, specifically for Princess. The newest cars, the elegant Glacier Bay, and the Wrangell - St. Elias were custom built from the ground up in Denver especially for Princess Tours.

The tracks begin in **Fairbanks, mile 470**, and wind through the low taiga of the river lowlands for almost a hundred miles. Next is the rugged Alaska Range - the tracks follow the Nenana River Canyon, higher and higher to Broad Pass, before winding down the wetter coastal side of the mountains, and eventually to Anchorage, and the (relatively) ice free port of Seward. A spur line runs over the mountainous divide and to the small port of Whittier, on Prince William Sound.

Surveyor returns to camp, Turnagain Arm, circa 1920. Building the Alaska Railroad was hard, cold, and dangerous work.

UW Nowell 112

Somewhere on the lower Yukon the Saidie *transfers a load of freight to the* Kobuk River bound John Reilly, *Sept 29, 1903.*

Hand - drawn charts were often the only way to keep track of the shifting channels. The settlement of Circle is indicated by the small boxes on this drawing made around 1910.

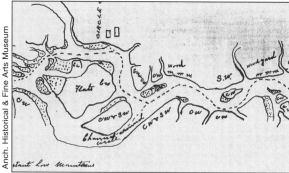

Anch. Historical & Fine Arts Museum

The River Country - Look for the big black and white wooden tripod (about 30' high), between the tracks and the river at Nenana, **mile 411**. Each winter this tower is dragged out onto the frozen river for the Nenana Ice Classic, a uniquely Alaskan lottery. What folks are betting on is 'Ice Out', the moment in spring when the frozen river breaks up.

It's entirely fitting that this be celebrated, for the rivers are the lifeblood for most of the towns in the immense drainage of the Yukon River.

Where there are no highways, the arrival of the first freight barge in the spring is always an exciting community event. This freight (usually in 40' containers or vans) usually begins its water journey from Seattle, stacked five and six high on a huge 400' ocean going barge, towed by a 5,000 horsepower tug. Somewhere near the mouth of the Yukon River, perhaps at St. Michaels, the containers would be hoisted onto a smaller barge, to be pushed upstream. Sometimes, for freight bound for communities on the smaller rivers, the container would be transferred a third time, onto a yet smaller barge, pushed by an even smaller tug.

Navigation is still tough - the river channels sometimes shift every few weeks; there are few buoys or navigational aids. Captains use hand drawn charts passed along from other captains and pilots. Sometimes the only way

Yukon Archives 5919

through is launching a skiff to sound out a particularly tricky channel before you entered it. Even then, groundings are routine.

The river as highway. Despite what you may hear, not everyone who lives out in the bush has a floatplane in their backyard. But the majority of villages and settlements in the vast country between the Alaska Range and the Bering Sea and Arctic Ocean lie along one of the many rivers with native and Russian names like Kitchatna, Tonzona, Kantishna, Hoholitna, and Chilikadrotna, Ugashik, Nushagak, and Kinak. When the ice is out, watercraft ranging from big tugs and barges to outboard jet boats move people and supplies around. When the ice is in, it is usually hard and smooth enough for vehicles.

It was during those in between months, the short spring and falls, that travel was difficult:

Winter was hard - sometimes the rivers froze quickly, trapping steamers far from any towns, forcing passengers to make their way overland, like this group, on the upper Yukon, in 1912.

"..My brother had a hunting lodge, way up the Noatak, with a native partner. One fall, I went up to help them, that first year when they were putting it up. 'Course there's no roads anywhere up there..all the stuff came in by barge to the village and then we had to lug it all up the river in the big Lund outboards, loaded right to the gills with sheetrock, 2x6's etc. It's almost forty miles up the river from the village to where the lodge is, and we really had to get the main lodge framed up

Steam ferry **Keewalik Flyer**, *near Candle, on the Yukon, 1903.*

UW Nowell 7829

Air boats are popular in the shallow sloughs and rivers. Also you may note outboard boats with their lower units replaced with jets (water pumps) for operating in shallow water.

and closed in that fall - we put in a barrel stove [wood stove made from a 55 gallon drum, fairly common in rural Alaska,] and kept working right through October. But then when we headed out to go home, the damn river was half froze up - maybe a hundred yards of ice, then fifty yards of water, then more ice! I thought we were screwed - that we'd have to leave the skiffs on the bank for the winter, and hike the 40 miles back along the shore.

"But my brother's partner, a native, he cruised back and forth when we got to the first of the ice, checking it out, then called over to us, 'If this works, follow me...' I didn't have the faintest idea what he was going to try, but he swung around, got up to full throttle and headed right for the ice. Then, just as he hit, he killed the engine, and pulled it up and that aluminum skiff slid right up on top of that ice and skidded almost all the way across to the next open water! So we swung around, got a good run at it, and up we went too...

"That first time we were a little hesitant, but then after a few more tries we got the hang of it, and we could slide maybe 50 yards if we could get a good run at it...and a lot of them frozen places were 50 yards or less, so we'd just slide all the way across and into the water on the other side and just keep on going.

"What a kick - we got back to the village without having to push those boats over the ice hardly at all. But you could tell - another two or three days and we'd have been totally screwed."
— A friend.

The big weird thing near mile 362, as the train emerges from the Nenana River canyon is the Usibelli coal tipple. Inside is the equipment for filling the coal cars that run north to Fairbanks, or all the way south to Seward to be loaded aboard ships for the Orient.

The country changes substantially here as the trees seem to swallow us up until it seems we're traveling in a leafy canyon. This is all the northern tiaga - a taste of the vast, low, mixed black spruce and birch forests that cover

UW Wilse 557

Several families of reindeer herders from Lapland in northern Finland were brought to Alaska in the 1930's to establish herds of these caribou-like creatures.

much of the Yukon basin that drains interior Alaska. Plants and trees don't get very big here; the growing season is short and the ground has great frozen areas (permafrost) just below the surface.

Look for the Early Warning Missile Site, at Clear, mile 392. This one and two others, are all that remain of the DEW line - the array of radar sites, built during the Cold War across all of northern Alaska and Canada. Before sophisticated satellites, their job was to watch for Russian missiles coming in over the north pole at North America.

Keep an eye peeled for river rafters in the Nenana River Canyon near here. Also moose are sometimes seen on the hillsides.

The country is so flat here that the Nenana, barely thirty yards wide in places in the gorge, and rushing along faster than a man can run, breaks into many branches like Seventeenmile and Lost Slough, and almost seems to just disappear into the flats before finally rejoining to enter the Tanana River at Nenana. Early travelers on rafts often had to pole tediously through miles of shallows here.

Worse were the mosquitos - when the river was wide, there was frequently a breeze, but when it got narrow and windless - watch out!

The forest here is known as taiga, very different from that of Prince William Sound and Southeast Alaska. Gone are the tall hemlocks and cedars, replaced by low white and black spruce, poplar, birch, aspen and larch. Where the trees seem particularly stunted is a sign of either wet muskeg or frozen permafrost close to the surface.

The Denali Princess Lodge, located on a bluff overlooking the Nenana River is at the entrance to Denali National Park.

Denali National Park

The park was orginally established in 1917 as Mt. McKinley National Park, a wildlife preserve that didn't include the mountain for which it is named. Finally in 1980, the protected area was tripled in size, to include the entire mountain massif and caribou herd winter range and calving grounds, and renamed Denali National Park and Preserve.

Travelers expecting the wide range of visitor services available in many 'Lower 48' national parks might be disappointed here. For the park's true grandeur lies in its being, as much as is possible with the limited visitor access, an intact subarctic ecosystem. For many, Denali Park is experienced in a bus with a naturalist/driver. For others, a visit might include camping at Wonder Lake, with backpacking through the wilderness.

Excursions from the Denali Princess Lodge:

Bird's-Eye View of Denali by
   Airplane
Denali Wilderness Lodge
Denali Wilderness Rafting
Denali Heli-Hiking
   Adventure
Denali Helicopter
   Fightseeing
Denali Horse Trail
   Adventures
Natural History Tour
Nenana River Rafting
Mt. McK's Roadhouse Revue
Tundra Wildlife Search
For more information,visit the lodge information desk.

"..Important Bear Notice ..now before we get out of the bus and walk around, listen up for some bear etiquette. If we should happen to encounter a bear in our little walk, the first thing you do is circle up and surround the bus driver."

—Heard on a Denali Park
tour bus.

"**In the bus, Denali National Park, Sept 17, 1997**: We didn't have to wait very long to see wildlife; just five minutes after entering the park, we stopped to watch two very big, brown, and somewhat dishelveled looking moose wandering through the low bushes perhaps 25 yards from the bus. Big is the operative word here. Everyone is concerned about bears, but I wouldn't want to meet a moose face to face on a narrow trail either.

A little later our sharp-eyed driver pulled over again and directed our attention to a place on the hillside where something brown could be seen moving. This was nature in the raw - you needed binoculars to see it, but a big 'griz' was chowing down on what looked like a side of Dall sheep.

The next stop was a ranger's log cabin, and a presentation of winter life in the park, when rangers depend on dog teams for travel (motorized travel is restricted in much of the park during the winter.)

The bus continued, skirting the south side of Primrose Ridge, and a wide valley drained by the Savage River.

Here was no Yosemite Half Dome, Old Faithful, or yawning chasm of the Cororado River. But rather a stark, Arctic, almost other worldly landscape, in which we humans felt very much like only visitors.

Our turnaround was an overlook with a view across to the already wintry looking Alaska range. There was coffee and home made banana cake from the back of the bus. On the ride back, our drive spoke of his past, growing up in rural Oregon, and his Alaska dream - of coming North to share, in some way, his strong naturalist interests and abilities. His commitment to this land and to the Park's values were very evident; one felt fortunate to have him as guide."

Brenda Carney

Caribou, like moose, are large members of the deer family. Both males and females have antlers. Caribou are much more likely to be found in groups than the more solitary moose.

Jim Brandenburg, Minden Pictures

Moose - these are big, big critters - keep your distance!

The interior tribes of this part of Alaska are mostly Athabascans. The harsher climate forced them into a much more nomadic and difficult existence than the Indians from the coast.

The Seventy Mile Kid: When the park was created in 1917, it was entirely fitting that Harry Karstens, known as the 'Seventy Mile Kid,' was the first superintendant. Barely 19 when he came north with the Klondike Gold Rush, he got his nickname after he and a buddy pulled a dogsled themselves on a 40 day trip back into the Seventy Mile River country of the upper Yukon. A few years later he got the 900 mile dog sled mail run contract from Gakona on the Copper River to Fort Gibbons on the Yukon, through the unmapped Alaska interior. His bitterly cold trips along this route became an Alaska legend.

Denali

Early explorers sometimes got a glimpse of a very high mountain to the north of Cook Inlet, a peak the natives of the region called Denali, which meant "The High One". An early prospector named it Mt. McKinley, but most Alaskans today refer to it as simply Denali.

At 20,320, it is the tallest peak in North America. If this mountain were in California, or perhaps Peru, it would be a world class climb, but it wouldn't have the particular challenges that comes with its high latitude.

The Alaska Range is a wall between Yukon - Arctic highs and North Pacific lows. The result is a highly volatile microclimate, and a mountain that can basically create its

own weather very rapidly. Most fatalities here are caused by weather changes, combining wind, cold, and snow.

> "On the northern side of the range there was not one cloud; the icy mountains blended into the rolling foothills, which in turn melted away into the dim blue of the timbered lowlands, that rolled away to the north, growing bluer and bluer until they were lost at the edge of the world. On the humid south side, a sea of clouds was rolling against the main range like surf on a rocky shore."
>
> —Belmore Brown, *Conquest of Mt. McKinley*

Many climbing parties have had the bitter experience of getting close to the top, only to be turned back, sometimes just a few hundred yards short of the summit by wind and cold. Experienced Denali climbers know that they can only get near the top and hope that the mountain gods will allow them to tread on the top of the continent.

The Pioneer Climbers - for the first climbers, in the early 1900's, just getting to where they could start their climb was an immense task in itself. The 1912 Browne - Parker expedition left Seward on February 1, with dog teams, and took almost 5 months to reach within a few hundred feet of the summit, only to be turned around by weather on two different days. When they finally gave it up, and turned to leave that desolate spot, their last memory was of the continual roar of wind from the summit somewhere in the clouds above them.

An Imposter's Claim - One of the oddest episodes n Denali's history was the 1906 claim by Dr. Frederick Cook, a very experienced Arctic explorer, that he and a companion had made it to the top of the mountain, the first to do so, bringing down photographs for proof. Climbers familiar with the mountain doubted Cook's claims, but it wasn't until 1910 that a group, climbing to

Few mountains experience such dramatic weather changes as Denali, perched between two very different climate zones.

Enjoy the views of the mountain when it's 'out', for sometimes the clouds may hide it for several days in a row.

UAF, Rasmuson Library, 81-208-03

Alfred Lindley and Harry Liek, after their successful ascent of Denali, May 1932. On their way down the mountain they encountered tragedy - two members of a scientific expedition had fallen to their death in the treacherous crevasses.

Voices from Denali

"...The storm now became so severe that I was actually afraid to get new dry mittens out of my rucksack, for I knew my hands would be frozen in the process. ..The last period of our climb is like the memory of an evil dream. La Voy was completely lost in the ice mist, and Professor Parker's frosted form was an indistinct blur above me... The breath was driven from my body and I held to my axe with stooped shoulders to stand against the gale; I couldn't go ahead. As I brushed the frost from my glasses and squinted upward through the stinging snow, I saw a sight that will haunt me to my dying day. The slope above me was no longer steep! That was all I could see. What it meant I will never know for certain - all I can say is that we were close to the top."

— Belmore Brown, *The Conquest of Mt. Mckinley*

"I was snowshoeing along about fifty feet back of the sled, with Harry (Liek) right behind me when, without warning, the snow fell away under my snowshoes. I plunged into sudden darkness.

I had time to let out a feeble shout. Then for a couple of long, long seconds I plummeted downward. I remember thinking, 'This is it, fellow!' Then my pack scraped against the slide of the crevasse, my head banged hard against the ice wall and I came to a jarring stop.

When my head cleared and I could look around in the blue darkness, I saw I was on a plug of snow wedged between the ice walls. On either side, this wedge of snow fell away into sheer blackness.

About forty feet above me I could see a ray of sunlight, slanting through the hole I had made in the surface crust. The crevasse was about twelve feet wide up there, it narrowed to two feet down where I was. Below was icy death."

— Grant Pearson, *My Life of High Adventure*

"But in half an hour, we stood on the narrow edge of the spur top, facing failure. Here, where the black ridge leading to the tops of the pink cliffs should have flattened, all was absolutely sheer, and a hanging glacier, bearded and dripping with bergschrunds, filled the angle in between...I heard Fred say, 'It ain't that we can't find a way that's possible, taking chances. There ain't *no* way.'

Climber Emilio Gunther towing a sled with extra supplies.

We were checkmated with steepness, at 11,300 feet with eight days mountain food on our hands. But remember this: also with scarce two weeks provisions below with which to reach the coast and winter coming. The foolishness of the situation, and the fascination, lies in the fact that except in this fair weather, unknown in Alaska at this season, we might have perished either night in those two exposed camps."

— Robert Dunn, *Shameless Diary of an Explorer*

"We tried to take some snaps, but had to give it up. For four minutes only did I leave my mittens off, and in that time, I froze five tips of my fingers to such a degree that after they had first been white, some weeks later, they turned black, and at last fell off, with the nails and all. Not till now, six months later, do they start to look normal again."

— Erling Strom, *How We Climbed Mt. McKinley*

"... My mind was racing. I had to grab the rock near Dave with my left hand; it was bare, no mitten or sock. It would be frozen. I had to. Suddenly my bare hand shot out to grab the rock. Slicing cold.

Climber Belmore Browne made three attempts on Denali, but was defeated each time.

I saw Dave's face, the end of his nose raw, frostbitten. His mouth, distorted into an agonized mixture of compassion and anger, swore at me to get a glove on. I looked at my hand. It was white, frozen absolutely white."

—Art Davidson, *Minus 148 degrees, The Winter Ascent of Mt. Mckinley*

UAF Rasmuson Library 81-218-07n

On Denali, 1932. When we look at all the high tech equipment today's climbers consider essential, our respect for the feats of the pioneer climbers grows.

specifically dispute Cook, found his supposed summit: 10,000 lower and 20 miles away from the actual summit.

First to the Top - In 1910, a group of hardy Alaskan prospectors, tired of the the controversy stirred by Cook's claims, decided to prove that Alaskans could do the job. This was the so-called "Sourdough Expedition." They reached the top of the North Peak, (the South peak was slightly higher but they didn't realize it at the time) put up a 14' pole and flag, and then went back down, and got back to prospecting!

Of course, many folks doubted their claim (until another expedition, years later, saw the pole,) and the credit for being the first to climb McKinley went to Alaskans Hudson Stuck, Harry Karstens, and their party in 1913. They were fortunate in having a window of clear and calm, though bitterly cold, weather at the top:

> "There was no pride of conquest, no trace of that exultation of victory some enjoy over the first ascent of a lofty peak, no gloating over good fortune that had hoisted us a few hundred feet higher than others who had struggled and been discomfited. Rather...that a privileged communion with the high places of the earth had been granted...secret and solitary since the world began. All the way down, unconscious of weariness in the descent, my thoughts were occupied with the glorious scene my eyes gazed upon, and should gaze upon never again."

> —Hudson Stuck, in *Mt. Mckinley: The Pioneer Climbs,* Terris Moore

Denali today - The mountain has become a very popular climb, sought each summer by expeditions from all over the world.

Todays expeditions almost universally begin at the Talkeetna airstrip and a flight to a base camp at Kahiltna Glacier at 7,000 feet. This base camp is a busy place, with a ranger station and aircraft and climbing parties coming and going. How very, very different from the rigors faced by the mountain's true pioneers.

Don't surprise bears, don't run from a bear (but walking backwards rapidly is OK!), and being careful with food are rules in bear country.

"In the Hot Tub, Denali Princess Lodge, Sept. 17, 1997, evening: The Nenana rushes by in the canyon below; across it the aspens are all bright orange, and the upper slopes dusted with snow. I feel the shadow of those who struggled in the high country beyond the ridge. Belmont Browne and his group - five months of hard traveling, only to be turned back just a few hundred yards from the top. Art Davidson and his friends - caught in a 130 mph blow, in winter, out in the open, at 18,000 feet, chipping out a cave in the ice and managing to survive. And the many who didn't make it, swallowed up by the sea of crevasses, or simply disappeared. One feels humbled."

"Well it won't stop a bear, but you can shoot yourselves with it if one comes after you..."
- advice from a pilot to some greenhorn campers who showed him their bear gun - a .32 caliber pistol!

"Waiting for the Midnight Sun Express, Sept 17, 1997: Our breath is white before us, whipped away quickly by the wind. We stand wrapped in coats, the last leaves, orange and yellow whirling around us. Fall is but a few short weeks in the Alaska Range; the heavy snows are waiting. Then the long mournful horn echoes from the hills across the river and the Northbound pulls into the station. Glad to get in, out of the cold, get a hot "Mt. McKinley" - coffee and Yukon Jack liquer and just sit, watching the landscape flow past.

"The silty Nenana boils and rushes through the canyon below us. I imagine the little mining camps back in the draws, the men working all winter, to dig out the frozen earth, and pile it to wait for the spring thaw, when they can process the ore in the sluice boxes. The weather warms and the water begins to flow down through the riffles in the sluices , lifting away the dirt, until only the gold remains. Finally the gold is in the pokes (small canvas bags) and the men pack to go to town, drag the boats down to

Away, away - the last northbound Midnight Sun Express of the 1997 season at the Denali Park Station, Sept 17.

the shore, tie everything down, and slide out into the current, to let the bucking Nenana take them to Tanana, or Fairbanks, with money to spend, maybe even a trip "outside" before winter.

"Our train squeaks and squeals around the sharp bends above the river; if these bends were any sharper these long cars couldn't make it. Seven winding miles, and then the mountains flatten, become foothills, and the low taiga forest surrounds us."

Denali Park to Talkeetna the railway follows the Nenana River toward The **Continental Divide** which crosses Broad Pass somewhere in the Summit Lake area, near **mile 312**. This is a significant geographic locale - streams a hundred yards south drain eventually into Cook Inlet, near Anchorage, 140 miles south. But just a hundred yards north the streams drain into the Nenana River, which empties into the Tanana, which, many miles later, flows into the mighty Yukon, to flow to the Bering Sea, 800 river miles away.

Low and treeless **Broad Pass** at **mile 304** was the major north and south route through these mountains long before roads or trains. Look for little cabins along the lake - they're shelters for stranded travelers and pilots.

Look for the 918' Hurricane Gulch Bridge, at **mile 284**.

Look for the little airstrip, through the trees to the east at Talkeetna. This village is the staging area for almost all expeditions to the top of Denali, and for most it begins with a flight to Kahiltna Glacier at 7,000', where base camp is established and the climbing begins. For many years well known pilot Don Sheldon honed his glacier landing skills here, and gave invaluable assistance to many climbing parties.

Motorcoach - Talkeetna to Mt. McKinley Princess Lodge - Roughly an hour trip, paralleling the Chulitna River. The lodge is on the bluff on your right, just before the highway crosses the river.

Look for the gravel road leading off to the west at **Trapper Creek**, about halfway to the lodge. If you were to jump into a four wheel drive vehicle and follow the road, winding through the alder and spruce lowlands, past small lakes and crossing dozens of streams for forty miles or so, you'd come finally to a little valley scattered with miners cabins, a landing strip or two, and in the hills above, a half a dozen placer mines.

The folks here have the sort of life style many came to The North to seek - a combination of semi-wilderness living and a business for cash needs, in this case gold mining.

But as Alaska grows, even these remote folks aren't immune from its impacts. Presently state agencies are considering this area for an entrance to Denali State Park, setting up the classic battle of old timers vs. developers.

Trumpeter swan and two cygnets (young swans) on Byers Lake. Photo by Toby Riddell, Susitna Expeditions.

Trumpeter Swans - the bus driver's tale:

"..I live on a lake, back off the road a bit, just two other cabins on the whole lake. There's always been a pair of trumpeter swans there, each summer as long as I can remember. They mate for life, and they're sort of solitary, so usually you'll just get one pair on a lake.

"But for the last couple of days there's just been one swan out there, honking like crazy. So finally this morning, I went out to where they nest, and found wolf tracks and a bunch of feathers..."

Princess Cruises

The big lounge at the The Mt. McKinley Princess Lodge offers a panoramic view of Denali and the Alaska Range.

"Mt McKinley Princess Lodge, September 14, 1997: Took mule ride tonight with a friend from the ship. Our 'mule skinner' was a rough hewn fellow, and as we meandered through the hills behind the lodge, he spoke of his years of experience hunting and trapping in the bush. He promised a Denali view we wouldn't forget, and he was right.

But for the dimmest color in the aspens, the low country was dark when we came to the view point. The sun was way off to the west, and its low slanting light putting all the valleys and low places in shadow. But we could make out Ruth and Tokositna Glaciers, Avalanche Spire, Windy Corner and Karsten's Ridge, all those places that had brought so much difficulty and heartbreak to climbers.

Beyond, and high above, a long snow-capped ridge, touched pink at the top with the sun's rays, rising to a marked high peak at its north end, was Denali, looking like the top of the continent that it was. We dismounted, set up a tripod to catch the moment, and then it was time to go, for the night was coming swiftly.

But on the way down, the mountain was always there, pink, in the fading light, above the trees. And I was reminded of the journals of the early travelers to Tibet and Nepal. Of how wherever they were, Everest was always there, seeming to loom over them."

Mt. McKinley Princess Lodge Excursions:

Byers Lake Kayaking
Byers Lake Nature Hike
Chulitna River Rafting
Glacier Helicopter Flightseeing
Historic Talkeetna Walking Tour
Mt. Mckinley Flightseeing
Mt. McKinley Princess Lodge River
 Shuttle

McKinley View Jetboat Safari
Salmon Sportsfishing
Susitna Valley Fly-In Fishing
Talkeetna River Raft Trip
Talkeetna Mountain Horse Train
 Adventures
Tokositna River Rafting &
 Flightseeing: "The Grand Slam"

Kay Riddell

"Mt. McKinley Princess Lodge, September 15, 1997: Up at first light, to climb just a half mile, to a high clearing. The sun had yet to crest Curry Ridge behind me, but like the night before, shone full and pink on the long snow covered ridge that was Denali, and only a long winding mist cloud showed where the Chulitna River threaded through the forest below the lodge.

"In the early afternoon, took kayaking excursion to Byers Lake. I've been around the water for decades, but in larger, powered craft. This business of sliding along, effortlessly, barely disturbing the water was an unexpected treat. There were just three of us, the lake glassy still, and now and again the haunting cry of the loon and the trumpeter swan. The magic of the afternoon was tangible; we spoke little, preferring to glide along the shore, on water as transparent as air. Near the lake's outlet, a school of sockeye salmon rippled the water, their bodies brilliant red against the mottled browns and greens of the bottom. And there were Denali and her sisters, rising from the forest of yellow alder and dark larch and spruce, to reflect across the stillness.

"Lingered after dinner, with friends, the big fire to our backs and the last pink light on The High One out the tall windows to the west. We stayed until late, but when it was time to go, we went out to the wide deck for one last time, and there they were - splayed across the sky above the Alaska Range - the northern lights: pale greens and yellows, a boldly moving and changing pattern.

"There are some things you can only remember - pictures can't truly show, words can't fully describe, and this was one."

On Byers Lake - Denali loomed from the water above the trees, and the still-ness was only broken by the drip of our paddles and the cry of a loon.

The cry of a loon is a particularly haunt-ing sound. Young loons are sometimes carried on their par-ent's backs while swimming.

Land a floatplane here? In a true feat of bush flying, Talkeetna pilot Don Sheldon landed in the rapids in a river canyon to save a surverying party whose boat had been destroyed by the rocks and churning white water.

Sometimes the train slows near mile 224, to let travelers get a good view of the Alaska range across the Susitna River: Denali at 20,320', and her lower sisters, Mt. Hunter, 14,573', and Mt. Foraker, 17,400'.

The Susitna is normally placid, but about 65 miles northeast of here the river turns violent in a five mile rapids named Devil's Canyon. It was here in August of 1955, that one of the more remarkable feats of Alaska flying took place.

Talkeetna pilot Don Sheldon saw the wreckage of a US Army survey boat in the canyon on a charter flight to a nearby lake, and upon returning, spotted survivors huddling on the rocky shore with almost no way out, unless he could somehow land in the river canyon. The rapids in the river created 6 foot waves - certain death to land on, but after a couple of passes through, Sheldon found a little strip of calmer water, just above the survivors, where he thought it might just be possible to land. Sheldon made his approach, swallowed hard, and set his little Aeronca down. Once he was in the water, he had to let the river carry him backwards, into the rapids, for him to get to where the survivors were:

> "As the plane backed into the first of the combers, I felt it lurch heavily fore and aft. It was like a damned roller coaster. The water was rolling up higher than my wingtips, beating at the struts, and I could barely see because of the spray and water on the windows. All of a sudden the engine began to sputter and choke, and I knew it was getting wet down pretty good..."
>
> —Don Sheldon, in *Wager With the Wind*, by James Greiner

Somehow the engine kept going, and Sheldon managed to maneuver close enough to shore for one of the men to clamber aboard. Getting out was almost as hard -

backing the plane down the rapids, until he came to another stretch just barely long enough to effect a take off. Sheldon had to repeat this remarkable performance three more times to get all the survivors out.

> "Fer Cris'sake, all it would take is for one of those Alaska Airlines jets to cream into Mt. Juneau and it'd take the the whole legislature with it..."
> — Heard around Alaska

Racing sled dog team, circa 1920 Does it sometimes seem like there are two Alaskas - Southeast and the vast interior? It does so to many Alaskans who want to have the capital moved closer to the Anchorage Fairbanks corridor.

Once you take your cruise, you'll probably notice that there are basically two Alaskas - the drizzly, grey one down there with Ketchikan and Juneau, and the wide open one up here with Anchorage, Fairbanks and the whole really, really, big rest of the state. It will probably also occur to you that the capital, Juneau, is way down there, and well, really isolated from the whole rest of the state?

Don't think that this same thought hasn't occurred to many Alaskans. In the 1970's when the state was flush with oil revenues — just the oil lease sale, in 1969, 8 years before a drop of oil flowed down the pipeline, brought in 900 million dollars, — **'Move The Capital' was a bumper sticker seen all over the state.**

The only problem was where to move it. In true Alaska fashion, Anchorage and Fairbanks were such rivals that neither would accept the other as capital. So why not pick some centrally located spot in between, and make that the capital? Brillant! So, in 1976, Alaskans voted to build a new capital near **Willow, mile 185.7.** So where is it, you say? Cooler heads prevailed a few years later, when the first cost estimates came out, and the capital remained in Juneau.

Now and again, through the trees, you'll glimpse a road, the George Parks Highway, just to the west, or left of the train. Between this highway and the Bering Sea coast, 500 miles to the west, there are no roads. (Well, O.K.,

On the back of the Midnight Sun Express — The lakes and marshes north of Anchorage are all part of the Northern Flyway for migrating birds. Be ready with your binoculars.

The red -necked Phalarope is common on lakes and marshes here.

there are a few exceptions - the 20 miles of bumpy pavement between Naknek and King Salmon, on Bristol Bay, a few miles around Dillingham and a few more around Nome. But, basically it's pretty lonely out there.)

"Aboard the Midnight Sun Express, Knik Flats, Sept 14, 1997: my tablemates must think me a little odd. When our car emerged from the forest of quaking aspen and paper birch, and out onto the flats bordering Knik Inlet, I stopped talking, probably in mid sentence. The marsh grasses moving in the breeze, the flocks of ducks and even Arctic Terns, feeding in the shallows but so obviously waiting for that north wind to follow south, the snowy ramparts of the Alaska Range rising up above, the beauty and the drama of it all overwhelmed me.

"For this is part of the northern flyway. To these thousands of acres of shallow wetlands, braided with the streams of the Knik and Matanuska Rivers, tens of thousands of birds come each year, to feed, and rest, to wait for weather.

"When the traveling weather - a still morning or that high pressure that heralds a northerly - comes they're up and away. I suspect they're like we mariners, in our little boats, seeking the most sheltered routes. Instead of heading down Cook Inlet to the outside coast, they'll pass Anchorage, turn east, up Turnagain Arm, and then up Portage Creek, the valley between the mountains, then over the low divides into Prince William Sound. If the wind is too easterly in the sound, they might lay over in the marshes and flats at the head of Pigot Bay. But if the breeze was westerly there or sou'west, they'd just pause there, and then be on the wing once again, making time when they could, just like us, perhaps a very long day, 190 miles to the welcome flats and marshes of the Copper River Delta. They'd overnight, wait again and travel when they could - coming at dusk to the Situk, or even the Alsek, on the outside coast, another long day.

"I've had fishermen tell me about coming upon waiting flocks on the Alsek flats in the fall. Thousands of ducks and terns, just laying in the rippled sloughs, waiting for weather. Then when a morning came still, or with a breeze out of the north, they'd be off the water at very first light, some wheeling east, to follow the Alsek and the Tahshensheni through that icy wall of the Fairweather Range, and then south through the interior valleys. But others headed southeast, down the outside coast, following the shore towards Cape Spencer, bound maybe for the sloughs and flats up at the head of Idaho Inlet, or Tenakee Arm.

"And I remembered our own struggles to get south in our little boats. Traveling when we could, sometimes just harbor to harbor, two days of waiting for one of traveling, a long month of it from Skagway to Seattle. In some ways, I suppose we weren't that different from these birds, waiting, waiting, for weather."

Truly remarkable travelers, the Arctic Tern (black cap, red bill and feet, long forked tail) summers in Alaska then takes off each fall for a 10,000 mile journey to winter in the Antarctic. You might see them in the Knik marshes.

The Matanuska Valley Experiment

During the Great Depression, 202 families were chosen from the distressed northern Midwest, and brought by the federal government to found an agricultural colony and begin a new life in the rich bottomland of the Matanuska River valley, northeast of **mile 150.**

It didn't work out as the planners had hoped. The first summer was unusually wet; many children grew sick; the soil quality was uneven. The sizes of the plots wasn't really big enough to make a living from. Some families gave it up, but the remainder stayed, fighting the challenges of high latitude farming. Today the

They grow them big up North – cabbages at Fairbanks.

THE MIDNIGHT SUN EXPRESS.

The Midnight Sun Express has an open observation platform and great views from the enclosed upper deck.

valley farmland is a natural target for developers creating more suburbs for Anchorage commuters, but the long hours of summer daylight still produce some spectacularly large vegetables, most notably the legendary 90 pound cabbages.

"**Anchorage, September 14, 1997, 7:45 a.m.**: Our train sits waiting on a siding, near the water. The other passengers board quickly, their breath white in the chill morning air, but I stand aside, let the bus leave, to take in the surroundings. The days get shorter quickly in the fall this far north and the sun is still behind the Chugach Mountains to the east, yet just illuminating the volcanoes along the snowy wall of the Alaska Range, across Cook Inlet. The shiny sides of the coaches are yellow and pink, reflecting the sky, while all around is almost dark. Here and there along the waiting train, steamy air vents from beneath the coaches, cloaking all in a mysterious other world feeling. The last whistle finally blows, and I have to board. Yet I linger until the very last, unwilling to leave the drama of this moment."

Note: on the following pages is **The Dawn Princess Journal,** an account of a cruise up the coast from Vancouver to Seward, on a glorious week in September, 1997.

It covers the same itinerary that you will be taking, but **in reverse.**

Dawn Princess Journal
Gulf of Alaska Cruise
September 6-13, 1997

Humpback whale near Glacier Bay. Michio Hoshino, Minden Pictures

"Tracing shining ways through fiord and sound, past forests and waterfalls, islands and mountains and far azure headlands, it seems as if surely we must at length reach the very paradise of the poets, the abode of the blessed."

— John Muir, *Travels in Alaska*

Day 1 – Vancouver and the Winding Way North

Points of particular interest:
1. - Gulf Islands: sheltered waterways, popular recreation area.
2. - Yuculta Rapids: small craft route; even whales wait for slack water here.
3. - Desolation Sound: roadless, semi wilderness marine park.
4. - 'The Graveyard', site of a particularly nasty tide rip when a flooding tide is opposed by a strong southerly wind.
5. - Seymour Narrows: a gorge with swift currents; a legendary place. Safe passage is only possible at slack water, every six hours.

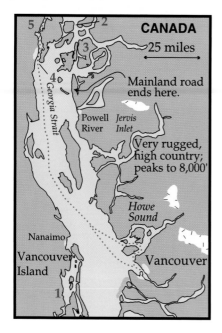

Above: Point Atkinson, Howe Sound.
Below: workboat, Johnstone Strait.

*Above: troller at Sara Point, Desolation Sound.
The steep mountains in this area dashed the
hopes of railroad men who hoped to bridge the
narrow channels to Vancouver Island.*

*Abandoned homestead, Yuculta
Rapids. The coast used to be dotted
with tiny settlements.*

*Looking across Georgia Strait from a
cove in the Gulf Islands. The dozens of
islands and protected waterways here
and in the American San Juan Islands,
further south, are a boater's paradise.*

Day 2 - The Wilderness Begins -
Up the British Columbia Coast

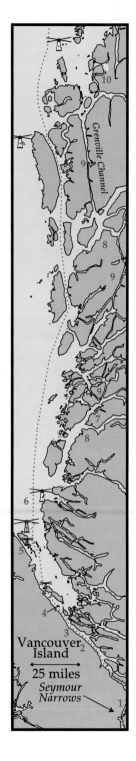

Points of particular interest:

1. - Routes: ships use Seymour Narrows, small craft prefer sheltered channels further east.
2. - Johnstone Strait and orcas: this is one of the best places in the world to see these big black and white killer whales.
3. - Mile 264 - Robson Bight: orcas like to rub their backs against the rocks here.
4. - Alert Bay: native village, look for the really tall totem poles.
5. - Mile 309 - God's Pocket: northbound small craft would wait in this tiny cove for good traveling weather.
6. - Queen Charlotte Sound: can be rough; small craft hurry across.
7. - Namu Cannery. Famous killer whale Namu captured near here, became aquarium star.
8. - The lonely north coast: few settlements.
9. - 'The Northern Canyons': small craft route, too narrow for large ships.
10. - Prince Rupert, regional center, connected by rail to interior British Columbia.

Johnstone Straits is particularly popular with orcas or killer whales. Naturalists and photographers from all over the world come each summer to study and photograph these whales.
Flip Nicklin, Minden Pictures

East of the deep and wide ship channels are the more winding and narrow channels used by fishing boats and other small craft.

For generations salmon fishing, and logging were the mainstay industries along the coast. Salmon like this gorgeous Columbia River king were caught in Hecate Strait and along the outside coast of Vancouver Island.

Native culture continues to be a strong element along the British Columbia coast.

Mainland mountains, Frederick Sound.

My neighbor, Flea, a hand-troller at Point Baker, 1974.

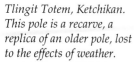

Tlingit Totem, Ketchikan. This pole is a recarve, a replica of an older pole, lost to the effects of weather.

Mt. Edgecumbe from a hill above Sitka. Island Princess *may be just seen behind the islands in the left of the photo.*

Day 3 - Islands Without Number - Ketchikan and Southeast Alaska

Points of particular interest:
1.- Misty Fjords National Monument.
2. - Myers Chuck, **Mile 626**: roadless settlement. Look for small fishing craft.
3. - Snow Pass, **mile 720**: look for whales.
4. - Entrance to Wrangell Narrows, constricted shallow passage to Petersburg and points north.
5. - Point Baker, **mile 745**: my island homestead was in the cove just behind the island with the light on it. Look for whales near the little island.
6. - Chatham Straits, many bays with abandoned salmon, herring, or whale processing plants.

*Salmon trolling, ocean coast, at Cape Addington, **mile 700W**.*

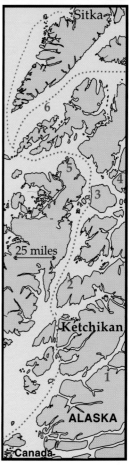

Skagway, tucked into the folds of a river gorge, at the head of a long fjord, is rich with the history of those who passed through, headed to the Klondike in the Gold Rush.

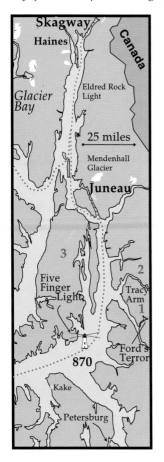

Day 4 - Juneau, & Day 5 - Skagway

Points of particular interest:
1. - Ford's Terror: <u>very</u> narrow entrance leads to spectacular remote basin.
2. - Tracy Arm - long fjord with glaciers.
3. - Admiralty Island National Monument.

*The first ice, from Tracy Arm or Le Conte Bay is sometimes seen in the vicinity of **mile 870.***

A tug tows a long raft of logs through the winding passages of Wrangell Narrows near Petersburg.

Floatplanes wait at Juneau to load visitors for flightseeing. In this largely roadless region, these aircraft are used for everything from hauling groceries to law enforcement.

Gallery at Port Chilkoot, near Haines. Known for a nearby fall and winter concentration of bald eagles, Haines is connected to the Alaska Highway.

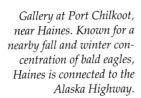

Calving ice at Hubbard Glacier. Some of the pieces that fall off weigh hundreds of tons, creating very large waves - small craft stay clear! © 1998Mark Newman/Alaska Stock

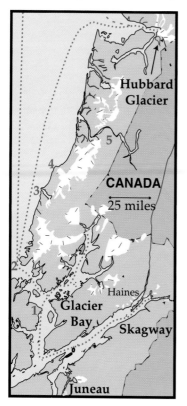

Day 6 - Into The Ice:
Glacier Bay and the Outside Coast

Points of particular interest:
1. - Point Adolphus, **mile 1000**: humpback whales often congregate here.
2. - Cape Spencer, end of Inside Passage.
3. - Lituya Bay: a 1958 earthquake made a tidal wave 1800 feet high.
4. - Lonely and remote coast; no towns.
5. - Alsek - Tatshenshini Rivers - popular with kayakers. After your trip a float plane flies you back to civilization.

Humpback whale breaching. The bay and the waters adjacent to it are also the summer feeding grounds of a number of humpback whales. Have your binoculars ready! Michio Hoshino, Minden Pictures.

Dawn Princess in Johns Hopkins Inlet. The walls seem to tower over us and the sounds of the glaciers are very loud.

Early morning, **Dawn Princess,** *off Cape St. Elias, Gulf of Alaska. In the mists beyond the cape are the high peaks of what has been nicknamed 'The Roof of North America'.*

Day 7 - Prince William Sound, A Jewel in Alaska's Crown

Points of particular interest:
1. - College Fjord with many active glaciers.
2. - Bligh Reef, site of ***Exxon Valdez*** oil spill.
3. - Alaska pipeline to Prudhoe Bay.

The 150 foot spruce trees of College Fjord give a clear sense of the massive size of Wellesley Glacier

Harvard Glacier calves, creating a splash almost reaching to the top of its 300 foot high face.

For almost 70 years, square rigged sailing ships served the canneries here. Tongass Historical Society photo.

The outside waters along this part of the coast are subject to bitterly cold winds in winter. Such winds can build up dangerously heavy loads of ice on vessels large and small.

Interior Alaska Scrapbook

Above: The Chugach mountains reflect off the windows of the Midnight Sun Express at Anchorage.

The riverboat Discovery III *pauses beside a fish wheel on the Tanana River near Fairbanks.*

Last trip of the season - looking out at fall foliage along the Tanana River from the Midnight Sun Express.

Deep in the heart of Denali National Park, a moose feeds in the shallows of Wonder Lake. *Michio Hoshino, Minden Pictures*

This is bear country; follow a few simple rules to stay out of trouble.

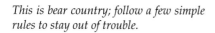

Along the Chena River, near Fairbanks.

On Ruth Glacier. Michio Hoshino, Minden Pictures

Today the land and the waterways in Alaska are much as the original explorers found them. This is not by chance. The history of Alaska, especially in the 20th century has been a tug of war between those who wish to develop and change the landscape and those who wish to preserve it.

We are fortunate that people like John Muir, Adolf and Margaret Murie, and many others successfully championed the cause that wilderness should exist for its own merit. Due to these efforts, a vast area of National Parks, Preserves. and Forests were created to preserve the heritage and beauty of Alaska and The North, hopefully forever.

Traveler's Guide to Birds

BALD EAGLE. Size: wingspan to 6 feet and larger. Range: Oregon to Bering Sea. Distinguishing features: Large soaring bird, adult marked with white head and tail, juveniles dark brown or mottled. Notes: Uncommon in Puget Sound, these very noticeable large birds are common throughout coastal British Columbia and Alaska. While scavenging dead fish, they will also attack live fish and small animals.

BONAPARTE'S GULL. Size: to 14 inches. Range: Peru to Bering Sea. Distinguishing marks: smaller than most gulls, easily recognised by black head and bill and white wing tips. Notes: Nests and breeds in interior, migrates south in late summer, returns in spring.

ARCTIC TERN. Size: to 10 inches. Range: Circumpolar. Winters in Antarctic, summers in coastal Alaska and British Columbia. Distinguishing features: Terns are noted for their smaller size, slender shape, and distinctive long forked tail. Arctic terns have a prominent black cap on their heads. Notes: These remarkable birds migrate some 8,000 to 10,000 miles each spring and fall.

COMMON LOON. Size: to 20 inches. Range: California to Bering Sea. Distinguishing features: Large diving bird with sharp bill and noticeable white and black checkerboard pattern on dark back. Notes: Dives when approached. Feeds on fish. Requires long flapping takeoff run on windless days. Haunting, whoooo call.

Traveler's Guide to Birds

RAVEN. Size: to 24 inches. Range: Central America to Bering Sea. Distinguishing features: Crow-like, but substantially larger. Jet black, almost glossy purple color; call is a distinctive *klok* sound. Notes: The raven is a central figure in Haida and Tlingit mythology; raven figures appear on totem poles and dance masks.

MARBLED MURRELET. Size: 10 inches Range: California to Alaska. Distinguishing marks: Very short neck, marbled white markings on brown. Winter plumage is dark above, white below. Notes: This species, seen commonly in all seasons in Southeast Alaska, may be the next Spotted Owl. Nesting in old growth timber, its numbers are declining.

STELLER'S JAY. Size: to 12 inches. Range: Washington to Bering Sea. Distinguishing features: Bright blue and black coloring with distinctive black crest. Very visible and busy; likes to taunt larger birds, such as eagles. Notes: Named for German naturalist Georg Steller, who was with explorer Vitus Bering, whose 1741 expedition discovered Alaska.

SPOTTED SANDPIPER. Size: to 8 inches. Range: California to Arctic. Distinguishing marks: Easy to identify in summer plumage with large spots underneath. Fall and winter plumage is brown above and white below with no spots. Notes: This little bird is seen over most of the Alaskan coast. When surprised, flies away from the shore with short, jerky wingbeats, and returns nearby.

So now that you've had a really comfortable ride down through the Heart of Alaska in the Midnight Sun Express, you should think a bit about transportation in The North, in the days before the railroad. In those days, the only link between some towns in winter was the weekly horse drawn sleigh.

It was a long, cold, and risky ride. Crossing the thawing rivers in the spring was only one of the hazards. The writer is Margaret Murie, remembering a trip when she was sixteen:

Look for salmon, like these coho, or silver salmon, in the streams and rivers that your train passes over. The angler who caught these has tethered them in the stream to keep them alive.

"Out of the trees—there was the Delta River, snow covered still, but somehow looking pretty soggy and gray and at least half as wide as the Tanana at Salcha. Roy stood up and looked across. I rose to my knees and peered over too. Over against the oppo-site shore was a black streak, about thirty feet wide. The lead horse snorted. Roy said nothing, settled the reins in his hands, turned and looked the lashings over, and said very calmly: 'Ish!'

"As we went out onto the ice, through slushy snow, he spoke again, 'Remember what I told you before—stay with us. They may have to swim a few feet, you know, but just hang on to those ropes.'

"Now we were reaching that black streak, and as if in a daze I heard the sound of water, and Roy's voice talking softly, urgently to the team. But they were old stage horses; they plunged in. I felt the whole sled lift and float; a terrific churning, a great heave and a thump, and up the steep bank we went in a rush. The horses stopped as soon as they were up on the level again. They knew they rated a rest there."

–Margaret Murie, *Two in The Far North*

You might get a close up view of F-15 fighters as you pass Elmendorf Air Force base, just north of Anchorage. Although showing their age, they can still climb *vertically*, and accelerate at the same time with their afterburners lit.

Orca whale mural on J.C. Penny building, Anchorage.

Anchorage - Downtown Alaska

The old saying, "You can see Alaska from here." basically describes the relationship of Anchorage and the rest of the state. While some 40% of the entire state's population resides in the greater Anchorage area, it's a good bet a lot of them blast out of town each weekend, judging from the number of planes, campers, snowmobiles, 4 wheelers, kayaks, etc, in the back yards all around town. Don't be surprised to see a moose meandering around town, though wandering bears are more unusual.

Though Anchorage overlooks **Cook Inlet** and **Knik Arm**, it's hardly a waterfront town in the mold of Ketchikan or Juneau. There's no place for boats to tie up downtown - the rivers draining into the inlet bring a big silt load and the there are extensive tide flats making it difficult to even get to the water in most places. Most marine activity is centered in Ship Creek, north of town.

The eight mile long, paved Tony Knowles Coastal Trail, starting at the end of 2nd, Avenue, is a great walk, and opportunity to watch shore birds.

The newest and shiniest high rise office buildings usually belong to Big Oil in this town. The revenue from this industry basically redefined Alaska economics, and gave its citizens the unique distinction of getting the only state dividend checks in the country. Far sighted leadership in the early days of the oil boom established a large and so far untouched 'Permanent Fund' which yields enough income for checks typically in the 1000$ range annually for each of Alaska's citizens.

Cheating on the Permanent Fund. There's a lot of P.O. Box addresses in a state as rural as Alaska. There's also a lot of people who like to get that check, regardless if they qualify as a resident or not (Alaska's residency definition is pretty strict). Fish and Wildlife Protection officers (game wardens) who enforce the state's many fishing and hunting regulations, and other law officers, are usually alert to ID's with post office box addresses:

"We were way back up the Koyukuk, fishing, and this fish cop appears out of nowhere in his boat and asks to see our licenses and our photo ID. I mean, that's lonely country up there - we hadn't seen anyone for days...

"So anyway, when he asks for my photo ID, I gave him my Alaska driver's license. He checks it out, then sez, 'Hey, pal, this here says you live in King Salmon. Well, I've lived in King Salmon for the last 10 years. How come I've never seen you?' I finally had to admit I spend most of the year in Idaho..

"Shit...I had to go to court, and got fined a thousand bucks for falsifying a residency and another hundred bucks for not having a fishing license... and way up the Koyukuk."

— A sportsfisherman

Downtown Resolution Park with a statue of Captain Cook offers a view of the inlet and a fitting tribute to this remarkable and lucky explorer.

Take a few minutes and walk to the **Captain Cook Memorial**, overlooking the water at the end of 3rd Ave. You can get a clear sense of the very different shoreline below, but also it's an opportunity to reflect on the many unusual deeds of this English sailor, who charted much of the vast reaches of the Pacific Ocean.

Bad Friday, 1964 - Most folks were just settling down to supper when the most powerful earthquake to hit North America this century struck. Anchorage was mostly built on unstable clay, which is particularly susceptible to movement in a 'quake'. So move it did - splitting apart, dropping whole blocks and tumbling expensive waterfront

Belugas and orca whales are occasionally seen right in front of town.

UW 14501

When the earth shook. Some sections of town were so shattered that survivors could only be reached by helicopter.

homes down steep bluffs. Within minutes, much of the downtown core was a ruin of fallen storefronts, crumpled streets, and shattered businesses.

Property damage was extremely heavy, but fortunately only nine people died.

Shopping - if your cruise is over and you haven't done all your shopping, it's all here in downtown. Take an evening to explore these shops and especially the galleries of native art and crafts. There are pieces here that would be hard to find anywhere outside Alaska.

Galleries and other notable places - **Alaska Center for the Performing Arts**, 6th & F; **Wolf Song of Alaska**, inside J.C. Penney Mall, 6th & E; **Reeve Aviation Picture Museum**, 343 W. 6th; and **Anchorage Museum of History & Art**, 121 W. 7th.

Anchorage Excursions:
Anchorage City Tour - 2.5 Hours.
Best of Anchorage Tour - 5.5 hours.
Brown Bear Flightseeing Expedition - 2 hours.
Classic Airlines Flightseeing - 1.5 hours.
26 Glaciers Cruise - 12 hours.
Glacier Flightseeing with Lakeside Inn Visit - 3 hours.
Flightseeing Over Alaska via Floatplane - 3.5 hrs.
Kenai River Sportsfishing - 12 - 13 hours.
Turnagain Arm Helicopter Flightseeing - 2 hours.
For more information, visit the hotel excursion desk.

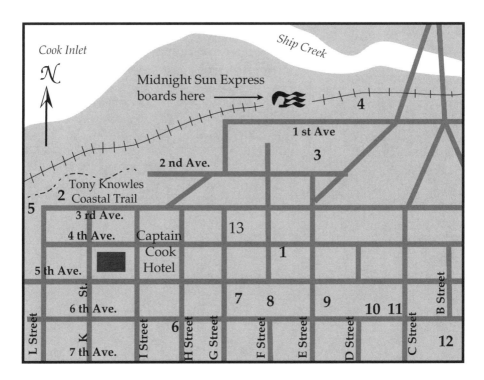

Downtown Anchorage

1. Log Cabin and Visitor Information Center
2. Tony Knowles Coastal Trail - ten mile trail that follows the shore with great views.
3. Alaska Statehood Monument
4. Alaska Railroad Depot
5. Resolution Park with Captain Cook Monument
6. Oomingmak Musk-ox Producers Co-Op - unique garments from some pretty strange creatures.
7. Alaska Center for the Performing Arts
8. Town Square Municipal Park
9. Reeve Aviation Picture Museum
10. Alaska State Trooper Museum
11. Wolf Song of Alaska - large wolf exhibit; free.
12. Anchorage Museum of History and Art - excellent collection; gift shop and cafe.
13. Alaska Public Lands Information Center

Be sure to save some time for the shops and galleries here. This 9x9 framed replica Yup'ik Welcome Mask was less than $100.

Coach to Seward - 127 miles, typically four hours. Almost all two lane road, winding through valleys, past several lakes and many salmon streams. There is usually at least one rest stop, at a particularly scenic spot of the driver's choice.

The volcanoes across Cook Inlet - you'll glimpse three of the region's active volcanoes as you travel along. Minor eruptions are a regular part of contemporary Alaskan life.

Most recently, in 1992, the tallest at 11,070', **Mt. Spurr,** erupted, disrupting air travel, and covering a wide, but mostly uninhabited area, with fine ash. When the wind changed direction and brought the ash to Anchorage, the local remedy for keeping car engines running was a homemade filter of ladies panty hose wrapped around the air cleaner. The ring of fire continues out the Alaska peninsula, where **Mt. Aniakchak** continues to vent steam through its year round snow cover and others like **Mt. Pavlof** and **Mt. Shishalden** occasionally cough up steam and hot ash. (see story below)

Little visited, seldom climbed, lonely Aniakchak volcano rises from the tundra west of Ugashik Village, on the Alaska Peninsula. Note steam vent on left slope.

"We were crabbing in the Bering Sea, maybe fifty miles offshore, nighttime, the usual rotten weather, freezing spray flying, you know, everyone's pretty much got their hoods up and heads down, just sorting crab and trying to stay dry.

"Then the skipper slows way down and starts blowing the horn for something. As soon as we looked up we could see it -

Steam Vent

one of those old volcanoes out on the chain or the peninsula was clearing its throat - just blasting out red fire and smoke and lighting up the whole sky. Man, what a sight! We just idled there, just a 'gawking at it - I never even seen anything like it - just like this Roman candle, ten thousand feet high and sixty miles away. Blew for maybe ten minutes, then that was it. We waited for a bit, but she didn't blow any more that night anyway.

"But, god, what a sight!"

—Fisherman Russell Fulton

While most recent Alaska eruptions are of the "throat clearing" variety - fireworks and a bit of ash, the 1912 Mt. Katmai blast was more along the lines of a nuclear bomb. The explosion was heard in Juneau, 750 miles away and sulphuric fumes drifted all the way to Vancouver, B.C.

In Kodiak, the ash fall was so heavy that houses collapsed, and much of the town's population took shelter in a Coast Guard cutter. For two days there was no sun and only constant lightning pierced the black clouds.

It was to be almost three years before anyone ventured into the area of the volcano. When the first visitors arrived in the Katmai area, they found a desolate moonscape with so many smoking fumaroles that they named it **The Valley of 10,000 Smokes.** Today few of the fumaroles are active and the area is more known for its bears.

The volcano in the ocean - in 1883 observers were awed by a smoking volcano emerging from the icy waters of the Bering Sea, to become Bogoslof Island.

UW Nowell 5718

The Bears at Katmai

Waiting for that perfect fish. The bears don't catch the jumping fish with their paws, but actually grab it out of the air with their mouths! At the peak of the run, some 200-300 fish a minute are leaping these falls, so the bears have a pretty good chance.

The Valley of 10,000 Smokes is pretty quiet these days (most of the old fumaroles have stopped smoking), but this the-size-of-Rhode-Island national park is well known for another feature: the bears.

If you are near this part of Alaska (Katmai is about 250 miles west of Anchorage) in late June or July, and want to see bears, up close and personal, this is the spot.

For the bears the attraction is the salmon. The park encompasses several major salmon producing lakes, and in spawning season, the streams that feed them are full of literally hundreds of thousands of fish.

The visitor center is at Brooks Lodge, built in the 1930s as a sportsfishing camp. Today it is a classic Alaska lodge, with individual log cabins overlooking the lake and the mountains.

I flew in there in July of 1997, with my son, and some friends, after just finishing our commercial salmon fishing season in Bristol Bay, 80 miles to the west.

The only way in is by floatplane; it pulls up to the beach, and you walk up to a small log cabin that is both the park headquarters and gift shop. Our group crowded in to watch the 'Bear Etiquettte Video' a presentation on how to avoid those unpleasant one-on-ones with bears.

As we were watching there was a clatter outside, and we looked out to see a brown bear about the size of a Volkswagon, rattling the bolted-down, bear- proof trash cans.

As we walked the paths to the viewing platforms, we were accompanied by a walkie-talkie equipped park ranger, who was monitoring bear movements. Several times on the way to the viewing stand at the falls on the Brooks River, we had to move off the trail to let bears pass. (They have right of way!)

Then we got to where we could see the falls through the trees, and my feet stopped walking. There, in plain sight were at least six very large brown bears, very intent on the business of catching the fish that were leaping up the four foot falls, oblivious to we humans.

We climbed the ramp to the viewing platform, our guide latching the gate behind us. In front, arrayed across the falls, and in the stream below were the bears, wading, chasing fish in the pools, snatching them out of the air as they leaped the falls.

In a tree, just twenty yards from the platform, were two 100 lb. bear cubs. When they got bored and began climbing down, their mother would amble quickly over from the stream and indicate to them in no uncertain terms that they were to remain where they were.

When a bear got a fish, it would walk into the shallows, hold the fish down with one paw, and neatly strip off a fillet with the other, flip the fish and do it again - an impressive performance.

The park ranger said there hadn't been a bear incident in 12 years, but we forgot to ask what the park's definition of an incident was - did you have to get stitches, or would a few scrapes and bruises do it?

Several 'viewing stands' afford an excellent opportunity to watch and photograph the bears. This is not for the squeamish - sometimes the bears are literally rubbing on the posts that support the elevated platforms.

Anchorage Convention & Visitors Bureau

Close to Anchorage, Portage Glacier is a popular attraction.

When the road narrows and parallels a steep rocky hillside, the water on your right will be **Turnagain Arm**:

> "Turnagain Arm is noted for the violent winds which blow out of it whenever the wind is easterly, and is locally referred to as the Cannon, which expresses the opinion held of it."
>
> —*US Coast Pilot 9*, 1964 edition.

Quicksand and Bore Tides in Turnagain Arm. Aside from the violent winds, this shallow, funnel shaped arm has a bad reputation for the combination of forces waiting for the careless traveler - deep, unstable sands and quickly rising tides. Imagine, you're out on the flats at low tide, hunting or beachcombing. An unexpectedly soft patch of sand suddenly swallows your leg up to the knee. You struggle, but can't free it. Then you hear an odd sound, like a faraway roaring, and realize it's the tide, coming up the arm, a low wall of water.

Small craft operators and travelers on beaches and mud flats should exercise particular care here due to powerful tides and areas of quicksand.

It turns out that the particular glacial silt here has a large number of triangle-shaped grains. When the right amount of liquid is present, they float loosely in suspension, but when disturbed, by a leg, for example, seem to lock together. Struggling only locks the grains tighter.

In a few particularly tragic episodes, rescue personnel arrived in time to try without success to extricate the vic-

Flip Nicklin, Minden Pictures

tim, who quickly drowned as the tide rose.

The tides in this area are among the biggest in the world - in the larger tides up to 35 feet of water must move into this arm in the six hours between low and high. The size of the tides is governed by the relative position of moon, earth, and sun. But what happens in Turnagain Arm on these larger tides, is even more dramatic. The water actually enters as almost a wall, moving at up to 10 mph.

Look for beluga whales chasing salmon here. Belugas, white, or cream-colored, (young may be gray) are a toothed whale, typically 15 - 18' in length. They seldom travel much further south than Cook Inlet on the Pacific Coast, and especially seem to like the shallow rivers in western and northern Alaska. It is not at all uncommon to find these whales almost nudging the riverbank in just four or five feet of water, miles upriver. They are popular with aquariums as they are particularly vocal, and early sailors nicknamed them sea canaries, after hearing their many sounds through the hulls of their ships.

Belugas have a more developed acoustic sounding sense than many other whales, allowing them to find leads in the ice floes they often prefer to swim among.

Anecdotal evidence seems to indicate that the population might be substantially larger than presently thought. Fred Kraun, an Alaska Native and retired airline pilot living in the Bristol Bay area, did a aerial survey of a school

Belugas stranded on gravel bar. Young, with black rimmed fluke, seems to be trying to nurse. Belugas, accustomed to shallow water, and among the smallest of whales, routinely survive strandings, swimming away when the tide floats them again. They have, however, learned to remain still while waiting, to avoid attracting the attention of predators.

Brenda Carney

Big fishing on the Kenai Peninsula. Most out of state anglers freeze or smoke their fish and have them shipped home.

of belugas feeding on salmon in the Kvichak River in the spring of 1997. By carefully counting, he figured that school alone at between 1,500 and 2,000 whales.

At the very head of the arm, where the highway swings around to the west, you're on a ten mile wide narrow neck of land that seperates the Kenai Peninsula from the rest of Alaska. Just ten miles across the mountains to the east is Passage Canal and the town of Whitter, on Prince William Sound. Once a major trade route for Indians, gold prospectors and fur traders wound across the mountains. There's no road to Whittier yet, (but construction is beginning) - you get there by driving your car onto the train! Look for the railroad siding on the left, with ramps for loading cars. This is quite a trip. If you take the 26 Glacier Cruise excursion from Anchorage, you'll take it. The train travels through two tunnels, one of which passes beneath a 3100' mountain with a glacier on top. In its early days as an Army port, much of Whittier life took place inside one huge army building.

About 8 miles east are **Portage Lake and Glacier.** An excellent visitors center and its proximity to Anchorage make it one of the most visited glaciers in the state.

The **Sterling Highway** branches off to the west, 31 miles north of Seward, to cross the Kenai Peninsula to reach the west side of Cook Inlet, including Homer, Nikilski, Ninilchik, Kenai and Soldotna.

The **Sterling Highway** branches off to the west, 31 miles north of Seward, to cross the Kenai Peninsula to reach the west side of Cook Inlet, including Homer, Nikilski, Ninilchik, Kenai and Soldotna.

Look for cars driving onto railroad flatcars, near mile 70.

Kenai Lake, on the right, around 15 miles from Seward, zig-zags west through the mountains (you see the eastern end of the lake from the road) 22 miles to Cooper Landing, a sports fishing and river rafting center, popular with many Anchorage residents. The Kenai and nearby Russian Rivers are known for some of the best king salmon fishing in all of Alaska. But if you seek solitude while you're fishing for those big kings, look elsewhere. The secret's out, especially about the Kenai, and locals have come to refer to the king salmon season as "Combat

Princess Cruises

Kenai Princess Lodge is perched on a bluff above the Kenai River with spectacular views and excellent facilities. Excursions include:

Kenai Upper River Sportsfishing
Kenai Lower River Sportsfishing
Kenai Fjords National Park Cruise
Resurrection Bay Wildlife Cruise
Kenai Airplane Flightseeing

Kenai River Scenic Float Trip
Kenai Canyon River Rafting
Kenai Nature Hike
Back Roads of Cooper Landing

Whatcom Co. Museum of History and Art, Moran 74

Mailman and dog team, circa 1900. Roadhouses on established routes provided lodging for travelers and their dogs .

In fall or spring, look for migrating birds along this route.

Fishing," with anglers lining up almost hip to hip in the most popular spots. If your neighbor hooks a fish - haul your line in if you want to avoid a tangle!

This last part of the road runs over a series of low divides among the Kenai Range. To the east and west are several substantial ice fields and dozens of large and small glaciers. The highway also travels past a number of lakes, giving a glimpse of the sort of stream and lake fishing that attracts so many anglers to Alaska.

Look for spawning salmon in many of the streams that you will be passing over, especially Salmon Creek, whose tributaries cross and recross the highway in the first five or six miles above Seward.

The winter storms - it's easy going now, but the low passes form a highway for the powerful weather systems that march back and forth between the Arctic highs to the north, and the North Pacific lows out in the Gulf of Alaska. The glaciers that seem to ooze out of every crack in the nearby mountains are testimony to the amount of moisture that pours off the ocean and onto the coast when the winter weather systems begin tracking in. The power of these storms became part of the lore of The North as soon as early Alaska novels became popular reading:

"It was early in the afternoon when the Indian stopped and began testing the air; Balt also seemed suddenly to scent a change in the atmospheric conditions.

"What's wrong now?" Emerson asked, gruffly.

"Feels like wind," answered the big man with a shake of his head. The native began chattering excitedly, and as they stood there, a chill draught fanned their cheeks. Glancing upward at the hillsides, they saw that the air was now thickened as if by smoke, and, dropping their eyes, they saw the fluff between their feet stir lazily. Little wisps of snow vapor began to dance upon the ridges, whisking out of sight as suddenly as they had appeared. They became conscious of a sudden fall in the temperature, and they knew that the cold of interstellar space dwelt in that ghostly breath which smote them. Before they were well aware of the ominous significance of these signs the storm was upon them, sweeping through the chute wherein they stood with rapidly increasing violence. The terrible, unseen hand of the Frozen North had unleashed its brood of furies, and the air rang with their hideous cries. It was Dante's third circle of hell let loose - Cerberus baying through his wide, threefold throat, and the voices of tormented souls shrilling through the infernal shades... There was no question of facing the wind, for it was more cruel than the fierce breath of an open furnace, searing the naked flesh like a flame."

— Rex Beach, *The Silver Horde*

Coach stops along the road to Anchorage may include viewing salmon in streams many miles from the salt water.

Early travelers in the high passes would rush down into the trees to get out of the wind when a storm approached.

Dawn Princess at Seward. If this bay looks familiar to you, it may be because the opening scene from The Hunt for Red October, with Sean Connery on the conning tower of the Russian missile submarine cruising down a wintry fjord, was filmed here.

Seward

The Good Friday Earthquake - If town looks fairly new, it's because it is - much of the port and downtown was destroyed in the violent events of March 27, 1964. When the ground started shaking, it created sort of an underwater landslide and most of the waterfront immediately dropped around 6'. Next the big fuel storage tanks east of town ruptured, allowing burning oil to spread out over the bay in front of town, setting the stage for the next disaster - a tidal wave. As the shaken residents began to take stock of their situation, a few noticed that the sea had receded substantially from the shore. A little later a tidal wave in the form of a 30 foot wall of water, carrying the burning oil with it, blasted into town to shatter and burn much of what was left. Fortunately the death toll was light, but the port and basically the entire waterfront were destroyed and took a decade to recover. Not only did 107 coastal Alaskans lose their lives, but the tsunamis killed people as far away as Oregon and California.

Fishing, sport and commercial, and tourism, are the engines that run the economy here. Look just south of the small boat harbor for the big parking lot for campers and motor homes. Every Alaskan is entitled to a subsistence catch of salmon. Originally intended for natives and other

rural residents who traditionally depended on fish, today many city dwellers take advantage of its provisions to load up on salmon either frozen or home canned in jars.The **Alaska SeaLife Center**, opening in 1998 is part rehabilitation center for species damaged in the spill, and part aquarium/visitor's center.

One of Seward's biggest attractions for visitors is the **Kenai Fjords National Park**, a dramatic series of narrow bays and glaciated fjords to the west of town. The land in most of the fjords has only recently emerged from the ice - actually the Harding Icefield, which once covered much of the entire Kenai Peninsula.

As most of the park is rugged, roadless country, most folks visit it by boat. Several vessels operate out of Seward on daily excursions to the park.

Got just a few hours in town? There is a glacier you can drive to - Exit Glacier, just 8 miles west of town. Use care here and don't walk where you'd be at risk from falling ice - a visitor was killed in 1987 this way.

The Seward waterfront looked as if it had been through a shredder after the Good Friday Earthquake and tidal wave of 1964.

Sportsfishing is a major activity around the Seward waterfront.

Seward Excursions:
Alaska's Glaciers via Helicopter - 1.3 hrs.
Alaska Sealife Center - 1.5 hrs.
Best of Seward and Exit Glacier - 3.5 hrs.
Deluxe Resurrection Bay Cruise & Sealife Ctr. - 6.5 hrs.
Resurrection Bay Wildlife Cruise, 3.5 - 4 hrs.
Seward Town & Homestead Cabin Tour 2 hrs.

See ship's excursion desk for more information.

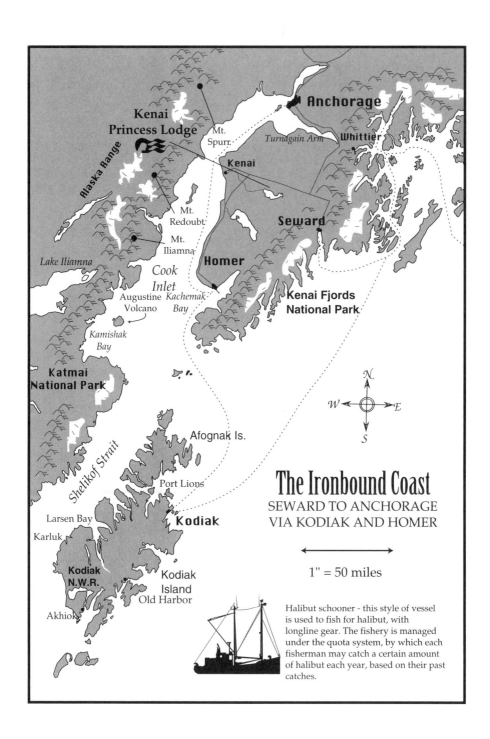

Kenai
Princess Lodge

Mt.
Spurr

Alaska Range

Turnagain Arm

Anchorage

Whittier

Kenai

Mt.
Redoubt

Mt.
Iliamna

Lake Iliamna

*Cook
Inlet*

Augustine *Kachemak*
Volcano   *Bay*

Homer

Seward

**Kenai Fjords
National Park**

*Kamishak
Bay*

**Katmai
National Park**

Shelikof Strait

Afognak Is.

Port Lions

Larsen Bay

Karluk

**Kodiak
N.W.R.**

Kodiak
Island

Old Harbor

Kodiak

Akhiok

N
W   E
S

The Ironbound Coast
SEWARD TO ANCHORAGE
VIA KODIAK AND HOMER

1" = 50 miles

Halibut schooner - this style of vessel
is used to fish for halibut, with
longline gear. The fishery is managed
under the quota system, by which each
fisherman may catch a certain amount
of halibut each year, based on their past
catches.

CHAPTER 2

The Ironbound Coast

ANCHORAGE, MILE 1870CI, TO SEWARD, MILE 1600S, VIA HOMER AND KODIAK

"It was good money allright - two season's in a row I made over eighty grand on deck. But don't ever think we didn't earn it. Our skipper, for example, he kept a little toothpick on a string in the wheelhouse and when coffee and pills wouldn't keep him up no longer, he'd stick that toothpick into his mouth. That way, see, when he nodded off that toothpick'd jab him in the cheek and wake him up. The cook'd make cakes and leave them on the table right by the porthole that gives out onto the deck, so we could reach in and get a piece. Twenty hours straight on deck, thirty hours sometimes. Sure it was big money, but I know you'd take two years off your life for every one you were up there"

—*A king crab fisherman*

DAY ONE, EVENING

Seward to Vancouver Passengers: YOUR TRIP BEGINS ON P. 123.

Your journey begins in **Cook Inlet**, named for its discoverer, British Captain James Cook, who passed through in May of 1778 looking for the Northwest Passage back to the Atlantic Ocean.

Look carefully at the water here. Near the head of the inlet, the water becomes in places more like liquid mud due to the glacial silt from the several rivers that drain into it. This can be very damaging to salt water pumps·and other machinery.

Shortly after leaving Anchorage, you'll see a wide bay to the east at **mile 1850CI**, This is Turnagain Arm, mostly shallow and widely covered with mud flats. At times the incoming tide rushes over these flats as a moving

Russian Orthodox grave in native village. The influence of this church is widespread throughout the Kenai Peninsula and Western Alaska.

wall of water. In places the surface of the exposed tide flats contain a quicksand-like mud, and in rare instances people have been trapped, and drowned by the incoming tide. See. P. 76

Cook continued his exploration west and north, through the Bering Strait into the Chukchi Sea, where he was blocked by the permanent ice pack. He eventually made his way to Hawaii, where he was needlessly killed in a squabble with natives. Two of Cooks officers, William Bligh and George Vancouver were to become famous in their own right, Vancouver as the Northwest coast explorer extraordinaire, and Bligh as the captain of the *Bounty*, during the famous mutiny.

Tidal currents in Cook Inlet are especially strong, due to its funnel-like shape. In a large tide, the current in places may reach up to 8 knots. (9.8 MPH!) Also as the glacial sheet retreated centuries ago, it dropped many boulders which form hazards to mariners traveling in shallow waters. Fortunately the tide is usually so strong that these can be seen by wakes created by the current:

> "Heavy swirls with overfalls should be avoided, and any disturbance which has a recognizable wake in the water should be avoided as indicating a dangerous rock or shoal."
> —*US Coast Pilot 9, Pacific and Arctic Coasts*

Belugas, cream colored whales, typically 12-18 feet long, are frequently seen here in summer.

The current posed quite a challenge when a substantial body of oil and gas was discovered underneath the lower inlet. Drilling platforms not only had to contend with the strong current, but the ice that sometimes moved with it in winter. Platforms were developed resting on a single pillar, which reduced the chances of ice damage.

As an added precaution, powerful tugs were stationed at the rigs in the winter to push the bigger ice flows away before they could cause damage.

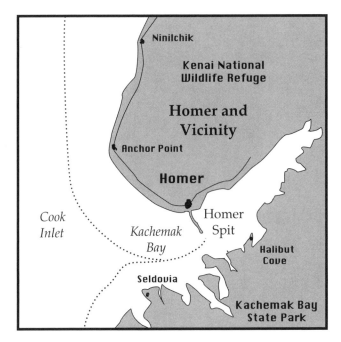

All of the communities in this part of the Kenai Peninsula have economies that depend on commercial fishing and visitor activities.

<u>DAY ONE</u>
<u>EVENING</u>

PLEASE NOTE:
<u>THESE TIMES ARE</u>
<u>APPROXIMATE. YOUR</u>
<u>SHIP'S SCHEDULE MAY</u>
<u>CHANGE DUE TO WIND,</u>
<u>TIDE, FOG, OR OTHER</u>
<u>FACTORS.</u>

Four noticeable volcanoes lie along the Alaska Range on the west side of Cook Inlet. Each has erupted in recent history. Volcanic activity is part of life in thispart of Alaska. These aren't extinct by any means! See Page. 73

The town at **mile 1760CI**, is **Ninilchik**, first settled by Russians and now a fishing settlement. If you see what looks like hordes of people on the beaches in this vicinity, they might be clamming. The first good low tides of the spring (the range of the tide varies in a 28 day cycle, according to the relation of the moon and the earth) are popular with those seeking razor ond other clams.

Fishing with tractors - there are many salmon fishermen operating set nets along this part of the estern shore of the inlet. These are usually set along a beach or mud flat at low tide. As the tide comes in, it floats the net, and any passing fish are caught. Several fishermen with several sites to tend, use tractors to pull the nets.

The town to the east at **mile 1795CI** is **Kenai**, well known for its salmon fishing and recreational activities.

The western shore of Cook Inlet is for the most part unpopulated, except for a few very small seasonal fishing settlements, and an ARCO oil facility at Drift River, opposite Kenai. The area is popular as a destination for fly-in fishing and camping.

Look for salmon gill-netters operating in Cook Inlet.

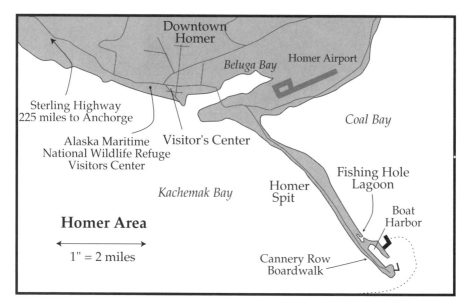

Downtown Homer

Beluga Bay

Homer Airport

Sterling Highway
225 miles to Anchorge

Coal Bay

Alaska Maritime
National Wildlife Refuge
Visitors Center

Visitor's Center

Fishing Hole
Lagoon

Kachemak Bay

Homer
Spit

Boat
Harbor

Homer Area

1" = 2 miles

Cannery Row
Boardwalk

Homer

Once a remote coal mining settlement, today Homer is a town of 5,000 set in a truly exquisite location. Looking south across Kachemak Bay to the snow covered mountains on the Kenai Peninsula, it is becoming a well known arts community as well. Commercial fishing is the lifeblood here and in the surrounding small communities. Like Seward, Homer is at the very end of a road from Anchorage

The Spit - Homer's most unique feature is a four mile sand spit sticking out into Kachemak Bay. At the end of the spit is the harbor as well as marine support facilities, a few eateries and gift shops.

The headquarters of the Alaska Maritime National Wildlife Refuge is in town. Its 3.5 million acres are spread across much of the coast of Alaska to the west. The visitors

Homer Excursions
Glacier Flightseeing by Floatplane - 1.5 hrs.
Gull Island & Halibut Cove Expedition - 3.5 to 4 hrs.
Homer Fishing Adventure - 5 hrs.
Homer Highlights - 3 to 3.5 hrs.
Kachemak Bay Guided Nature Hike - 3.5 hrs.
Touch a Glacier Helicopter Landing - 2 hrs.
For more information, visit your ship's shore excursion desk.

center has exhibits and displays of the wildlife found in the refuge.

Homer overlooks a four mile long spit, Kachemak Bay, and the lower Kenai Peninsula.

Sport fishing, as you may have guessed, is excellent here. One of the local hot spots is the lagoon just north of the boat harbor - hatchery raised fish are moved to cages in the lagoon, causing them to imprint the lagoon's location and return there as adults to try to spawn. Sometimes, toward the end of a runs, 'snagging', or dragging a bare hook through the water, is allowed to harvest all the rest of the fish. Kids especially like this - catching is easy!

Halibut Cove, on the opposite shore of Kachemak Bay from Homer, is a roadless fishing settlement with a strong arts flavor. Not having a road creates a community that is very different from any of the places visited by most cruise ships. One's schedule tends to revolve around the weather and the tides. The **Gull Island & Halibut Cove Expedition** offers an opportunity to see such a community.

DAY TWO
AFTERNOON

Seldovia, 20 miles west of Halibut Cove, is another commercial fishing oriented community, accessible only by charter plane or boat.

After leaving Homer, you will proceed out into Cook Inlet, and swing toward Kodiak Island, some hundred miles over the horizon to the south.

Homer is off the beaten track for cruise ships. Your ship is a rare visitor here.

Neils Thomsen

Is this a boat? - The Expansion *iced up at Seward. Icing up was a constant problem for vessels traveling the western Alaska coast in winter.*

Tales of 'Cap' Thomsen and The Aleutian Mailboat

In the 1950's, the only outside contact for 19 isolated native villages on the Alaska Peninsula and Aleutian Islands was the 114 foot mailboat *Expansion*, which made regular round trips from Seward. Neils 'Cap' Thomsen was one of those entrepreneurs that Alaska seems to attract. (We met 'Cap' a few chapters earlier, running a freight boat into Ketchikan.)

About the first thing 'Cap' noticed on his stops was how some native villages seemed to have a lot of single young men, and another village, maybe a hundred miles away, single women, but neither knew of the others:

"So I bought a Polaroid camera and took pictures of the unmarried natives. I'd write their names and towns on them: 'Nona Polapalook from Gambrel Bay,' etc. I put the pictures up on two bulletin boards, one for single women and another for single men. Pretty soon after that the word was out, and any time we'd round a point to come into a harbor where a native village was, the singles would be jumping into their boats and rowing out as fast as they could to meet us even before we got the anchor down! They'd come aboard and head right for the singles bulletin boards. Also back in those days, to be legally married, the natives had to go to Cold Bay, a long way away. So I got a Justice of the Peace license, so I could marry them right aboard the boat!"

— 'Cap' Neils Peter Thomsen

'Cap' Thomsen's boat also served as a general store, many times taking furs in trade for rifles, flour, etc. He also was a traveling branch of the Bank of Kodiak for the native villagers, some of whom had taken to burying the money they made fishing in jars in their back yards until they needed it.

Neils Thomsen

'Cap' Thomsen aboard the iced-up Expansion *after a difficult trip up Shelikof Strait to Seward in wintertime.*

   An early cruise ship? "FOR ROMANTIC ADVENTURE , Sail to The Aleutian Islands, 'Land of the Smoky Sea,' See majestic steaming volcanoes, Witness the drama of life at sea, See roaring sea lions, precious sea otter." So went the pitch on Thomsen's brochure, seeking travelers wanting an off the beaten path experience. He might have added, 'Help the Captain work on his crab processor.' for on each trip, Thomsen managed to lay over in remote Dutch Harbor, for three or four days, long enough for the passengers to see the local sights, as well as doing a little scraping and painting on Thomsen's floating crab processor, the BETHEL I.

   These were the days when the king crab fishery was just starting. Most of the activity was in the Kodiak area, but wherever 'Cap' anchored the *Expansion*, he set a crab pot over and noted how many of the big spiny fellows he caught. A few years later, when his crab processor was ready to go, he recruited some boats from Kodiak by telling them that he knew most of the good crab fishing spots in the Aleutian Islands. Thomsen was able to ride the king crab boom to the peak, eventually selling his little company for some 5 million dollars, and heading to the Caribbean to build a resort!

   Neils also wrote a remarkable book, *The Voyage of The Forest Dream*, about some of his early sailing days as a lad of 18, aboard a big square rigger loaded with lumber on a trip across the Pacific.

In the late evening you'll pass near the **Barren Islands, mile 1690.** West of the Barrens is the 25 mile-wide entrance to Shelikof Strait, the passage between Kodiak Island and the mainland. This area has long had a particularly bad reputation among mariners, because of the violent and cold winds that blow out of some of the passes on the Alaska Peninsula during winter gales.

Caution: tide rips in the Barren Islands area can be hazardous to small craft.

"Anchorages in Puale Bay are indifferent to poor...Williwaws are frequent. Even in westerly weather the winds funnel through the low passes to the west of the bay with greater velocity than that encountered in Shelikof Strait."
- United States Coast Pilot - Pacific and Arctic Coasts. 1964 edition.

Author's Note - when I was 21, I took a job on a brand new 104' steel king crab vessel. We left Seattle in early March for the 2000 mile trip to Dutch Harbor in Alaska's Aleutian Islands. It was a difficult journey. I have included some journal entries from that trip. Note that our trip was in <u>winter</u>. In the summer, when your ship passes here, the weather is fine.

'West'ard' is the term used by northwest mariners to describe the Alaska coast that lies to the north of the sheltered waters of Southeast Alaska and the Inside Passage.

A Journey to West'ard

Joe's Log

"**March 17, 1971, Shelikof Strait** - By day we saw no other boats, by night, no lights. Inhospitable ice mountains rose from every shore. I yearned to see another boat, a town, but there was nothing.

"In the evening, in the below zero degree dusk, we anchored up right next to the beach in Uyak Bay, on the southwest side of Kodiak Island.

"An hour later, the wind came on, slamming into us. When the big gusts hit, all conversation in the galley would cease, and we'd listen to the shriek, audible even through the insulated steel hull, seeking any weakness.

"At 3 a.m. an unusually violent gust of wind followed by rattling pops and cracks had us all in the pilothouse.

'Rocks and pebbles picked off the beach by the wind, and

we're almost a quarter of a mile away,' said our skipper, George Fulton. 'One winter I saw a boat whose whole bow looked as if it were sandblasted - the paint gone right down to the bare metal, just from anchoring too close to the beach.'

His brother, Russell, stepped into the circle of light over by the chart table, tapped a thick finger on a narrow bay across the straits from where we lay.

These are open and exposed waters, where temperatures drop much lower than in Southeast Alaska (the Ketchikan - Juneau area). Our crab boat, similar to the above, was brand new, strongly built, and very able. Yet many times, we had to anchor up and wait, knowing that to travel in such bitter temperatures and driving wind was to court disaster.

'See this spot? Puale Bay - its the windiest bay on the whole coast. Sure, you look at it, and think it's a great anchorage, you think you're safe if you manage to get in there, especially if it's your first time. But see these lakes up here, frozen maybe twenty feet thick, and this river valley? Well, you get the right conditions and it's worse than the Copper River flats. Thirty, forty, fifty below up there, and all that air gets real heavy and dense, and just starts running like water down that river valley, speeding up, picking up saltwater over the bay, makes kind of an ice mist, and you'll ice up unbelievably fast, even when you're <u>anchored up</u>, even close to the beach.'

"In the morning the wind seemed to have eased a little. Russell and suited up once again and with shovels and baseball bats, beat the ice off the anchor winch, got the heavy anchor aboard, and we set off around the point into Shelikof Strait.

"We gave it up after just fifteen minutes - every sea drove freezing spray onto our hull and house, and in just that short time we could feel the boat rolling noticeably slower from the added weight of the ice.

"After we got back into the harbor it took us <u>an hour</u> to "beat the ice off the anchor winch and bow just so we could even operate the anchor winch to lower the anchor."

A Fisherman's Tale

"Blow? We anchored up in one of those Shelikof Bays once, just once that that was enough for me. We anchored as close to the beach as we could with all the anchor wire we had out so we wouldn't drag. Then the wind started. First it blew our antennas off. After that it was howling so loud, I didn't dare go up into the pilothouse - I thought it was going to blow the windows out - just the wind!"

- a friend

Seattle Historical Society 17588

Where it all began - large King Crab with Bertha and Clarence Anderson, circa 1950. Anderson was captain of the pioneering crab boat Deep Sea. *The very sweet meat of these large crustaceans created a boom fishery that remains legendary in the Northwest to this day. Many fortunes were made by the fishermen who managed to contend successfully with the very difficult weather and sea conditions of the North Pacific and Bering Sea. The remarkable part about king crab is that when abundance is high they travel in* <u>herds.</u> *Sometimes fishermen encounter such volumes of crab that they wonder how many are being killed each time a heavy pot hits the ocean floor.*

Kodiak Island

One of the largest islands in the US, its early residents were the Koniag Indians, whom the Russians found to be particularly strong, cunning, and aggressive.

In the summer months, many Kodiak residents travel in small boats to remote locations to commercially fish for salmon.

Kodiak today is the home of a particularly hardy group of Alaskans, most of whom depend on fishing and live in or near the main town, also named Kodiak.

This town has had its share of natural disasters. On June 6, 1912, residents observed a curious looking fan shaped cloud, getting closer, higher and darker, with flashes of lightning inside the cloud. This was the tipoff that something very unusual was ocurring as lightning was a rare event. The sky got even darker and then small earthquakes could be felt, and finally ash began falling from Mt. Katmai, some 100 miles away.

Visibility dropped to almost nothing - people groped their way toward the foghorn of the Coast Guard Cutter *Manning*, and some 500 sought refuge aboard as the cutter steamed away from the shore and anchored in total blackness.

Flunking the bear test at Katmai National Park. After being briefed on bear etiquette, (Don't run; they'll think you're food!) this momma bear and two cubs appeared out of the woods, maybe 20 feet in front of my 14 year old son and myself. I began walking backwards, rapidly, but when I turned to check on my son, he was a hundred yards down the trail, kicking up dust and sprinting as fast as he could!

DAY THREE

Two days later, it seemed safe enough to return. The town was buried in almost two feet of ash and many roofs had collapsed. Ash piles may still be seen today in many parts of the Alaska peninsula.

Then in March of 1964, as the town was getting ready for the salmon season, it was shattered, like Seward and Anchorage, by the Good Friday Earthquake. After five minutes of terrifying shocks, the radio station broadcast warnings of possible tidal waves. Many people moved to higher ground, and watched in horror as a huge tsunami roared into the harbor, snapped mooring lines, threw boats up into the streets and knocked houses off their foundations. Over 200 vessels were lost or destroyed and canneries and cold storage plants simply disappeared. Fortunately, there were few fatalities.

After the earthquake devastated the town and essentially swept all the crab and fish plants into the bay, processors had to do something quickly. The easiest solution was to bring up ships and beach them with processing facilities built inside. The *Star of Kodiak*, an old WW II liberty ship, right by the docks, had a new life in Kodiak as a cannery.

Did you know? - At the time of the California gold rush, some entrepreneurs set up an ice company on Woody Island, on the east as you enter the harbor, and hired natives to cut and store some 10,000 tons of ice each winter in buildings with sawdust insulation. Before the Woody Island venture most of the ice used in California came around Cape Horn from Boston. The Alaskan ice cutters had horses to haul the ice and the first road ever built in Alaska was here to exercise the horses during the summer.

The business went well until mechanical refrigeration developed, but the makers of that machine paid the Alaskans not to ship ice for a while!

The most dangerous job in Alaska - crewing on a king crab vessel. The money was great, but the risks were high. Especially in the early years of the fishery, many older wooden vessels simply were no match for the weather of the Bering Sea in winter. Here a crewman throws a coil of buoy line. The other end is attached to a 700 pound crab pot. If the crewman's arm or clothing were to snag in the line, he would be quickly pulled overboard and dragged down to his death.

The King Crab Fishery

In the 1970s Alaskan fishermen found a truly remarkable concentration of these spidery crabs. When fishing was good, the big pots would come up with up to 2,000 pounds of crab after less than 24 hours in the water. Boats would get a 200,000# load in 48 hours! It was legendary money, but legendary work as well - when you were on the crab, 18 - 20 hours on deck a day were routine.

The heaviest concentration of crab was found in the Alaska Peninsula - Bering Sea - Aleutian Islands area. In the winter, this area has some of the stormiest weather in the world, and many, many able vessels and crews were lost to violent winds, big seas, and low temperatures.

Of the many disasters in the king crab fishery, none was more tragic and puzzling than the loss of the 123 foot sisterships AMERICUS and ALTAIR, in good weather on Valentine's Day, 1983. Both vessels, loaded with some 230 king crab pots, left Dutch Harbor, in the Aleutian Islands, and were never heard from again. Only the capsized hull of the AMERICUS, which sank shortly thereafter, gave a clue to their fate.

It took months of detective-like work to find the cause. After offloading some 28,000 gallons of fuel, and loading the heavy crab pots, the vessels,

Bart Eaton

The sea claims another. While riding out a severe Bering Sea Storm in 1978, several crab pots broke loose on deck aboard the brand new 150' Key West. It was too rough to try to secure the heavy pots, and one broke off a 12" air vent pipe, allowing water to flood into the vessel. Fortunately another crab boat was able to rescue all aboard.

unknown to anyone aboard, had such a high center of gravity that they were rolled upside down by mild seas.

Today all crab vessels operating in these waters carry a certificate specifying exactly how many pots they may carry and in what conditions. (In summer, with no danger of icing, they may carry substantially more pots than in winter.)

After almost two decades of spectacular growth both in catch and fleet size, the crab population crashed in the early 1980's. For a while the joke in Alaska banks was that when you started a new account, you got a crab boat free as a premium.

Fortunately it was in this period that foreign fishing effort in the rich waters of the Bering Sea was being reduced, creating much needed opportunities for the crab fleet to convert to trawling - towing funnel shaped nets for cod, pollock and other species.

Today the crab fishery continues, but at a much lower harvest level than in the boom days of the '70s and early '80s.

When it was big - crab fisherman Walter Kuhr and friends. For many, this was nothing less than another gold rush. Many crewmen worked their way up from deck work to owning large crab vessels, in just a few years.

Jo Keers, Kodiak Hist. Society P633.45 w/n

Most of the Kodiak fishing fleet ended up in the streets of town after the 1964 earthquake and tidal wave.

Kodiak native peoples, like those all along the northwest coast, had no immunities to the diseases brought by the first white visitors and suffered badly.

Most of Kodiak Island is unsettled and wild, with seasonal fishing settlements located in several of the larger bays. With less than a hundred miles of roads, many residents get around by boat or floatplane.

In the winter much of the rest of Kodiak Island is little visited. However, in the summer, men and women spread out all around the coast to persue various fishing activities, primarily for salmon. The primary method of salmon fishing in the Kodiak area is purse seining, and seiners here are generally shallower and smaller than the seiners used in Southeast Alaska - the Ketchikan - Juneau area.

Editor's Choice: *Working On The Edge* by Spike Walker is a fascinating tale of a young man working in the Kodiak king crab fleet. Walker chronicles the boom years and the Gold Rush sort of opportunities that changed the life of many a young crewmember. He also somberly notes the loss of many fine boats and crews.

Commercial fishing today - Kodiak area fishermen, like those all throughout Alaska, enjoyed high prices and strong salmon runs during much of the 1980s as much of their harvest was purchased by Japanese buyers. In recent years, however, the slump in the Japanese economy has produced a ripple effect in salmon prices. Most fishermen are receiving substantially less for their salmon than a decade ago.

Did you know? Tidal wave is a misnomer. The proper name is tsunami, and they are essentially shock waves emanating from an undersea earthquake. In deep water they are tiny - perhaps a foot high - and travel at high speeds - up to 500 MPH. It is when they reach shallow waters that they become giant waves sometimes 100 feet high or more.

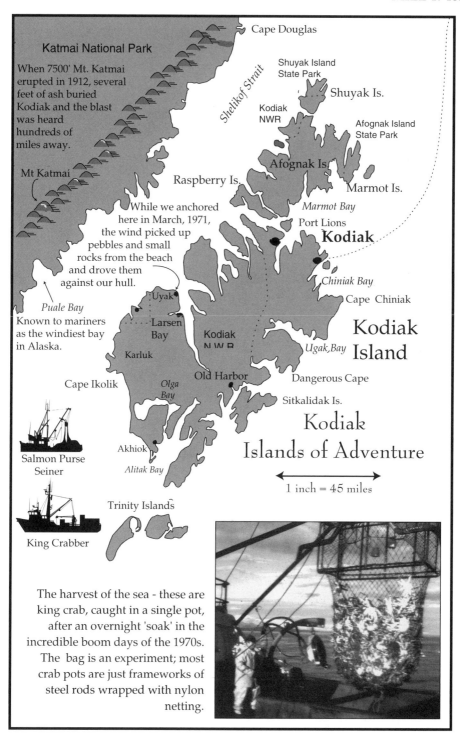

Katmai National Park

When 7500' Mt. Katmai erupted in 1912, several feet of ash buried Kodiak and the blast was heard hundreds of miles away.

Mt Katmai

Cape Douglas

Shelikof Strait

Shuyak Island State Park

Shuyak Is.

Kodiak NWR

Afognak Island State Park

Afognak Is.

Marmot Is.

Raspberry Is.

Marmot Bay

Port Lions

Kodiak

While we anchored here in March, 1971, the wind picked up pebbles and small rocks from the beach and drove them against our hull.

Chiniak Bay

Cape Chiniak

Puale Bay
Known to mariners as the windiest bay in Alaska.

Uyak

Larsen Bay

Kodiak N W R

Ugak Bay

Kodiak Island

Karluk

Cape Ikolik

Olga Bay

Old Harbor

Dangerous Cape

Sitkalidak Is.

Salmon Purse Seiner

Akhiok

Alitak Bay

Kodiak Islands of Adventure

1 inch = 45 miles

Trinity Islands

King Crabber

The harvest of the sea - these are king crab, caught in a single pot, after an overnight 'soak' in the incredible boom days of the 1970s. The bag is an experiment; most crab pots are just frameworks of steel rods wrapped with nylon netting.

The traditional bidar-ka, used by natives both in Kodiak and the Aleutian Islands. Note rain gear made of seal intestines sewn together, and shelf for coiled line.

UW NA 1995

Kodiak Area tribes have joined together to create a cultural center in downtown Kodiak.

Russian Kodiak - this town was a major base for the early Russian merchants and settlers who were primarily interested in sea otter pelts. This was not a gentle period in Kodiak history - if the hunters of a particular village resisted hunting sea otters, the village might be destroyed by the Russians.

Of course, like other native groups up and down the coast, the Alutiiq people of Kodiak Island had no immunities to the diseases brought by the Russians and other traders. This combination of disease and murderous tactics to induce sea otter hunting took a heavy toll on the native population.

Kodiak became the first capital of Russian America (the capital was later shifted to Sitka). Today the biggest reminder of the Russian period is the Russian Orthodox religion, a major influence throughout much of western Alaska.Look for the blue onion domes of the Holy Ressurection Orthodox Church, just a block from the

Kodiak Excursions
Custom Kodiak and Russian Heritage Tour - 3.5 hrs.
Kodiak by Kayak - 2.5 hrs.
Kodiak Island Overview - 3.5 to 3.75 hrs.
Kodiak Island and Bear Viewing Flight - 3.25 hrs.
Kodiak Island Fishing - 5 to 5.5 hrs.
Kodiak Wildlife Quest - 3.75 to 4 hrs.
WWII "Grumman Goose" - Flightseeing - 2.25 hrs.
For more information, please visit your ship's excursion desk.

docks. It is one of many active Russian Orthodox parishes in the state.

A Native Cultural Renaissance - in 1995, the eight Kodiak Island area native groups formed the Alutiiq Heritage Foundation as part of an effort to celebrate and preserve their native traditions.

The Foundation created the Alutiiq Museum and Archaeological Repository, located on Mission Road, just two blocks from the docks. Featuring an excellent display gallery as well as a gift shop, it is well worth visiting. If your schedule allows, you may also wish to see the Kodiak Alutiiq Dancers perform. Dancing, once discouraged by missionaries, is now part of this cultural renaissance, as these tribes celebrate their past.

Downtown Kodiak has most attractions within easy walking distance. In addition to those listed above, the Baranof Museum, just across the street from the visitor information center has a good display on Kodiak's Russian and early American history.

How far did the the tidal wave carry boats? Three blocks from the harbor on Mill Bay Road, is a plaque marking where the 86' power scow *Selief* ended up after the water receded. Patched up and refloated, she is still working and fishing up and down the coast.

Want to see sea lions up close? You'll probaby find a few hanging out near around the shore, just outside the harbor. Don't expect cute - these brutes are big, smelly and sometimes aggressive. Keep your distance!

If you haven't been flightseeing yet, consider doing it here. As well as having an excellent chance at seeing some bears, you'll get a unique perspective on this spectacular area.

DAY THREE

Since being protected by Federal law, some sea lions have become aggressive toward people - be careful!

Traveler's Guide to Work Boats

TUG. Size: 40 to 150 feet. Range: all waters. Distinguishing features: High bow, low deck aft with tow winch behind deckhouse. Gear: none. Crew: 3 to 8. History: Many supplies arrive in Alaska by barge and tug, especially in Southesat Alaska. During the rush to get pipeline and drilling supplies to Prudhoe Bay in 1975, tugs were chartered from as far away as Louisiana.

SELF-LOADING LOG BARGE. Size: 200 to 400 feet. Range: Puget Sound to Southeast Alaska. Distinguishing features: Twin cranes on tall wide supporting structures. Gear: none. Crew: 2 to 4. History: For long distances or rough water, towing logs in traditional rafts is unsuitable. These barges and their cousin, the self dumping barge (ballast tanks flooded so that logs slide off) are used to reduce losses on these routes.

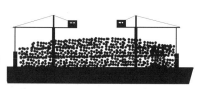

WOOD-CHIP BARGE. Size: 200 to 300 feet. Range: Puget Sound to Southeast Alaska. Distinguishing features: High-sided barges with chips heaped and spilling over, sometimes loaded so that barge is almost awash. Gear: none. Crew: none. History: A generation ago all sawmills had sawdust burners. Today environmental regulations and the demand for chips for paper making and chemical production have changed this waste into a valuable product.

TRACTOR TUG. Size: 100 to 160 feet. Range: Puget Sound. Distinguishing features: Pilothouse is more amidships than other tugs. Gear: none. Crew: 4 to 6. History: This unusual tug doesn't have a propeller. Rotating vertical fins beneath the vessel propel it and allow it to move sideways or turn in its own length. Used frequently for oil tanker escort duty in Puget Sound.

HALIBUT SCHOONER. Size: 60 to 100 feet. Range: Washington coast to Bering Sea. Distinguishing features: Two masts, setting chute, baiting shack on stern. Gear: longline for halibut or black cod. Crew: 5 to 8. History: Some of these fine vessels were built in the 1920s or earlier. They fish by setting strings of baited hooks in deep water.

KING CRABBER. Size: 80 to 160 feet or more. Range: Bering Sea and Aleutian Islands, occasionally in Southeast Alaska. Distinguishing features: articulating cranes for moving pots. Gear: large metal pots (up to 8-by-8-by-3 feet) fished in deep water for king crab. Crew: 4 to 6. History: In the early 1980s some crewmen made $100,000 in a three-month season. Today fewer crab mean harder times.

POWER SCOW. Size: 70 to 100 feet. Range: throughout Alaska. Distinguishing features: Boxy shape, pilothouse and living quarters aft, twin booms. Gear: used as salmon tenders. Crew: 3 to 7. History: Many were built for World War II Aleutian Campaign. Popular for their shallow draft and large capacity. One, the *Balaena*, even has room below decks for a salt water hot tub.

PURSE SEINER. Size: 35 to 58 feet. Range: throughout Alaska. Distinguishing features: Round power block hung on boom, carries or tows large skiff. Gear: encircling net. Crew: 3 to 7. History: Used for herring in spring, salmon in summer. Many vessels built to Alaska-limit rule: 58 feet maximum overall length.

Traveler's Guide to Work Boats

SALMON TROLLER. Size: 30 to 50 feet. Range: northern California to Yakutat, Alaska. Distinguishing features: tall trolling poles. Gear: lures and baits. Crew: 1 to 2. History: In the 1980s, Alaska established two different troll licenses. Power trollers have mechanical gurdies or winches to raise and lower the lines. Hand trollers, which display HT plaques, must crank lines up and down by hand.

SALMON GILL-NETTER. Size: 28 to 45 feet. Range: Columbia River to Bristol Bay, Alaska. Distinguishing features: Net drum or reel mounted in stern with vertical rollers aft. Gear: surface drift gill net, 16 feet deep by 900 to 1,200 feet long. Crew: 1 to 4. History: Many gill-netters bring their families for the season, especially in Southeast Alaska.

DRUM SEINER. Size: 50 to 75 feet. Range: Puget Sound to northern British Columbia. Distinguishing features: Large steel drum or reel mounted aft, sometimes recessed; large skiff towed astern or aboard. Gear: encircling net. Crew: 4 to 7. History: Prohibited in Alaska. In British Columbia, fishermen may not have engines in skiff.

SCHOONER-STYLE TENDER (HOUSE AFT). Size: 60 to 100 feet. Range: throughout British Columbia and Alaska. Distinguishing features: Carries no fishing gear; usually displays fish company identifying sign, such as "Icicle Seafoods." Gear: none. Crew: 2 to 5. History: Vessels vary; some date to the 1920s, when they were built to service fish traps (outlawed in 1958).

FLOATER (FLOATING PROCESSOR). Size: 150 to 600 feet. Range: Gulf of Alaska and Bering Sea. Occasionally seen in Southeast Alaska. Distinguishing features: Cluttered superstructures with cranes, housing trailers, and so forth. Sometimes has vessels unloading alongside. Gear: none. Crew: 20 to 200 or more. History: Much Alaska fishing occurs remote from town-based processing plants. Floating processors can move from fishery to fishery.

FACTORY TRAWLER. Size: 120 to 400 feet. Range: Bering Sea and Aleutian Islands. Distinguishing features: High sides, large gantry and net reel aft. Gear: trawl nets for cod and pollock. Crew: 20 to 150. History: Before the mid-1980s, foreign factory trawlers dominated the Bering Sea. Today, American-owned vessels have displaced the foreign fleets.

HOUSE-FORWARD TENDER. Size: 50 to 100 feet. Range: throughout Alaska. Distinguishing features: No fishing gear, but has weighing or pumping equipment aboard as well as fish company sign. Gear: none. Crew: 3 to 5. History: During the July peak of the salmon season, hundreds of tenders of all sorts work the waters of Alaska. Look for "CASH" signs, signifying buyers who don't have their own fleets.

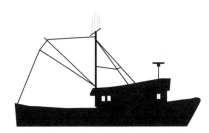

HOUSE-AFT CRABBER. Size: 80 to 200 feet. Range: Bering Sea and Aleutians. Occasionally in Southeast Alaska as tenders. Distinguishing features: Tall house aft with deep well deck forward and articulated cranes for handling crab pots. Gear: large metal pots (up to 8-by-8-by-3 feet) fished in deep water for king crab. Crew: 4 to 8 or more. History: Popular design allows skipper to see crew working; evolved from halibut schooners.

Halibut Longlining

Iron men in wooden ships were the mainstays of the halibut fishery. For generations, Norwegian-descent fishermen set out from northwest ports in graceful halibut schooners for long trips, sometimes almost to Siberia. Baiting and hand coiling miles of gear set out along the bottom, hauling it back, and cleaning the fish as they came aboard made for 18- and 20-hour days on deck. The stamina of these men was legendary along the waterfront.

In the early 1990's the joke in the fishing business is that "all you need to be a halibut fisherman is a few free weekends." By 1994 the halibut season had been reduced to a few 12- to 48-hour "openings," or periods vessels were allowed to fish. This wasn't because of a shortage of fish, but rather that a huge fleet was taking the quota.

A traditional Halibut schooner.

It was a poor system. The catch, coming all at once, overwhelmed processors, and gear tangled on the grounds. Finally in 1995, fishermen were given quota shares according to their catch history, and were allowed to fish whenever it was convenient for them.

The northwest halibut resource is strong. On occasion, during a 24-hour or 48-hour opening, vessels have caught more than 50,000 pounds. Today fishermen receive prices in the $2 to $3 a pound range for their catch. Several species of cod are also targeted by longline fishermen.

LONGLINER'S DICTIONARY:

BECKET: a short piece of line knotted into the ground line, into which the gangion is attached.

CHICKEN: small halibut.

CIRCLE HOOK: efficient style introduced in 1980s.

GANGION (pronounced ganyon): leader between ground line and hook.

SKATE: unit of longline gear, usually 300 fathoms long (1,800 feet) with hooks every 21 feet.

SNAP GEAR: system using friction snaps to attach leaders to ground line.

STRING: 10 skates tied end to end, with anchors and buoys at either end.

WHALE: very large halibut.

Purse Seining

Each spring thousands of college-age young men walk the docks of Puget Sound ports seeking their ideal summer job—a crew job on an Alaska-bound purse seiner. The lucky ones begin work in late May or early June—painting and readying the graceful 58-footers, overhauling and building their expensive nets, and sailing north.

The end of a set; hauling the bag aboard.

Seining is a complicated operation requiring coordination between the seiner, the large skiff, and a four- or five-man crew.

"Let 'er go!" cries the skipper and the crew pulls the pin on a shackle, releasing the skiff, which begins towing the net off the seiner's stern. The seiner then makes a wide curving turn, typically "hooking" the net off a point, to catch fish traveling with the tide.

At the appropriate time the skiff will circle back, passing the end of the net to the larger vessel. Next the crew winches in both ends of the purse line, pulling up the net's bottom and transforming it into a sort of basket from which there is no escape. As the net is hauled aboard with the power block, the basket becomes smaller, until the fish can be easily dipped aboard.

In the late 1980s, when fish prices were booming, a crewman might make $5,000 to $10,000 in a good season on a top boat.

Salmon purse seiners catch primarily pink and chum salmon.

PURSE SEINER'S DICTIONARY:
BUNT: the end of the net where the fish become concentrated.
HUNG UP: net hung on object or snagged on bottom.
MONEY FISH: sockeye salmon, much more valuable than pink salmon.
POWER BLOCK: hydraulically operated, boom-mounted pulley or sheave which pulls the net from the water, to stack on deck. Revolutionized seining.
WATER HAUL: a no-fish set.

Salmon Gill-netting

Imagine taking your family commercial fishing in Alaska in a nicely fitted out 40-footer — gill-netting three or four days a week and having the rest to explore, sports-fish, beachcomb, and so forth. This is what many men do, fishing the simplest of nets — a floating vertical wall whose meshes are sized to snag just behind the gills of traveling fish. A gill-netter will roll the net off his drum into the water in a likely spot, wait for a few minutes to several hours, and then wind it back onto the drum, standing in the stern and stopping the drum to "pick" fish as they appear.

Although the gear looks simple, fishing it in the tides of the region is tricky. The best fishermen know where to set their nets at each stage of the tide.

To fish for salmon commercially in Alaska you must buy a "limited entry permit" from someone who wants to leave the fishery. Permit prices range from about $65,000 for a southeastern Alaska gill-net permit to $350,000 or so for a False Pass (Alaska Peninsula) gill-net permit. Permit prices fluctuate with the prosperity of each fishery.

GILL-NETTER'S DICTIONARY:

A FRONT ROW SEAT: setting your net right on the district boundary just as the fish are coming in with the tide.

BACKLASH: when a net snags and rips as it comes off the reel.

GETTING LACED OR CORKED: having another fishermen set his net too close to yours.

GETTING TRASHED OR KELPED UP: getting a net full of kelp or driftwood.

HITS: fish visibly hitting and becoming gilled in the net.

SOAKER: keeping one's net in the water for several hours or more.

Salmon Trolling

More than any other Alaskan fishery, salmon trolling is an art. The fisherman must choose among many styles and colors of lures or bait for the one just right for the particular time of day, depth of water, color of sky, and other factors.

Identified by their tall trolling poles, vertical for traveling, lowered to 45 degrees for fishing, these ubiquitous craft use hooks and lines to catch king, silver, sockeye, chum, and pink salmon. Some of the larger boats are "freezer trollers," able to make longer trips, not limited by how long their ice lasts. Most boats, however, make trips of up to a week and deliver a premium-quality iced fish. Most trollers use small power-operated drums to haul in their lines. Some smaller vessels, displaying "HT" signs, may use only hand power for this task.

Although net-fishing vessels are restricted to certain areas, trollers pretty much have the entire region to choose from when their season is open.

The troller's life is solitary, at times even spiritual. These fishermen, especially those who fish offshore, become much more separated from the cares of the land than their net-fishing brethren.

TROLLER'S DICTIONARY:

BIG SCORE: good catch.

FAIRWEATHER GROUND: popular offshore trolling area northwest of Cape Spencer.

FLASHER: a large (to 12 inches long) rectangular, shiny, metallic device to attract fish.

HOOTCHIE: plastic squid lure, available in many colors.

SKUNK DAY: no fish.

SMILIE: very large king salmon.

Traveler's Guide to Marine Mammals

BELUGA WHALE. Size: to 18 feet. Range: Arctic waters to Bristol Bay, Cook Inlet and Turnagain Arm, Alaska. Distinguishing features: Adults are pure white; juveniles are gray. Likes coastal waters, especially rivers. Especially likes codfish, but also crabs and mussels. Frequently seen in groups. History: Nicknamed "sea canary" because of extensive vocalizing.

BOWHEAD WHALE. Size: 45 to 60 feet, weight to 100 tons or more. Range: Arctic waters. Distinguishing features: Very large head, black with white chin. Plankton eater, skims schools with top of head just above surface. History: A staple of Eskimo diet. Once hunted extensively for its baleen, used in corsets.

HUMPBACK WHALE. Size: 30 to 50 feet, weight to 40 tons. Range: Throughout Alaska and British Columbia in summer. Winters in warm waters. Distinguishing features: Black with white throat and belly, long tail flipper with irregular edges. Knobs and bumps on head and flippers. Likes to breach, or jump dramatically. History: Much studied, commonly seen, sings hauntingly.

GRAY WHALE. Size: 30 to 50 feet. Range: coastal Arctic to Mexico. Distinguishing features: Black with white spots and blotches. Only large whale with overhanging upper jaw. Sometimes pokes head vertically out of water; also breaches. History: Calves its young in one of several lagoons in Baja California after annual migration. Whale watchers count them on their journey.

ORCA, OR KILLER WHALE. Size: to 30 feet. Range: global, especially coastal. Distinguishing features: Bold black and white markings, dramatic tall dorsal fin, especially on male. History: Before 1970s thought to be dangerous to man. Captured whales showed remarkable intelligence and docility. Many in aquariums. Travel and live in pods, or groups.

STELLER'S, OR NORTHERN SEA LION. Size: to 13 feet and 2,400 pounds. Range: California to Alaska; often found in large numbers at remote rookeries. Distinguishing features: Large size, visible ears, bad breath, and occasional loud roaring. History: Now protected by law, these large mammals are commonly seen along the Alaska coast. Eats fish, particularly salmon, to the annoyance of man.

HARBOR SEAL. Size: 4 to 6 feet. Range: Throughout most of the northwest coast. Distinguishing features: Grayish with spots; the most common seal in Alaska. Has no visible ears; clumsy on land. History: Fish and shellfish eaters, they frequently steal salmon from fishermen's nets and lines. Protected by law..

DALL PORPOISE: Size: 4 to 7 feet. Range: Throughout most northwest waters. Distinguishing features: Black body with dramatic white markings, small triangular dorsal fin. Sometimes mistaken for killer whales, but are much smaller with lower dorsal fin. Usually travels in groups. History: Likes to ride the bow waves of fishing and other craft.

Alaska History Time Line

30,000 B.C.	Migratory hunters from Asia move across the land bridge from Siberia to Alaska, spread, and settle North America. They evolve into three main groups: Aleuts, Eskimos, and Indians.
8,000 B.C.	As the Ice Age ends, the rising ocean covers the land bridge. An ice bridge forms. Migration slows.
1741	Vitus Bering and Aleksei Chirikov land in Alaska on an expedition from Russia and bring back 800 sea otter skins. Bering is lost on the return trip. The fur traders—*promyshlenniki*—begin outfitting trading expeditions, and the rush is on.
1778	British Captain James Cook explores the Alaskan coast, seeking a Northwest Passage to the Atlantic.
1791-5	British Captain George Vancouver with two ships explores and charts the Northwest Coast exhaustively but finds no Northwest Passage.
1799	Aleksandr Baranov consolidates Russian possession of Alaska with a fort and trading base at Sitka.
1867	Secretary of State William Seward buys Alaska from Czarist Russia for 2 cents an acre: $7.2 million. The fur resource has been used up. Purchase is hailed as "Seward's Folly."
1879	Naturalist John Muir canoes throughout Southeast Alaska and discovers Glacier Bay. (When Vancouver had passed through there was no bay; it was full of ice.) Muir's reports inaugurate tourism to the territory.
1896-1900	Gold strike on a Yukon River tributary brings 100,000 people to Alaska and the Yukon Territory.
1922	Roy Jones makes the first floatplane flight up the Inside Passage; small aircraft revolutionize travel in the bush.
1925	A 674-mile dogsled relay brings diphtheria vaccine to Nome.
1942	Japan invades the Aleutian Islands. The Alaska Highway project is begun to move defense supplies.
1959	Alaska becomes the 49th state.
1964	Good Friday earthquake.
1968	10 billion barrels of oil are discovered at Prudhoe Bay.
1977	First oil flows through an 800-mile engineering feat, the Alaska Pipeline.
1980	Alaska National Interest Lands and Conservation Act (ANILCA) is passed, establishing new parks and settling Alaska Native land claims.
1989	Tanker *Exxon Valdez* rams Bligh Reef, Prince William Sound, creating a massive oil spill and years of work for hundreds of lawyers.

Living With Whales

Once hunted for oil and bone, today the whales of the northwest coast are recognized as being unusually intelligent, even gentle creatures. The most common whales you are apt to see on your cruise are orcas, or killer whales, and humpbacks. From a distance, whales are apt to be spotted by the distinctive white spout, as they exhale when surfacing. Flip Nicklin, Minden Pictures

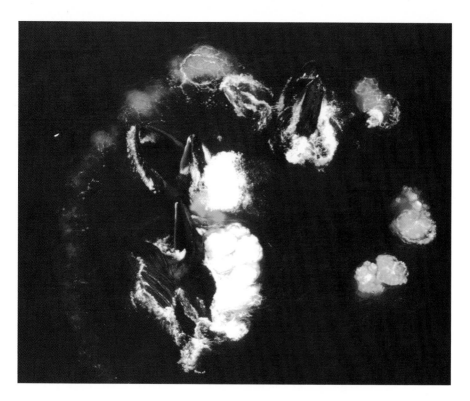

Bubble feeding - by circling around a school of fish, and exhaling, a curtain of bubbles is created, which serves to herd the fish into a compact bunch. The whales then surface through the middle, mouths open to eat. Mitsuaki Iwago, Minden Pictures

Humpbacks

Commonly seen throughout British Columbia and Alaska in summer, they migrate south and west in the winter, frequently to Hawaii. Adults are up to 50 feet long and 40 tons in weight. Distinguishing marks are white throat and belly, and knobs and bumps on head and flippers.

Gregarious, they frequently are seen in groups, sometimes using a technique called bubble feeding to herd and feed on herring or other small fish.

Their most dramatic behavior is breaching, or jumping clear out of the water. A 30 or 40 ton whale hitting the water makes a huge splash which may be seen at long distances.

They seem to particularly congregate at places where the current runs rapidly around a point. Traditional places for seeing whales are Clarence Straits, north of Ketchikan, Snow Pass, **mile 725**, Point Baker, **mile 745**, Frederick Sound, Stephens Passage, Point Adolphus, **mile 1000**, and Glacier Bay. Look for their distinctive white spout.

Mother and calf, in waters off Hawaii. Flip Nicklin, Minden Pictures

Whales are very gregarious, often traveling and feeding in groups and singing to each other with their haunting melodic sounds. Flip Nicklin, Minden Pictures

Orcas

Easily recognized by their tall black tails, orcas are seen throughout the Alaska cruise area. The best places to look for them are in western Johnstone Strait, where they seem to congregate to feed on salmon in the summer. Frans Lanting, Minden Pictures

Orcas travel in family groups called pods. They can be aggressive feeders, often almost beaching themselves as they chase young seals or other prey into shallow water. Frans Lanting, Minden Pictures

Over the past 25 years a number of orcas have been captured from the British Columbia - Puget Sound Area for sale to aquariums all over the world. Recently a growing awareness of the intelligence of these remarkable mammals has led to the banning of such captures. Frans Lanting, Minden Pictures

Somewhere on the Arctic coast, a stranded beluga waits for the tide to come in. These whales particularly like shallow rivers and strandings are not uncommon. They have learned to rest quietly while waiting, so as not to attract the attention of bears and other predators. Flip Nicklin, Minden Pictures

Belugas

Nicknamed sea canaries for their extensive vocalising, these small (to 20') whales are usually found along the shores of the Bering Sea and Arctic Oceans. However, they frequently stray as far south as Cook Inlet and Turnagain Arm during the summer, and can often be seen chasing schools of salmon.

Christine Cox illustration

John Muir and Dog, on Brady Glacier, 1880

"...He looked up along the row of notched steps I had made, as if fixing them in his mind, then with a nervous spring he whizzed up and passed me out on the level ice and ran and cried and rolled about fairly hysterical in the sudden revulsion from the depth of despair to triumphant joy."

— John Muir, *Travels in Alaska*

Christine Cox illustration

Skagway, Winter 1897

For some, the challenge of the north - the cold, the difficult conditions, was simply too much:

"It was a real cold night. We walked along in the snow and we come to a fellow setting on the back of a Yukon sled. Yep, he was setting there in the middle of the road talking to hisself. His head was down on his hands. He looked plumb played out. He never seen us; he just went on talking to hisself. Over and over he'd say: "It's hell. Yes; multiply it by ten and then multiply that by ten, and that ain't half as bad as this is. Yes, it's hell..."

—Martha Mckeown, *The Trail Led North*

What You'll Catch

At most stops in Southeast Alaska, charter boats are available to take parties sportfishing. Typically these boats are modern, comfortable cruisers, able to take parties of up to six. Depending on the season and where the "bite" is, vessels may run an hour or more to get on the fish.

Most fishermen like to target on king and silver salmon. Kings, running in size up to 60 pounds and larger, are caught from May through August with the best fishing generally in the first half of the season. Silvers run smaller, typically 6 to 10 pounds, and are available from mid- June through September. Pink salmon are smaller still, 3 to 5 pounds, but run in great numbers, beginning around mid- June.

"Will I catch a fish?" If you just want a king and won't settle for anything less, the answer might be maybe. But especially in July and August when the silver and pink runs are strong, many people easily catch their limit (6 fish per person). If for some reason, the salmon aren't running that particular day, many skippers will shift over to target on tasty lingcod, rockfish or halibut, so rarely would you come back empty-handed.

Suzanne Billings

A morning's outing—Alaska's abundant salmon resource means even the inexperienced usually catch fish.

"What if I'm not very experienced?" Don't worry—there are a lot of fish in Alaska, and charter skippers are quick teachers. Many people who have never fished before catch their limit.

"What's it like?" As much as anything else, going out on a charter boat for a day is a chance to get out and see, close and at first hand, some of the most abundant marine life and most dramatic scenery in the world. Whales, dolphins, seals, and eagles are all common sights to the charter fisherman. Bring your camera! Many skippers also throw in an informative harbor tour on the way out to the grounds.

"What do I do with the fish?" In most towns, services are available to freeze, store and ship your fish. Some cruise ships are able to freeze fish as well, and most will happily cook and serve a passenger's fish. Typical prices run from $100 to 150 per person for a day's outing.

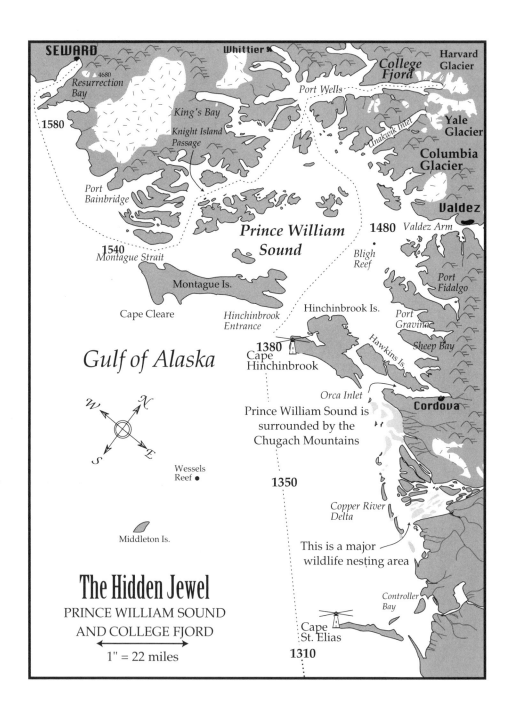

SEWARD

Whittier

College Fjord

Harvard Glacier

4680
Resurrection Bay

Port Wells

1580

King's Bay

Knight Island Passage

Anakwik Inlet

Yale Glacier

Columbia Glacier

Port Bainbridge

Prince William Sound

Valdez

1480   Valdez Arm

Bligh Reef

Port Fidalgo

1540
Montague Strait

Montague Is.

Cape Cleare

Hinchinbrook Entrance

Hinchinbrook Is.

Port Gravina

Sheep Bay

Hawkins Is.

Gulf of Alaska

1380
Cape Hinchinbrook

Orca Inlet

Cordova

W   N   E   S

Prince William Sound is surrounded by the Chugach Mountains

Wessels Reef

1350

Copper River Delta

Middleton Is.

This is a major wildlife nesting area

The Hidden Jewel
PRINCE WILLIAM SOUND
AND COLLEGE FJORD

1" = 22 miles

Controller Bay

Cape St. Elias

1310

CHAPTER 3

The Hidden Jewel

COLLEGE FJORD AND PRINCE WILLIAM SOUND

"Tracing shining ways through fiord and sound, past forests and waterfalls, islands and mountains and far azure headlands, it seems as if surely we must at length reach the very paradise of the poets, the abode of the blessed. "

—*John Muir,* Travels in Alaska.

DAY ONE
EVENING

Y our journey begins in steep sided Resurrection Bay, **mile 1590**. (For orientation purposes places along your route have been numbered in **miles from Seattle**.) If you've seen *The Hunt for Red October*, the landscape may seem familiar - the first scene of the submarine slipping out of a wintry fiord, was filmed here. About 45 minutes after leaving the dock, your ship will pass west of **Fox Island, mile 1590S**. Today the island has a small guest facililty on it used by a tour boat operator. But it was here that noted artist and author Rockwell Kent spent the winter of 1918-1919 with his nine-year old son.

Kent was a true renaissance man and adventurer. In addition to being a talented artist, he had a penchant for living close to the edge. His adventures, some of which they were lucky to survive, are in a powerful account, along with some of his excellent woodcuts and drawings, published as "*Wilderness, A Quiet Adventure in Alaska*" by Geo. Putnam & Sons, New York, 1920.

The Kents came to Seward seeking an isolated place to winter, and by chance encountered a rough hewn homesteader, who offered to share his island with them.

PASSENGERS FROM ANCHORAGE-HOMER-KODIAK: THESE TIME NOTATIONS ARE FOR SEWARD-VANCOUVER PASSENGERS. USE POSITION INFORMA-TION IN YOUR SHIP'S NEWSPAPER

There are several sea lion rookeries in the Resurrection Bay area

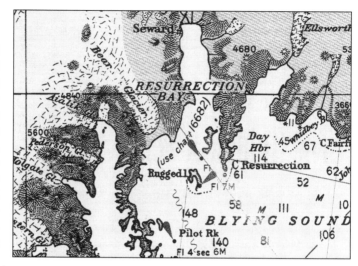

Seward (top) and surrounding rugged coast. Almost all the coast to the left or west of Resurrection Bay is part of Kenai Fjords Natinal Park. The park is largely wilderness with few visitor facilities. Most visitors visit the park in an excursion boat from Seward.

Their boat was a small dory and they had a few dicey moments on their occasional trips to Seward:

> "The aspect of the day had become ominous. The mountainous land appeared blue black, the sea a light but brillant yellow green. Over the water the wind blew in furious squalls raising a surge of white caps and a dangerous chop. I was now rowing with all my strength, forseeing clearly the possibility of disaster for us, scanning with concern the terrible leeward shore with its line of breakers and stern cliffs."
>
> — Rockwell Kent, WIlderness, *A Quiet Adventure in Alaska*

Mariners: use caution; Kent's experience is not unique. Resurrection Bay is well known for its violent williwaw winds.

During their winter on the island they learned the true meaning of cold. A bucket of water left in the kitchen of their small log cabin would be frozen in the morning, even though the wood stove was going!

Have a good look around when you swing east after passing **Cape Resurrection**. The next 35 miles of coast is a rugged landscape with glaciers coming close to the water in the bays and the land rising steeply to mile high peaks. This coast, like most you will be traveling past for the next week, is almost totally unsettled, a vast de facto wilderness.

60 miles after leaving Seward, your ship passes between Montague and Knight Islands and enters wide and many-armed Prince William Sound, an area about the size of some small states. Except for three towns, Cordova, Valdez, and Whittier, and a few settlements, the area is mostly

AUTHOR'S NOTE: THE FOLLOWING JOURNAL ENTRY, LIKE ALL THE *Dawn Princess* ENTRIES IN THIS BOOK, IS FROM A NORTHBOUND VANCOUVER TO SEWARD VOYAGE.

DAY ONE
EVENING

"Dawn Princess **Knight Island Passage, September 12, 1997,** 8 p.m. - Away, away! Tonight the last dinner with our evening group, once strangers, now friends. Yet still, beyond my balcony, the wild beauty of this land beckons. When all is packed, I turn off the lights, put on a jacket and sit outside on my balcony, watching the dark islands and channels slide past.

"The powerful images of the afternoon are sharply etched in my mind. The huge piece of Harvard Glacier, toppling slowly into the sea with a hollow, booming roar.

"I imagine a fall afternoon, decades before, with a big square rigger like the *Star of Shetland*, sliding down the channel with a full load of canned salmon in the evening breeze.

"Finally all is darkness beyond our ship, and I think of old John Muir, scribbling in his Glacier Bay journal, a century and a quarter ago: '..whatever the future might have in store, the treasures we had gained this glorious morning would enrich our lives forever.'"

PLEASE NOTE
THE TIMES GIVEN IN THIS BOOK ARE ONLY APPROXIMATE, DUE TO THE VAGARIES OF WEATHER, CURRENTS, AND OTHER FACTORS WHICH MAY AFFECT YOUR SHIP'S SCHEDULE.

uninhabited, a dramatic island archipelago wilderness with many active glaciers.

It was here that the square-rigged ships full of Chinese workers and Italian and Norwegian fishermen came to build canneries and harvest salmon in the earliest days of the salmon fishery in Prince William Sound.

There are a few isolated native villages in Prince William Sound.

"The Chinamen was always getting hurt bad, handling cans. The muriatic acid used in soldering cans will eat holes clear into the bone. So I always kept the carbolic acid ready. Then when a boy had an acid burn I'd mix the carbolic acid with sweet oil and test it on my own hand. When it would eat the flesh and burn my hand, I'd pour it into the places where the acid was eating on the boys. I've seen Johnny Troyer, of the Pacific Metal Works, take a knife and cut the flesh out of his boys' hands, but that's too blamed hard. It don't hurt so much to eat it out with acid."

— *Martha Ferguson McKeown,* The Trail Led North

Mohai 16233

Asian laborers frequently traveled from the San Fran-cisco area each sum-mer aboard sailing ships to work in fish processing plants. Many canneries had seperate bunkhouses and even cooking areas for Asian workers, and cultural artifacts like old opium containers may still be found at old cannery sites.

Not OSHA approved - of course, as the quote shows – working conditions in those days were rough. Injuries were common, but often the same crews of work-ers and fishermen would return year after year. Sometimes the ships would bring up building supplies as well. They would put into a bay with a promising fish run, but with-out a cannery and then the crew would build the cannery in time for the season. It was a remarkable enterprise, one that continues strong to the present day.

When the ships arrived, little processing settlements, inhabited in the winter by only a watchman, would come alive for the summer months with the rattle of steam oper-ated canning equipment and the chatter of many lan-guages. In September, when the salmon runs were over, the cans and workers would be loaded aboard ship and sail hoisted for the run south to San Francisco or Puget Sound.

This relatively easy life was well-suited for these older ships, who by the 1920's had been largely displaced by steam powered vessels on most world trade routes. It wasn't until the late 1940's that the *Star of Shetland* or one of her sisterships hoisted aboard her last case of canned salmon, raised her sails, perhaps off Cordova in Prince

UW 8326

William Sound, or Karluk Spit, on Kodiak Island, or Ugashik in Bristol Bay, and disappeared into history.

Headed north - the Alaska salmon trade was the last liveli-hood for many old square riggers. Based in San Fran-cisco, they made sea-sonal round trips to Alaska until the 1940s. For the Bris-tol Bay bound fleet, a steam tug waited at tide swept Uni-mak Pass in case they needed a little help.

Early Explorers - Captain James Cook briefly explored this area in 1778. Setting out from England in the spring of 1768, he made three voyages to become one of the most famous explorers in history. Much of his work was spent in filling in the vast blank space on the map that was the Pacific Ocean. Exploring this section of the coast was to be his last hurrah. Returning to Hawaii, he was killed in a scuffle with natives in February of 1779.

But when Cook's men beached and caulked his ship in Prince William Sound, they traded a few fishhooks and trinkets for sea otter pelts, which were made into clothes to protect themselves against the cold. A year later, returning to England via China, the crew was amazed at what the worn out clothes fetched - $10,000! - and nearly mutinied, wanting to get back to Alaska and get more furs.

But it wasn't until 1794 that George Vancouver, one of Cook's lieutenant's, returned with his own exploring expedition, and more thoroughly explored and charted this region.

The principal occupation of area residents is commer-

DAY TWO
VERY EARLY

The classic sea otter position - floating on their back.

Brenda Carney

Prince William Sound is one of the best places to look for sea otters on your cruise.

Before regular ferry or mailboat service, remote settlements, and fox farms were often served by trading vessels with irregular schedules.

cial fishing, much of which is centered in **Cordova**, in Orca Inlet, the easternmost arm of Prince William Sound. Access to Cordova is only by ferry.

When the Harriman Alaska Expedition stopped at nearby **Orca** in June of 1899, they found a bustling cannery, staffed with Oriental workers, brought up on the nearby anchored full-rigged ship sailing ship from San Francisco.

The Sound teems with **sea life** such as sea lions, seal, and frequently humpback whales. Sea otters in particular have made a remarkable comeback. After being hunted almost to extinction, their population has risen to over 100,000 statewide.

Like Southeast Alaska, the Sound's islands were an excellent site for raising foxes for the fur trade. So called blue foxes were most in demand, and to get started a person need only buy a pair of adult foxes, set them out on a small island, make sure there were no predators and plenty of food, and let nature take its course. Generally fox farmers either raised them in cages, or let them grow wild, and trapped them once a year. Sometimes trading vessels made regular runs through the islands, trading furs for supplies. Usually located far from the nearest town, these fox farmers relied on the visits of these trading vessels:

A Fur Trader's Tale

"When the Depression came, I knew a lot of them fox farmers were desperate for supplies. Of course no one had any money, but I was able to talk the Seattle merchants out of a boatload of trading goods on credit.

"So off we went, through Prince William and through the

Problems with Sea Lions

Twenty years ago, a fisherman encountering a sea lion eating salmon out of his fishing net might be tempted to get his rifle. Today, however, sea lions, like all marine mammals in the US, are protected by law, with severe penalites for violators.

This has given rise to problems, particularly with California sea lions, like the one above. No longer having the experience of being harassed by man, some have become quite bold, even aggressively charging unwary fishermen.

Although large (up to a ton), these mammals can be suprisingly agile. The individual above jumped three feet up of out the water to land on this barge's narrow side deck.

However, population levels of another species, the Stellar sea lion, is dropping substantially, especially in the western Alaska - Bering Sea area. This reduction has alarmed biologists. If the decline warrants, the Stellar sea lion could possibly be classified as an endangered species. Such a designation would possibly severly impact commercial fishermen by forcing them to reduce catches of pollock, a species Stellar sea lions are thought to feed on.

islands out to west'ard...everyone was glad to see me come, so I was just trading supplies - flour, bullets, nails, etc - for fox furs.

DAY TWO
VERY EARLY

"So pretty soon I'm low on supplies, and I just know furs were't worth much, so we were pretty much in a pickle. But then when we got to Dutch [Dutch Harbor in the Aleutian Islands] there were telegrams waiting for me from all the major fur buyers in Seattle.

"Turns out Eleanor Roosevelt wore some fur trimmed coat at some blamed play or dinner and just that turned the whole fur market around, and I was able to unload them all, pay off what I owed and even make a little money."
— Fisherman Mike Jacobsen

The old Kennecott copper mine on the northwest side of Latouche Island has been abandoned.

Near **mile 1530** your ship will make a wide swing to the north into **Knight Island Passage**. Once many of these bays and islands were home to fox farms, herring

In these remote reaches of Prince William Sound, fish were sometimes processed on a 'floater' - floating cannery or freezer-ship such as the Moku. *Life aboard these ships some-times has its own unique problems. See story on right.*

If you see a vessel with a big 'cash' machine, it's not a floating bank, but an independent fish buying vessel or tender.

plants, prospectors cabins and the like.

If you see lights off to the west, off the port side of your ship after turning into Knight Island Passage, it will be the settlements around **Sawmill Bay**. Site of several fish processing plants in the past, today the bay is the site of a major aquaculture project to enhance salmon runs in the area.

A little later, you'll pass the **small flashing light** on **Pleiades Islands**. Directly ahead, as you begin your swing starboard is Chenega Island. If you look sharp along the shore closest to you, you may get a glimpse of the ruins of the abandoned village of **Chenega**. Largely destroyed in the 1964 earthquake, its residents moved to the Sawmill Bay area.

If you see floating ice in this vicinity, most likely it will be from Chenega Glacier, 10 miles west, at the head of Nassau fiord.

A Cash Buyer's Tale (see photo and caption above)

"The main trouble with cash buying is you end up carrying so much cash around. It's not so bad in a small boat, when you know all the gang pretty well. But in '68, we were cash buying with a floater with thirty guys onboard, and we didn't have a safe. Well, usually we had at least sixty or eighty thousand bucks in the cash box, so each night when I hit the

sack, I'd hide it in a different spot. You can imagine how many places there are to hide a cash box on a 120' floater! Then one morning, I forgot where I'd put it. *I couldn't find the cash box!* I was wild! I spent the whole day hunting for that sucker before I turned it up. I got a safe after that!"

— Bob Holmstrand

Upstairs in a cannery the crew keeps the cans feeding smoothly to the machines.

After it gets dark (if it does - at this latitude in mid summer, night is more like a long twilight), make sure you go up to one of the upper outside observation decks, find a place out of the wind, let your eyes get accustomed to the dark, and look around.

If you see a light at all, most likely it would be a fishing vessel, or perhaps a yacht, or a sports fisherman camping on the shore.

So why aren't more homes on all this great view property? This is the magic - and frustration - of Alaska. The vast majority of the land in the state is protected in some fashion, be it National Parks, National Forest, Wildlife Preserve. etc.

The magic is that we get the unique experience of being able to travel along this vast and wild land, and see it almost exactly as the first explorers saw it.

The frustration, especially for Alaska residents, is that there is so little land available to purchase and live on.

Set your alarm early - tomorrow morning around 6:30 a.m. you'll be entering College Fjord, a true hidden jewel.

DAY TWO
VERY EARLY

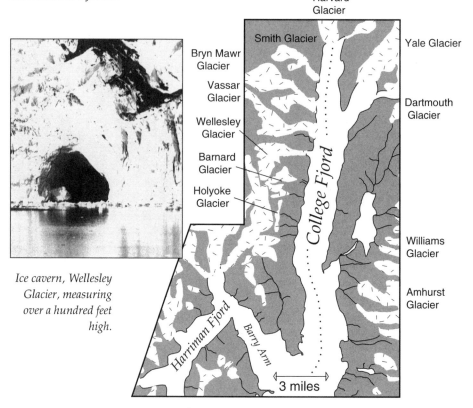

Ice cavern, Wellesley Glacier, measuring over a hundred feet high.

College Fjord

The hidden jewel of Prince William Sound is remote College Fjord. Within an eight mile stretch at the upper end of this fiord five major tidewaters reach the saltwater. While Glacier Bay has emerged from the ice so recently that substantial trees have not gained foothold close to the ice, College Fjord is a place where the forests and glaciers have coexisted for probably centuries.

"Dawn Princess **College Fjord, Sept. 12, 1997, 4 p.m.**
We slow for bears just after entering the fjord. They are halfway up a hillside eating berries, trying to stuff themselves before winter and hibernation. Four, perhaps five, depending on how good your eyes or binoculars are.

"We close the shore and approach Wellesley Glacier and a vast ice cave, perhaps a hundred fifty feet in diameter. But truly remarkable are the trees, growing close enough to the ice to give us a perspective we never got in Glacier Bay. This is big, big ice; the front of Wellesley must tower a good three hundred feet above the water just below it."

The result is a perspective on the great rivers of ice not seen in Glacier Bay. To see a glacier towering above the 100 foot tall trees of a spruce forest, like **Wellesley Glacier** is really impressive.

So where are the really big icebergs? By the time most of this ice gets to the saltwater, it has been fractured so much by those twisting mountain valleys, that most of the ice that breaks off is fairly small, say the size of a small apartment building at the most.

But remember that roughly 7/8 of an iceberg is below the surface of the water, so that something that looks small on top, like the size of a garage, still poses a significant danger to ships. (Small icebergs and so called 'bergy bits' are notoriously difficult to see on radar.)

"Dawn Princess Harvard Glacier, College Fjord, September 12, 1997, 6 p.m.** - We maneuver parallel to this wide ice face and wait for a very long while - does the Captain know something? Now and again there is a hollow crack, then a rumble and twenty or thirty tons of ice fall into the fjord. To be so close to the ice is mysterious, almost haunting - we all feel it, the upper decks and viewing areas are standing room only and we wait. An hour passes like this, but no one wants to leave.

"Then an unusually loud series of cracks erupts from near the western end of the glacier. Captain Warner moves us a little closer. A particularly tall spire on the very front of the wall begins to move, to topple ponderously forward. As one, the crowd gasps. Then the ice hits the fjord, throwing an explosion of water almost to the top of the glacier, 300' feet high! This is what we have come so far for."

Watching calving icebergs at Harvard Glacier.

DAY TWO
MORNING

UW - NA2098

The Harriman Expedition's chartered steamer George W. Elder receives visitors.

Much of the Alaska coast was not surveyed when the *Elder* made this trip; many times they had to sound carefully with the lead line.

The 1899 Harriman Alaska Expedition

After suffering a nervous breakdown, railroad magnate (Union, Southern, and Northern Pacific) Edward H. Harriman was ordered by his doctors to have a 'long vacation at sea'. Prohibited from taking railroad men, he instead assembled one of the most remarkable literary, scientific, and artistic expeditions ever to come to Alaska. Chartering the steamer *George W. Elder*, Harriman arranged for a well-stocked library and some of the leading naturalists, artists, and scientists of the day including naturalist **John Muir**, photographer **Edward Curtis**, and many others.

Perhaps their biggest contribution was their extensive observations in Glacier Bay in June of 1899, just 3 months before a huge earthquake shattered many of the glaciers.

Entering Prince William Sound, they again found what some have called the two Alaskas - the spectacular beauty of the land in stark contrast to the grubbiness and even squalor of those who lived there, or like gold miners or cannery workers, exploited the resources.

Several days later, as their ship approached what is

UW NA 2113

now known as College Fjord, they made a startling discovery - while the chart showed Barry Arm ending at Barry Glacier, in fact the glacier had receded enough for the ship to squeeze through, into the uncharted and unknown waters beyond. The reluctant captain was persuaded by Harriman to push into the unknown and it was a genuine thrill for the group to discover and map this new territory, that came to be named Harriman Fjord. A group including John Muir (naturally) spent two days camped in the new fjord while the ship returned to Orca for propeller repairs, after striking a rock.

Next was another unique opportunity - to name a fjord and its glaciers. As many of his party were 'Easterners', they surveyed many of the glaciers here, and named them for New England colleges like Dartmouth, Harvard, Wellesley and Vassar.

After leaving Prince William Sound, the *George W. Elder* proceeded 'to the west'ard', touching at many places that are still extremely remote almost 100 years later, including King Island, Alaska, and Plover Bay, Siberia, on the Bering Strait.

Plover Bay, Siberia. Note the whalebone structure over the fire for hanging pots.
After leaving College Fjord, the expedition worked their way west and north up the coast to Siberia and Bering Strait.

DAY TWO
MID DAY

Promenade deck,
Dawn Princess
Prince William
Sound, September,
1997.

"*Dawn Princess,* Prince William Sound, September 12, 1997, 1:00 p.m. Cloudless, with 100 mile visibility. Just after noon we slide through a scattered group of small icebergs. Blue-white, perhaps the size of garages, but hiding a much greater mass below the surface, they seem innocent, pristine. In the distance, hull down on the horizon is a southbound tanker, otherwise we are alone on this vast sound.

"Walked around the entire ship on the Promenade Deck for almost an hour, a fine and peaceful time. There is little wind here, and the sun shines hot and steady on the south side. The icebergs sliding past, the passengers reading, wrapped in steamer blankets on the graceful teak deck chairs - it is as if we had slipped back 85 or 90 years, and were on a classic liner, sliding across the Atlantic, somewhere near Newfoundland, in August of that last shining, timeless summer before the Great War".

After leaving College Fjord, you'll travel east, towards Valdez. Look for floating ice from the **Columbia Glacier** in the vicinity of **mile 1480**. This is a big one, even by Alaska standards - some 450 square miles - and with its towering (over 200 feet high in places) six mile-long face, it is as dramatic a sight as any in Alaska. It was ice from this glacier that the *Exxon Valdez* made its ill fated turn to avoid.

Actually this glacier is discharging so much ice that it is retreating rapidly up the bay, and it's expected to retreat

The face of the Columbia Glacier, accessed via excursion boat from Valdez.

as much as 20 miles in the next half century or so. So if you want to see it, do it now!

Did you know? - Probably the fastest moving glacier in history was the **Black Rapids Glacier**, north of Valdez. In 1927 it was big news when it began surging, hitting **almost ten feet an hour** at one point, headed for the road link to the outside world, the Richardson Highway. Reporters were disappointed when it stopped just short of the road and began a slow retreat.

Valdez - More Than the Tanker Terminal. This town of some 4,000 residents, backed by high mountains, has been called Alaska's Little Switzerland. Don't however, look for traces of its gold rush past. The entire town was essentially built after the 1964 earthquake and tidal wave destroyed what is now known as Old Valdez, four miles east. The only road into the Prince William Sound area, the Richardson Highway, follows the pipeline out of Valdez north toward Fairbanks, some 230 miles north.

Valdez' main feature, of course is the terminal for the Alaska pipeline. It takes roughly one supertanker a day to keep up with the flow through the insulated four foot diameter pipe that stretches 800 miles from Prudhoe Bay on the frozen Beaufort Sea. Look for the heavily laden tankers, usually bound for California or the Puget Sound ports of northern Washington State.

At times, when the ice fow flow from Columbia Glacier is particularly heavy, substantial amounts of ice move into this part of the Sound.

DAY TWO
MID DAY

Mariners should use particular caution in Prince William Sound due to substantial bottom changes caused by uplifting in the 1964 earthquake.

If you see small craft around what looks like a floating pen in the water, it is a herring pound or roe on kelp operation.

Halibut and friend.

The 1980s: Boom Times for Sound Fishermen

Herring Pounds - Spring visitors to Prince William Sound may see fishing vessels clustered around rectangular raft like structures. These are herring pounds, essentially pens in which a particular type of kelp is suspended. Once the kelp is hung in the pens, a seiner tries to locate a school of 'ripe' (i.e. ready to spawn) herring. These are then surrounded by a net, and fish and net are towed to the pen, into which the herring are released. If all goes well, the fish spawn and the eggs fasten onto the kelp fronds, producing "roe on kelp", a delicacy in high demand among Japanese consumers.

The very best kelp, however, is less abundant here than in Southeast Alaska, and during the short herring season, Alaska Airlines' 737's are sometimes pressed into service as 'Kelp Freighters', ferrying loads of kelp to Prince Willim Sound!

A decade or so earlier, divers used to harvest kelp on roe in Southeast Alaska. But competition was fierce and biologists worried about the resource, so wild harvest is today illegal.

But it is salmon that has been the bread and butter for most fishermen here. During the summer season, tenders or fish buying vessels spread out to the furthest reaches of the many fjords of the region, to buy fish from both purse seiners and gill-netters. These tenders acted like mother ships, often supplying groceries, water, and fuel for their boats.

A Fisherman's Tale:

"The best part of seining (salmon purse seining) Prince William is that there's basically only two ways for the fish to get in - Hinchinbrook Entrance and Montague Strait. If they're not in one place, then they're in the other.

"The most money I ever made in my life was 1988 - we were getting a buck a pound for pinks, and a buddy called me on the radio over to Danger Island. 'Better get over here' he said, 'It's big.'

"First set we totally loaded the boat, 60,000 pounds. We got a tender in there quick, unloaded, and set again, *another 60,000 pounds.* We deck loaded her..."

- Henry 'Ike' Issacson.

Happiness is a hot apple pie from the fish buyer when you deliver an extra big load. For Prince William Sound fishermen in the 1980's, prices were high, salmon were plentiful and life was good.

DAY TWO
AFTERNOON

In the hierarchy of salmon fishermen in Alaska, (there are many salmon fishing districts in Alaska, each with its different style of vessel and gear) the 'Prince William Sound Boys' in the 1980's were doing well. Salmon prices were high, and there were plenty of fish to be had. Life was good.

This comfortable world was shattered on March 23, 1989, when a long nightmare began - the oil spill.

John VanAmerogan

Pushed off course by drifting ice from Columbia Glacier, the Exxon Valdez *piles up on Bligh Reef, March 23, 1989.*

Ice, Oil, and the Exxon Valdez

"It was Sunday morning, I was just laying in bed, playing with the kids, trying to read the paper. The TV was on, some news thing about a tanker, but I wasn't paying any attention.. Then Nancy, my wife, said, 'Hey Ron, have a look at this - isn't that where you fish?'

"God! So I looked out and there's this tanker, with oil it seemed like for miles around it. And it was right at Bligh Reef, right where I put my herring pound!

"Yeah, we got some money, but the herring never came back."

— Ron Hames, fisherman

"The only guys that win are the lawyers."
— many fishermen

Look for Bligh Reef, mile 1475. Generally your ship will stop briefly in this vicinity for a smaller vessel to embark an pilot. This is where the *Exxon Valdez* oil spill occurred.

The evening of March 23 was calm, with a little fog, when the big ship departed the Valdez tanker terminal around 9 p.m. Two hours later the ship slowed near

John VanAmerogan

Oiled sea otter at washing station. These small, graceful critters suffered most from the oil spill. Many died from hypothermia, when their coats became oiled, losing its insulating property.

Rocky Point, about 15 miles out of town, to drop the pilot.

The *Exxon Valdez* was a huge (987 feet long by 166 feet wide) modern single skinned tanker carrying 211,000 tons of North Slope crude oil from Valdez to California refineries.

As was frequently the case, a substantial amount of ice - small icebergs and drift ice - was moving with the current across the shipping lane near Bligh Reef, just to the east of the channel, some 7 miles further south.

Captain Joseph Hazelwood elected to dodge the ice by crossing from the southbound traffic lane to the northbound lane (tanker traffic in this area is restricted to special traffic lanes), and then out of the channel entirely. Such a maneuver was neither dangerous nor uncommon, but required careful execution.

In a move he was to deeply regret later, Captain Hazelwood stepped into his stateroom to take care of some paperwork during this maneuver, leaving Third Mate Gregory Cousins in charge.

The problem with very large vessels like this one is that that they have such terrific mass and inertia. Even after the rudder is turned, the huge momentum of 211,000 tons of steel and oil tends to keep the ship traveling in the original direction.

DAY TWO
AFTERNOON

Many sea birds died from contact with the spilled oil.

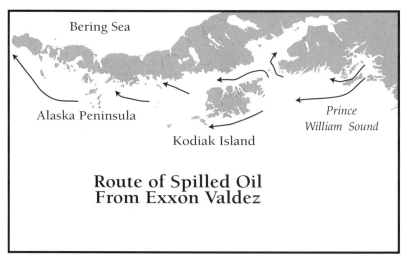

Bering Sea

Alaska Peninsula

Prince
William Sound

Kodiak Island

Route of Spilled Oil
From Exxon Valdez

The currents of the Gulf of Alaska carried the oil through many of the region's salmon fisheries.

Everything from old ferries to out of work cannery bunkhouse barges were pressed into service to house oil spill workers. To Exxon's credit, they spared no expense to try and get the oil spill cleaned up.

In this case the ship wasn't turned quickly enough and shortly after midnight, the *Exxon Valdez* slid up on Bligh Reef, instantly rupturing several of her crude oil tanks.

About three hours later, the first small Coast Guard cutter arrived on scene and its officers were stunned by what they found - the huge tanker aground on a well marked reef, with crude oil literally blowing out of the hull, bubbling almost two feet out of the water. It was their worst nightmare.

Within 24 hours some 10 million gallons of crude oil had spread into a slick that covered about 18 square miles.

Fortunately, the three days following the grounding were unusually calm - perfect weather for skimming and otherwise recovering oil from the surface of the water.

Unfortunately, much of the oil spill response equipment was temporarily unavailable. The reaction of fisherwoman Riki Ott after arriving on the scene the day after the spill said it all:

"I was stunned. There was no (oil spill) boom, no containment. Just a tanker on the rocks with two fishing boats coming up to it. Where was everybody?"

By the time a modicum of oil spill recovery equipment arrived on scene, the opportunity had been lost - the oil had thickened into a hard-to-skim 'mousse', and the wind and tide had started it on its journey to blacken literally thousands of miles of shoreline, and wreck economic

havoc on many of the state's salmon fishermen.

The spill was an unmitigated disaster for Prince William Sound and particluarly those fishermen who depended on the area's salmon and the herring stocks.

Of course the spill created a mini boom for thousands of scientists, technicians, reporters, and clean-up workers. Fishermen chartered their vessels at top dollar to work on the clean up, and marine suppliers gladly wrote up orders for tons of buoys, line, boots, foul weather gear, etc.

The remarkable recovery – in Prince William Sound, nature has shown itself to be remarkably resilient. Many affected sea life populations have returned to previous levels and the area appears to be as pristine as it always was. For salmon and herring fishermen however, the picture is not as rosy. Neither herring nor salmon have returned to pre - oilspill levels.

In the late afternoon you'll pass **Cape Hinchinbrook, mile 1380,** and pass into the open waters of the Gulf of Alaska. Ahead is a rugged and spectacular coast, fronted by the largest glaciers in North America flowing out of the Chugach and St. Elias mountain ranges. Be sure to have your bincoculars ready when the sun starts to go down! The low slanting light produces some gorgeous effects.

Salmon all over Alaska had to be thrown away after being contaminated with oil. Many cannery workers had no work.

DAY TWO
EARLY EVENING

Small craft travel with care in the open waters ahead, as it is a long distance between harbors.

Alaska Cruise Companion 143

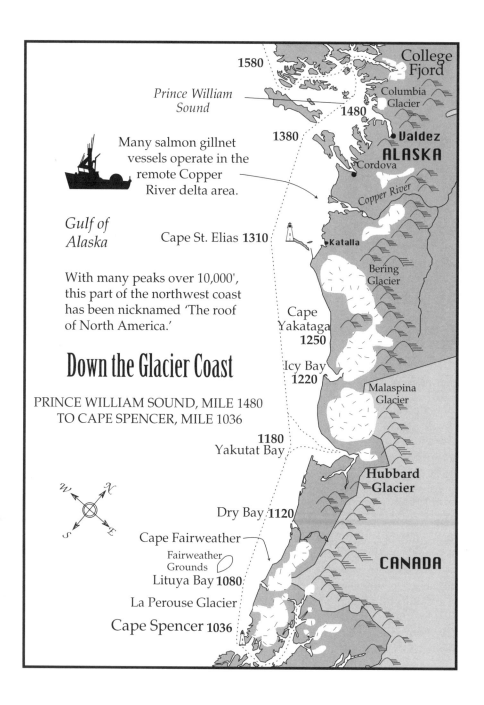

1580

Prince William
Sound

College
Fjord

Columbia
Glacier

1480

1380

Valdez

ALASKA

Cordova

Many salmon gillnet
vessels operate in the
remote Copper
River delta area.

Copper River

*Gulf of
Alaska*

Cape St. Elias **1310**

Katalla

Bering
Glacier

With many peaks over 10,000',
this part of the northwest coast
has been nicknamed 'The roof
of North America.'

Cape
Yakataga
1250

Down the Glacier Coast

PRINCE WILLIAM SOUND, MILE 1480
TO CAPE SPENCER, MILE 1036

Icy Bay
1220

Malaspina
Glacier

1180
Yakutat Bay

**Hubbard
Glacier**

W N
S E

Dry Bay **1120**

Cape Fairweather

Fairweather
Grounds

CANADA

Lituya Bay **1080**

La Perouse Glacier

Cape Spencer **1036**

CHAPTER 4

Down the Glacier Coast

CAPE HINCHINBROOK, MILE 1380, TO
CAPE SPENCER, MILE 1036 TO

"We thought it was an iceberg at first, way out past Spencer - you used to see 'em out there sometimes - but then when we got closer, we could see it was a big crab boat. But, God, weren't she iced over! Just like one big hill of ice, with some rigging and antennas sticking out of the top, and ragged pieces of plywood covering where the pilothouse windows were busted out. Pretty soon we could see the crew was all out on deck, knocking off the ice with baseball bats and shoveling it over the side as fast as they could. We all got up on deck to just stare at 'em - it was a wonder they hadn't capsized with all the weight of the ice. We heard about it later - a big cold northerly had caught 'em south of Kodiak. They busted their windows out trying to get back to the harbor, and finally just had to run before it, for three days, the spray freezing on 'em the whole time and the guys barely keeping up with knocking it off. It gits bad out there..."

—*Crab Fisherman Russell Fulton*

DAY TWO
EARLY AFTERNOON

Mariners: travel with caution - the next 350 miles is open ocean, with few harbors.

A head when you pass Cape Hinchinbrook, mile 1380, lies a very different landscape from that behind you.

Take your binoculars and have a good look around, especially at the shore before you get too far away. This body of water is called the Gulf of Alaska, but it's really part of the North Pacific Ocean.

This is the outside coast: bold, rugged, with few harbors, and backed by the stunning and rugged St. Elias

Alaska State Library

Busy days in Katalla - looking out toward the site of the new breakwater. The big fall storms of 1907 shattered the breakwater and dashed Katalla's hopes.

While hunting guides may have cabins in Katalla for seasonal use, no supplies or fuel are available here.

Range. In North America, only Alaska has a coast like this.

Along the coast, the **Copper River** emerges from the Chugach Mountains between Miles and Childs Glaciers. The river deltas and the myriad sand bars are the scene of considerable activity in the late spring and summer with shallow draft salmon gillnetters seeking the well known Copper River Red Salmon. Marketed as **Copper River Reds**, they are some of the first fresh Alaska sockeye salmon on the market and traditionally command a high price. Much of the fishing is in and among the sand bars on the flats, in and out of the breakers, a challenging fishery. Tenders (fish buying vessels) typically anchor in sheltered coves nearby.

The nearest town, which is the home port for most of these vessels, is **Cordova**, northeast of **mile 1380**. There is a native settlement, Alaganik, 10 miles up Alaganik Slough, the main channel of the Copper River.

A shallow channel for vessels with local knowledge exists over the shifting sand bars east of Hinchinbrook Island.

In the true Alaskan fashion, however, even this remote coast was not immune from the fever associated with mineral strikes:

The Perils of an Exposed Townsite

Today, Katalla, 25 miles north of Cape St. Elias, is little more than another ghost town. But around 1907 high hopes were raised when Eastern capitalists J. Pierpont Morgan, the Guggenheim Brothers and others formed The

Alaska Syndicate to develop the copper and coal resources along the Copper River to the northeast. The then tiny settlement of Katalla was picked as the place –"Where the rails meet the sails"– and between 5,000 and 10,000 construction workers poured into town.

Katalla's harbor, or lack of it was notorious among steamer captains. But when the "Googies" brought the famous railroad engineer M.K. Rogers to construct a 2,000 foot long breakwater, who could have doubted that a protected harbor bringing prosperity to all was just around the corner? Indeed two different railroad companies, each with its own plan for a breakwater and harbor, were literally racing down the river valleys from the copper country. However what looked good on paper was no match for the seas that a hundred mile per hour November gale drove in from the west on top of some of the highest tides of the year. When the three day storm finally blew off to the east, it had taken Katalla's prospects with it. All that was left of the 2000 foot breakwater was a few bent pilings and rock scattered along the beach. That was the end of Katalla's short lived boom as the railroad men quickly rerouted their track toward Cordova with its more protected harbor.

Without a breakwater, steamers would stop at Katalla only when the sea was calm, and load passengers and freight into small boats which either land on the beach, or proceed into the shallow river.

It was near here, when I was a young crewman on a crab boat, that we had an exceedingly close call:

A Journey to West'ard

"**March 6, 1971**: Sometime after midnight I awoke suddenly. The engine was only rumbling along at an idle, but it was something else that had woken me - the boat's motion - she took a roll, slow and loggy, seeming to hesitate at the end. I stumbled up into the pilothouse, instantly saw the problem: the wind had come up suddenly at Cape St. Elias and we'd iced up badly. Outside the window was a terrible sight - the two inch pipe rails around the foredeck were swollen into foot-thick bloated sausages, and in a few places they had already grown together into a solid wall of ice. The anchor winch was an unrecognizable white mound. I took a quick look out the back windows, and just as quickly looked away - What had been a neat stack of big crab pots, was now

Joe's Log

Alaska Cruise Companion 147

We found a house lot sized patch of partially sheltered water behind a dot of an island, and worked to break the pots free and put most in the fish holds, below the deck. But we were anxious, all the while fearful that the wind would change before we got done, that freezing spray would undermine all our hours of tedious work.

a lumpy hill of white ice, broken here and there by the black steel edges of the pots.

"It was easy to see how vessels died - after just a couple of hours, we'd accumulated enough ice to make the boat dangerously top-heavy - and we were only carrying 75 pots in a two layers on deck. Some vessels traveled north with several hundred pots stacked three high.

"Without a word, the engineer and I suited up with oilskins over insulated coveralls, grabbed the baseball bats and edged cautiously out onto the foredeck, clipping short safety lines around the rails, knocking the ice off as we went. It popped off easily, but it was awkward work - the boat rolling, the footing treacherous, the bitter wind turning the spray to slush on our oilskins. Once a sea larger than the others loomed suddenly out of the night, came right up over the bow - solid black water. It tugged at our knees for a moment and was gone.

"But it was a terrible feeling - the bow sinking, the water swirling around us, clutching at our legs. There was a white and strained face in the window, my hands fastened to the rail, but then the bow rose sluggishly and the water cleared.

"When we'd cleared off the tons of ice from the bow, we worked aft, knocking the ice off the rails as we went. An hour's work, just to clear the bow and boat deck area, but our little ship seemed to ride a little higher, roll a little quicker.

"The back deck was another story, for even the nylon

meshes of the pots had swollen with the ice, finally grown into an almost seamless mound of solid ice. Much of what we chipped fell on deck, had to be tediously shoveled over the side. And all the while the wind picked the water off the sea, froze it to every surface that we uncovered. It was blowing perhaps 25. No one spoke of it, but we all knew that it would only take another 20 knots of wind to make ice faster than we could chip it off, and it would only be a matter of time before we became too top heavy and simply rolled over. It had happened to other vessels in just those same conditions. We knew we had to find shelter and soon, to get as many pots below deck, into our holds, to reduce the area where ice could accumulate.

"It's the Copper River wind, boy," the skipper's brother told me in the galley when we were done and warming up. "It just sucks down off the flats and ice after a little sou'west breeze. All that ocean air just gets frozen up there, and all of a sudden decides to roll back to the sea. And I told that guy down in Seattle to put the pots into the hold when we loaded them. 'Oh, no,' he said. 'We won't have to do that...' Those guys down there don't even know what ice is except when they see it in their drinks...they think these new super boats can take anything"

"Even at less than a quarter throttle, we iced up again badly before we found a few acres of shelter behind a tiny dot of an island off the abandoned copper boom town of Katalla. We pulled the big steel hatch covers off, loaded as many of the heavily iced pots into the holds as would fit, laid the rest flat on the deck, lowered the boom and lashed it to the stern. The icy wind still clawed at us, but there was no sea. When we were finally done I looked around. We were probably the only humans within 50 miles and the vista - frozen islands, shore and mountains, now hidden, now revealed by moon and racing clouds was unspeakably bleak."

So beautiful, yet so sinister - the accumulation of ice on a vessel at sea can raise the center of gravity until capsizing becomes inevitable.

DAY TWO
AFTERNOON

CAPE ST. ELIAS

There's not even a ripple in the pool as the Dawn Princess *slides past Cape St. Elias on a perfectly still morning. The rugged high range behind the cape has received the nickname of "The Roof of North America", for its peaks, rising to almost 20,000 feet.*

The shore to the north, between Cape St. Elias, **Mile 1310**, and Cape Hinchinbrook, **Mile 1380**, is low and marshy in places, and is dominated by the deltas of several rivers, and a string of barrier islands, also low and grass covered.

"**Cape St. Elias, the south end of Kayak Island, is an important and unmistakable landmark.** It is a precipitous, sharp, rocky ridge, about one mile long and 1,665 feet high, with a low, wooded neck between it and the high parts of the island further north. About 0.2 mile off the cape is the remarkable Pinnacle Rock, 494 feet high."

—*US Coast Pilot 9,* 1964 ed.

"**Dawn Princess**, Cape St. Elias, 6 A.M., September 12: I am up at first light to see the day come off this remote and particularly unpeopled section of coast. Only a few of the staff are up, wiping the dew off the varnished rails, and beginning to set out the rows of chaises lounges. Once again, as one, we are all drawn to nature's canvas to the east. The sea is rippled - a pale purple cloth. Six miles off is the stark black silhouette of Cape St. Elias, with its 500' Pinnacle Rock clearly visible just offshore. Beyond, a lighter purple wall looming above the dark line that was the land, was the St. Elias and Chugach Mountains: Mt. Churchill, Blackburn, Sanford, and Bona, all over 15,000', and surrounded by their lesser brethren, with many 10,000 footers without having even been named or climbed.

"I slide into the hot tub, as the very top of the sun's red disc just peeps over the jagged horizon. Most of my fellow passengers are still sleeping; and I am able to savor this moment alone. There is no swell; even the pool's water is still.

"It is not always like this here; and as I soak, I remember clearly my very first transit of these waters. It was winter; we were perhaps in this very spot, when a change in the weather very nearly ended our lives."

A Journey to West'ard

"**March 5, 1971** - Underway from Yakutat at four A.M. The storm had blown out to sea in the night. The dawn, when it came, was truly awesome - first a faint yellow line, then a dozen peaks tinged with pink. But the sun when it rose, was red and angry, lighting up a couple hundred thousand square miles of bleak ice and rock with its eerie long-shadowed light before it disappeared into a strange, thin, hazy cloud cover.

"All day we steamed northwest, a few miles off the beach. The wind was offshore and light, our ride easy, but there was something about the day and place that made us all somber. The land to the north and east was a strip of beach, rising to icefields and mountains as far as the eye could see, range after range of cold, white peaks. The coast was broken here and there by little bays, all ice-choked and shallow, offering only limited shelter to shallow vessels.

"Night came early and inky black, but without a breath of wind. It seemed as if we were traveling through a featureless void. We ate early, and all gathered in the darkened pilothouse, anxious to make Cape Hinchinbrook, to put this long and exposed passage behind us."

Joe's Log

In that winter of 1971, this was such an isolated and remote part of the Alaskan coast, that even radio communication to the outside world in case of an emergency would have been difficult.

The Ruby Sands of Cape Yakataga

The tiny mining and hunting settlement at Cape Yakataga, **mile 1250**, is the only permanent settlement on the coast in the entire 150 or so miles between Cordova and Icy Bay. With patient effort, the 'ruby sands' (because of the high garnet content) around the Cape still yield a bit of gold.

The Cape House Lodge - more like a big log cabin - offers simple accomodations for the occasional hunter or traveler. Sometimes there was only a watchman at the old lodge, which had the only phone for many many miles:

Cape Yakataga is one of the few places along this stretch of coast where small craft may land on the beach, but only during rare periods of calm weather.

Brenda Carney

Bear tracks on beach, near Cape Yakataga. This was from a big one, probably a brown bear.

"A bush pilot told me about the phone, and flew me in there. I mean it's remote, there's just a few buildings and that's it. Anyway, there were a bunch of old magazines by the phone, you know, hunting and fishing magazines and such - the watchman who lived there subscribed to them, I guess. Anyway, I hadn't seen a magazine in a month or so, so I started reading, and then I notice the address the old guy had given himself: '122 Bearshit Drive, Cape Yakataga!' "

—Terry Johnson, fisherman

A Fisherman's Tale

"We were headed out to west'ard for crab. It started to blow up by Yakataga, so we decided to run back and duck into Icy Bay until it got better. Of course it was snowing, so you couldn't see that much, even with the radar, but we felt our way in, dropped the anchor and we just all sacked out, for we knew that once crabbing started, sleep could be a scarce commodity.

"This awful racket woke me up in the middle of the night, and I jumped out and went out on deck. 'Course in them rigs we always keep the generators running and the deck lights on all night, so I stepped out on deck, just as another couple hundred pounds of ice came crashing down from this big berg that was scraping down our side! Christ! This thing must have been sixty feet high - it just towered over us! Spookiest thing I ever seen - it dropped off another corner of itself, and dissappeared off into the snow. And them other guys never even heard it!"

— a friend

Mt. St. Elias marks the spot where the Alaska border changes from an irregular zigzag along the top of the coastal range to veer sharply north to follow the 141 degree west longitude line, arrowing across rivers, lonely mountains and tundra to Demarcation Point on the Beaufort Sea, some 650 miles north.

Icy Bay, to the north at Mile 1220, has the usual shallow entrance, though in recent years it has been the scene of considerable logging activity. One hundred years ago, the bay wasn't even there - it was filled with a glacier that extended several miles out into the ocean! These are active glaciers - there is often much ice in the bay, and sometimes icebergs will drift out of the bay and form a regular line of stranded bergs along the outside shore, all the way northwest to Cape Yakataga.

Alaska fishermen are remarkably plucky, heading up the exposed outside coast in all manner of small craft. But sometimes they get in trouble - see story below.

DAY TWO
EARLY EVENING

Shipwrecked

"Ah, I shouldn't have let Dad steer at night...that's how it all started - he was almost seventy then and his eyes were starting to go. We were headed up to fish Prince William, and I just laid down for a bit, and then the next thing I knew we were in the breakers - he'd just gotten in too close to the beach. The boat started to break up and that was way before survival suits, so we just ended up on the beach in our woolies, [long woolen underwear]...

"It all happened so quick there really wasn't any time for a radio call. The snow was right down to the water's edge in

There are no lights along this stretch of shore. Mariners should be especially cautious on dark nights to avoid the beach.

Alaska Cruise Companion 153

places - it was late April - so I figured our only chance was to try and make it back to Cape Yakataga - I knew there was at least a lodge or something there..

"It was really tough going - seemed like every mile there was a stream that we either had to wade across, sometimes up to our chest, and all snowmelt - just icy cold.

"We slept just huddled together, and then on the afternoon of the second day, Dad told me to leave him - that he couldn't go on any longer... The worst part of it was that we'd lost our snoose [powdered or so called 'smokeless' tobacco] and our chew both with the boat.

"If we hadn't stumbled across an old trapper's cabin, and found some old moldy pipe tobacco that we could chew on, I don't think we would have made it. But we spent the night in there, and each of us got a good chew in our mouths the next morning so life seemed a little more bearable...

"Turns out BP had some sort of drilling operation at the Cape back then, and the first building we came to was the mess hall. It was noon, and we walked in the door, all scratched up, just in bloody ripped woolies and our rubber boots. Everyone turned as we came in the door, and for a long moment, you could have heard a pin drop in there..."

—Dick Kietel, fisherman.

Even if it's dark, get your binoculars and look for these spectacular peaks. Many nights star or moonlight gives good visbility.

Did you know? - 'Snoose' (Copenhagen or Skoal brand smokeless tobacco) is extremely popular among the Northwest's many Norwegian descent fishermen. One notable spring, as the halibut fleet was getting ready to leave, there was not a can to be had anywhere around Seattle and the entire fleet waited at the dock until the snoose arrived.

Look for Malaspina Glacier, visible west of Yakutat Bay, and rising almost to 15,000' above sea level in places. Today the glacier has receded back from the shore, but just 100 years ago it was a very different story, with much of the coast along here a solid wall of ice extending out into the open ocean.

If it's clear, look for 18,008 foot Mt. Saint Elias, which will appear behind Malaspina Glacier as you leave Yakutat Bay. Sometimes visible further north and east, in the Yukon Territories, is Mt. Logan, at 19,850' almost a mile

higher than Puget Sound's impressive Mount Rainier, and just 400 feet shy of Alaska's Mt. McKinley.

The Roof of North America - East and north of Hubbard Glacier is an area that has been nicknamed 'The Roof of North America' - an immense rock, ice, and snow world with many of the continent's highest peaks. Ten thousand footers are common here, and there are at least four over 15,000'. Much of this area is the Wrangell St. Elias National Park and Wilderness. This mountain wall catches the eastward flowing moisture-laden air, which falls as heavy snow. The immense weight of the snow pack creates the largest glaciers on the entire Pacific coast. Hubbard Glacier is part of an vast ice mass that extends along a few miles behind the coast in an unbroken line (except for two places) almost to Anchorage, almost 400 miles away. Today the glaciers have all receded substantially back from the shore, but a century ago, the ice reached the ocean in many places.

Our crab boat seemed so big tied to the dock in Seattle. But the further north we went, the smaller she seemed to get. Our journey was a truly humbling experience.

DAY TWO
LATE EVENING

A Journey to West'ard

"March 4, 1971 - Tonight, 20 miles north of Yakutat, a wind came up. After five minutes it was blowing seventy. The temperature was fifteen degrees. The first spray over the bow

Joe's Log

froze instantly on the wheelhouse windows; we turned around with hardly a discussion. Our vessel was the best that the finest Northwest shipyard could produce, built for winter in the North Pacific, but turn around we did.

"In the outer part of Yakutat Bay, a sobering sight had us all up in the wheelhouse. The 140 foot trawler *Deep Sea*, pioneer of the whole king crab fishery, lay at anchor with a big covered barge in tow. The whole front of the structure on the barge was crumpled in, the top and sides mangled for a third of the way back and in places the aluminum sheeting was ripped like paper. Our skipper got the story over the radio - the barge was a floating shrimp cannery, headed for Kodiak, four hundred miles to the west. They had gotten within 10 miles of the shelter of Cape Saint Elias when the wind came up. Two hours later, the seas had punched in the front of the barge, forcing them to turn and run more than a hundred miles back to Yakutat.

Floating canneries, built on barges, old ferries, or ships, are used in the fisheries of western Alaska.

"We tied with frozen lines to a silent cannery wharf, and I walked up to the village with a shipmate in the blowing, drifting snow. In the whole settlement we saw only two lighted windows, and nowhere a footprint or car track. We trudged back to the boat through the knee deep snow with the trees only dark shapes on our left, and the cove on our right lit up by the brillant crab lights. Our boat, with the bark of her auxillary engine filling the night, seemed almost like a visitor from another planet.

"In the night, a blizzard swept in from the Canadian Yukon to the east. At the head of the harbor, in the lee of the great mountains, we lay sheltered from its force, but morning showed a grey and eerie world. Outside the windows of the pilothouse, a steady plume of snow settled down on us, drifting down from the wharf above. By noon, what little free deck we had was drifted rail to rail, almost waist deep with snow."

Headed for **Hubbard Glacier**? Your ship turns into Yakutat Bay here.

Three bare, light colored bluffs distinguish Ocean Cape, the entrance to Yakutat Bay, at mile 1162. This bay is the only really good anchorage for large vessels, in the 350 miles between Cape Spencer and Prince William Sound. Nevertheless, in very heavy weather, breakers or very high swells have been observed all the way across this 15 mile-wide entrance.

Yakutat, some 5 miles inside the bay from Ocean Cape, is the northernmost village of the Tlingit Indians, many of whom fish for salmon nearby. The same earthquake that shattered Muir Glacier in 1899 also hit this village pretty hard. It lifted part of the shore some 50 feet and created several tidal waves and waterspouts that left furrows in the sand 5 feet wide and 20 feet deep, according to some natives.

Russell Fjord, at the head of Yakutat Bay, contains Hubbard Glacier and Nunatak Glacier which both discharge ice into the bay.

Hubbard Glacier dams Russell Fjord

In April of 1986, Curt Gloyer, a pilot for Gulf Air Taxi, in Yakutat, returning from dropping off a climbing party noticed that Hubbard Glacier had surged all the way across the channel and essentially dammed Russell Fjord. He circled lower to make sure, amazed at the unusual sight.

This was an event without precedent in recent geologic history, and as soon as word got out, people and groups from all over the world converged on Yakutat to try and rescue the marine mammals trapped by the ice dam - primarily seals, sea lions, and porpoises. As the weather got warmer and the streams filled with snow melt, the water behind the glacier/dam began rising rapidly, eventually

Hubbard and the other glaciers in this area are created by moist Pacific air pushing up against the mountain wall to the east, and falling as heavy

DAY TWO
MIDNIGHT
HUBBARD GLACIER
PASSENGERS: YOUR
SHIP WILL APPROACH
THE GLACIER ON THE
THIRD DAY IN THE
EARLY MORNING.

Malaspina Glacier is a conspicuous landmark for mariners traveling this coast.

Alaska Cruise Companion 157

At times, when glaciers are very active, there is so much ice in the water that your ship must proceed very slowly.

reaching almost 90 feet higher than the level of Disenchantment Bay on the other side.

Finally, in the middle of an October night, the water pressure became too great and burst through the glacier wall. By the time the first pilots got out the next morning, the big lake in Russell Fjord was pouring out like a huge waterfall!

Surging Glaciers

Usually glaciers move slowly, say 3 to 10 feet a day. On occasion, however, they can surge forward at much higher speeds: 150 feet a day or even faster! They can also retreat (breaking off icebergs or simply melting back). John Muir's native paddlers, in 1879, almost didn't recognize Glacier Bay, as the ice had retreated so much since they had been there last.

Variegated Glacier, in Russell Fjord, has been an ideal site for studying these surges, as it surged regularly every 20 years.(give or take a few!) When the glacier finally surged in 1982-3, scientists were ready.

The surprising conclusion of these geologists was that normally, water is flowing in channels under the ice. When pushed by the weight of the snow and icepack in the mountains above it, the glacier speeds up, it fractures more readily and these water channels become clogged. This raises the water level to the point where it partially floats the glacier! The result - a fast glacier. Variegated Glacier hit 164 feet a day in June 1983! Of course this speed wouldn't crush your tent while you were trying to get out of your sleeping bag, but still, at over an inch a minute, it is actually noticeable motion - a good trick for something weighing millions of tons!

Naturally, as such a glacier surges forward, all that ice has to crack and flow to accomodate the twists and turns of its canyon or fiord. The result is a continuous rumbling and cracking that is truly awesome.

The 1898 Harriman Alaska expedition found this Tlingit seal hunters camp near Yakutat. Notice seal skins stretched on frames to dry.

Are those DC-3's? - If you think you see 50 year-old twin engined DC-3's circling to land at Yakutat airport, you're right. They haven't come for an air show - they're part of a fleet of so-called fish freighters that come to Alaska every year to move salmon out of remote areas to where they can be shipped out or processed. In Bristol Bay, 650 miles west, big four-engined DC-6's and 7's land and take off from sand bars to move fish. The DC-3's at Yakutat are probably transporting fish from the Dry Bay area.

Todays outdoorsmen, with radios and pre-arranged return trips with bush pilots, have it a lot better than some of the earlier residents, who were sometimes beset by unexpected bad weather:

A Trapper's Journal

"Oct 4, 1917: Getting sick packing, now looking for camping place. Cold in the lungs with a high fever."

"Dec 7, 1917: River froze except for a few riffles. Too much snow and too rough for sleighing. Snow getting deeper now."

"Dec 19, 1917: ...Can't travel. Don't believe there will be ice a man can run a sled over this winter. Very little grub, snow too deep and soft for hunting goats. Stomach balking at straight meat, especially lynx."

Hundreds of marine mammals were trapped by the sudden and rapid 'surge' of Hubbard Glacier.

Log cabin for dog, minus the roof. A trapper's life was a solitary one, often with just his dogs for company. A trapper would often build a number of simple cabins along his trap line for shelter in case of bad weather.

"Jan 8, 1918: ..River open as far as can be seen. Health very poor.. Wolverines been here eating my skins, robes, and moccasins, old meat, and also my goatskin door. They tried to run me last night, came through a stovepipe hole showing fight."

"April 3, 1918: Cooking my last grub, no salt, no tea."

"April 22, 1918: My eyes are useless for hunting. The rest of my body is also useless. I believe my time has come. My belongings, everything I got I give to Jos. Pellerine of Dry Bay; if not alive, to Paul Swartzkoph, Alsek River. "

— Courtesy of *Alaska Magazine* and *The Alaska Sportsman®*

About four months after this last entry, two prospectors found a body, apparently a suicide, in a rough and remote cabin near the Alsek River with the above journal nearby.

"**From Alsek River to Yakutat Bay**, the mountains are 5 to 15 miles from the coast, and between is a low wooded plain cut by numerous streams. The principal rivers between Alsek River and Yakutat Bay have shifting sand bars at their entrances and lagoons or tidal basins inside; they can be used only by small boats and launches at high water and with a smooth sea"

— *United States Coast Pilot*, Vol. 9, 1964 edition.

Small craft - use special care if you attempt to enter any of the bays along here. The entrances are all shallow, with shifting channels, and if you get into trouble, you're a very long way from anyone who can help you.

The Land - The 'low wooded plain' mentioned above is hardly a plain in the sense most travelers might think. A more apt description might be 'an almost impenetrable thicket of Devil's Club (a particularly sharp thorned bush), alder and other plant life'. Many mountaineering parties have begun their ascents of the peaks here by being transported to these shallow rivers by float plane. It is not uncommon for these experienced climbers to find that the most difficult part of their whole trip was just getting through the woods to a place where they could begin their climb! Climbers, sportsfishermen, and others usually reach this part of the coast by charter plane from Yakutat.

Lights at night? There are no navigational lights or settlements in the 110 miles of coast between the lighted buoy at Graves Harbor, **mile 1045**, and the Yakutat airstrip beacon (a green and white flasing light) at **mile 1155**. However, the rivers that meander behind the barrier beaches in this area are rich with salmon and trout, and fishermen come sometimes from all over the world to camp and fish this lonely region. Some choose to pay for a guide, who may even have a small cabin available for lodging. But many simply arrange for an floatplane to drop them off and come back for them later. For either style of traveling, a stay on this coast often leaves a lasting impression:

Brenda Carney

400 bucks a night for this shack? Some guides maintain remote cabins for their fly - in fishing clients. Some of these are on the spartan side...

"I just never had any idea of how much lonely country was out there until that trip. We were lucky - the weather was good - five days and no rain. Mostly we'd just fish, up and down all the streams. We were camped a little ways behind the beach, to get out of the wind, but after supper, we'd always go and sit behind some logs, and just look out. Behind us you could see the snow on the mountains, bright in the moonlight, but ahead and to both sides was just nothing, never a ship at sea, not another light anywhere, just nothing. Sometimes I'd get up early, bundle up, and go out and just walk the beach in the early morning light, with the surf in my ears and a lot of times fresh bear tracks..I tell you it was a very powerful experience. And we caught a lot of fish too!"

— A fisherman

DAY THREE
VERY EARLY

Caution: give this stretch of coast an offing of several miles, especially at night. There are no lights along the shore, and breaking seas have been reported as much as two miles out.

The land to the east, from the coast up over the Fairweather Range, and into the Yukon Territories of Canada, almost to the Alaska Highway, is for the most part a vast wilderness. It does present, however, an opportunity for kayakers or rafters willing to travel for

Looking south from near Dangerous River, mile 1140. The shore is wild and remote, little visited by man.

long distances far from any help or source of supplies.

For the truly brave hearted, the **Dezadeash-Kaskawulsh-Alsek route** includes the infamous **Turnback Canyon**. It was named after the 1898 gold prospectors who tried the Alsek as a route to the interior, had one look at the ten mile chute of churning 34 degree water and turned around.

This unforgiving canyon has become to kayakers what K2 or Everest is to climbers. A word of caution - sometimes high water and current conditions make this canyon truly impassable and kayakers are urged to have a contingency plan for a helicopter to shuttle them around the canyon.

The other route, via the **Tatshensheni River** involves less white water, but is no less of a wilderness

*Roughly 1200 people a year float through the vast wilderness east of Dry Bay and down the Alsek River in rafts like this. All but a handful take the Tatshensheni - Alsek Route.
A few hardy souls always try the infamous Turnback Canyon route.*

experience:

"..you almost have to do it to really sense what it's like back in there. We started off right from the Haines highway, and as soon as that bridge disappeared, it was like, except for our little group of four guys, humans had ceased to exist. It took us a week, and never did we see a plane, or a bit of trash, another kayaker..nothing. The amazing thing was that the river goes right through the middle of this range of mountains that go all the way up to 15,000'.

"Of course we just trashed the kayaks - they were just beaters to begin with, and we just left them on the beach when the plane came to pick us up. But the thing that I'll always remember was at the very end, when we had all our stuff on the shore at Dry Bay, waiting for the plane to come in and pick us up. It was a clear day, the river looked like it just came from a solid mountain wall, with no possible way through, and I just felt, 'Wow..we came through there..' "

—A kayaker.

"**Dawn Princess, September 11, 1997, 11:45 p.m.**: Just the staff is in the forward lounge, cleaning, as I pass through, climb up a deck, let my eyes get accustomed to the dark, and slowly make my way forward. Past the two sets of windbreaks until I'm on the sun deck, directly above the bridge. This area of the ship is totally dark, with unobstructed vision through perhaps 270 degrees. I find a place in the lee of the breeze, and wait, letting my eyes get fully adjusted. But for the palest line, perhaps surf along the beach or the high, snow country above, the land abeam is totally dark. But it is not the land that I have come for. Ahead, high up, and

The sun deck of a big liner is often deserted after dark. Find a place out of the wind and let your eyes get accustomed to the dark. You'll get a unique perspective on this vast land.

Day Three
Very Early

Caution: The entrance to Dry Bay changes frequently and should only be attempted in calm seas, at high tide, and with local knowledge, if possible.

A winter trip to Alaska was never easy in the old days, but having your vessel strand along this remote coast often meant trying to survive on the beach until help arrived. Sometimes it took weeks.

somewhat to the west is the greenish band of the northern lights. It is not brillant, nor multi-colored, but it shimmers, and moves slightly as I watch. Yes. Yes!

"The engines are so far aft and so well muffled that except for the murmur of the wind, it is totally quiet where I stand. Below me almost 3,000 people are sleeping, talking, working. Yet up here one only senses a great ship traveling silently through this remarkable night. I stay a long while; this is not an experience that comes along very often."

The Inaccessible Coast

Before the advent of helicopters, mariners unfortunate enough to strand along this coast usually had a particularly difficult time. When the little freighter *Patterson* beached herself near **mile 1090** in December of 1938, would be Coast Guard rescuers stood helplessly outside the surfline on and off for 10 days. As Christmas approached the story of the 18 survivors stranded on a remote Alaska beach made headlines all over the country.

But as pioneer Alaska aviator Shell Simmons circled the survivors, dropping supplies, he noticed that when a big sea was running, generally the 7th wave would run up the beach and slop over into a nearby creek, adding just enough water to allow him to land......quickly. He circled, watching and waiting, and finally timed his landing perfectly and was able take out the two injured seamen. But it was too risky to repeat and finally the other 16 survivors walked far enough toward Lituya Bay to be met by rescuers on foot.

UW Thwaites 0024-F25

Note how the left middle ball has a pattern etched onto it by the wind blowing the sand against the netting that was originally on the glass. The tubular glass on the bottom is an unusual find!

Hunting for Glass Balls? For generations Japanese fishermen used handblown glass balls of various sizes as buoys for their gillnets. Today the buoys are plastic, but many of the old glass balls eventually drifted ashore along the Northwest coast. The easy to find ones have been in stores, homes, and restaurants for decades. Today a glass ball is a rare find along most beaches.

There are parts of the shore along here that see few if any visitors. Places like these remote Alaskan beaches are where glass balls are still likely to be found, particularly in the grass and debris above the high tide line.

Did You Know?- Tlingit legend has it that several canoes capsized in the entrance to Lituya Bay just before Russian explorer Vitus Bering passed in July of 1714 and that the cargo - sea otter pelts wrapped in waterproof halibut skins - was found, and sold in Kamchatka, sparking the fur rush which led to the Russian fur era.

Just north of **Cape Fairweather**, a low, bare headland at **mile 1096**, vessels may seek shelter from moderate southeasterly or southwesterly winds. In heavy gales, vessels are advised to give the coast from Cape Fairweather to Ocean Cape, **mile 1162**, a wide berth as seas have been observed breaking several miles from shore.

Dry Bay, at mile 1120 is the shallow mouth of the Alsek River. Although a fair run of salmon enters this river, the entrance is shallow. Over the years several entrepreneurs have tried canning fish here, but in the end were

Early travelers reported that the Tlingits were able to travel from Dry Bay to Yakutat in their large, 40 - 50' canoes, without ever going out into the open Gulf. They followed the shallow lagoons and streams behind the beaches.

always defeated by the rough seas and shifting sand bars at the bay's entrance. After a particularly tragic mishap in 1944, when six Coast Guardsmen were lost as their surf-boat capsized in the breakers trying to reach two stranded fishing boats, vessels tended to stay away from Dry Bay. Recently, a small salmon processing plant has operated seasonally on the northern shore of Dry Bay, but owing to the difficulty of entering the river, the fish are transported by plane to Yakutat.

Lituya Bay is known as one of the most scenic on the entire coast.

Tragedies in Lituya Bay

"At the entrance of this harbor perished twenty-one brave seaman. Reader, whoever thou art, mingle thy tears with ours."
— part of 1786 memorial to sailors lost from French explorer LaPerouse's expedition, anchored in Lituya Bay.

Look carefully shoreward near mile 1080 for a bay with a narrow entrance and a high island in its middle. This is Lituya Bay, whose history is pockmarked with tragedy that continues even to the present day.

Mariners: use extreme caution when entering Lituya Bay, especially against an ebbing tide.

"Ebb currents, running against a southwest swell, cause bad topping seas or combers in which no small boat can live. Small powered vessels in the bay should stay away from the entrance on the ebb to avoid being swept through. The ebb current follows a narrow path for several miles out to sea and can be seen for some distance."
- *United States Coast Pilot* (1964 edition)

Lituya Bay offers a secure anchorage. But first you have to get in. The problem is simply this: all the tide for this roughly 25 square mile bay has to pour in and out of a narrow entrance. When the tide is ebbing, the current pours like a river out of the entrance and against the typical westerly swell, creating whirlpools and breaking seas.

The first white man to anchor within the bay was French explorer LaPerouse, in 1786, who had been at sea for 11 months without losing a man to disease or accident. Then in a single hour he lost almost a quarter of his crew when two exploring parties were swept into the tide rip that today still bears his nickname - "La Chaussee" - (The Chopper).

Those who sucessfully enter the bay (normally safe passage can be accomplished without problems on the flooding, or rising tide) find a place of particular beauty, with three tidewater glaciers. Though it is probably the least visited bay in Glacier Bay National Park, it creates a lasting impression with those willing to accept the challenge of getting there. Many who visit call it the most scenic bay in Alaska.

However, the loss of the French seamen wasn't the first tragedy in that stunning bay whose history gives mariners a good reason to seek shelter elsewhere. Native legend has it that angry gods have inexplicably wiped out

The Hermit of Cenotaph Island

Sometime around 1917, a prospector named Jim Huscroft settled on isolated Cenotaph Island in Lituya Bay to raise foxes. His simple cabin was known as 'Hotel Huscroft' to the members of mountaineering expeditions that started their trek to the high country in the bay. Once a year Jim would catch a boat ride to Juneau, to sell furs, perhaps a little gold, and stock up on supplies. The Juneau Elks Club would save the year's papers for him, and once safely home at Lituya Bay, he would read them one day at a time, just a year late. At times, in the winter, Jim probably was the only human being in the entire 125 miles between Cape Spencer and Yakutat Bay.

When the freighter *Patterson* stranded in December, 1938, Jim was instrumental in showing the rescue parties the trail from Lituya Bay to the remote beach where the shipwrecked survivors were waiting for help.

Bradford Washburn

Jim Huscroft, Cenotaph Island, 1933

whole villages in the past. White men tended to discount the old Indian stories. Until August 9, 1958.

The Giant Tidal Wave of 1958

Tlingit legends of whole villages being wiped out by an angry god seems to coincide with evidence of regular tidal waves ocurring here.

The evening of August 9, 1958 was gorgeous in Lituya Bay - several salmon trollers had come in to anchor for the night as was their custom, and turned in early. Around 10:20 Howard Ulrich, on his troller *Edrie*, was awakened by the sudden pitching and rolling of his boat. Still half asleep, he jumped up into the little pilothouse to see what was going on. What he saw became etched into his mind forever:

"These great snow -capped giants [the mountains at the head of the bay] shook and twisted and heaved. They seemed to be suffering unbearable internal tortures. Have you ever see a 15,000 foot mountain twist and shake and dance?

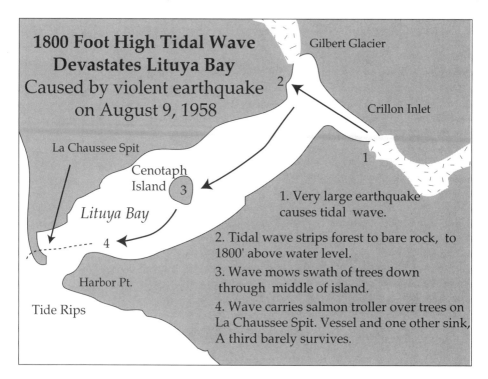

1800 Foot High Tidal Wave Devastates Lituya Bay
Caused by violent earthquake on August 9, 1958

Gilbert Glacier

Crillon Inlet

La Chaussee Spit

Cenotaph Island 3

Lituya Bay

1

2

4

Harbor Pt.

Tide Rips

1. Very large earthquake causes tidal wave.

2. Tidal wave strips forest to bare rock, to 1800' above water level.

3. Wave mows swath of trees down through middle of island.

4. Wave carries salmon troller over trees on La Chaussee Spit. Vessel and one other sink, A third barely survives.

At last, as if to rid themselves of their torment, the mountains spewed heavy clouds of snow and rocks into the air and threw huge avalanches down their groaning sides.

During all this I was literally petrified, rooted to the deck. It was not fright but a kind of stunned amazement. I do not believe I thought of it as something that was going to affect me.

This frozen immobility must have lasted for two minutes or longer. Then it came to a dramatic end. It so happened that I was looking over the shoulder of Cenotaph Island toward the head of the bay, when a mighty seismic disturbance exploded and there was a deafening crash.

I saw a gigantic wall of water, 1,800 high, erupt against the west mountain. I saw it lash against the island, which rises to a height of 320 feet above sea level, and cut a 50-foot-wide swath through the trees of its center. Then I saw it backlash against the eastern shore, sweeping away the timber to a height of more than 500 feet.

Finally, I saw a 50-foot wave come out of this churning turmoil and move along the eastern shore directly toward me."

— Howard Ulrich, as told to Vi Hayes, in "Night of Terror", courtesy of *Alaska Magazine* and *The Alaska Sportsman*® October 1958.

This was an earthquake so severe that it knocked the needle completely off the seismograph at the University of Washington in Seattle.

Ulrich put a life jacket on his six year old son, started the engine, ran all his anchor chain out (there wasn't time to pull it in) and headed into that wave as his only chance. Fortunately the chain snapped and the giant wave carried the *Edrie* on a wild ride over what had been dry land and forest just minutes before. Ulrich got off a quick radio call: "Mayday!, Mayday!, This is the *Edrie* in Lituya Bay. All hell has broken loose in here. I think we've had it..Good-by."

Dancing and weaving for survival among heaving seas, icebergs and thousands of floating trees, the *Edrie*

After 1958, few vessels would ever anchor in Lituya Bay without wondering - Can it happen again?

According to an eyewitness, Lituya Glacier was lifted at least several hundred feet up out of the water for a brief period during the earthquake.

finally escaped the wave and managed to stay afloat.

The two other vessels in Lituya Bay that night weren't so lucky. The *Badger* was carried by the wave over the trees and the land on the north spit, finally to sink outside the bay, her crew safe in a tiny skiff. The third, the *Sunmore,* was last seen running full speed toward the bay's entrance before the wave engulfed her, never to be seen again.

Bill Swanson, who with his wife Vivian survived the sinking of their troller *Badger,* saw a sight that gave geologists a clue to the almost unbelievably powerful forces at work that night in the mountains behind Lituya Bay:

"....The mountains were shaking something awful, with slides of rock and snow, but what I noticed mostly was the glacier, the north glacier, the one they call Lituya Glacier.

I know you can't ordinarily see that glacier from where I was anchored. People shake their heads when I tell them I saw it that night. I can't help it if they don't believe me. I know the glacier is hidden by the point when you're in Anchorage Cove, but I know what I saw that night, too.

"The glacier had risen in the air and moved forward so it was in sight. It must have risen several hundred feet. I don't mean it was just hanging in the air. It seems to be solid, but it was jumping and shaking like crazy. Big chunks of ice were falling off the face of it down into the water. That was six miles away and they still looked like big chunks. They came off the glacier like a big load of rocks spilling out of a dump truck. That went on for a little while - it's hard to tell just how long - and then suddenly the glacier dropped back out of sight and there was a big wall of water coming over the point. The wave started for us after that, and I was too busy to tell what else was happening up there."

—Courtest of Alaska Magazine and *The Alaska Sportsman* ®

Out on the Fairweather Ground, Ingvald Ask on the *Scenic* was still trolling when suddenly his boat lurched and shuddered as if it was hitting a rock, and whales began jumping out of the sea around him.

Near Cape Spencer, fishermen said dust and smoke covered the mountains, and one was reminded of a passage in the Bible: "And every mountain and island were moved out of their places."

Eightly miles away, in Lynn Canal, the Alaska-Seattle undersea cable broke in four places.

Today, no one who is familiar with the history of Lituya Bay anchors there without wondering about when such an earthquake and subsequent tidal wave might happen again.

DAY THREE
VERY EARLY

To the west at mile 1090, is the Fairweather Ground, an area of legendary king salmon fishing. Here the ocean floor humps up to form a ridge, 75 feet deep at the shallowest, pushing nutrient rich water up and creating a feeding ground for the big king salmon. It was discovered by accident in 1954, by a commercial salmon fisherman 'prospecting' or looking for new fishing grounds. See Page. 85 for more information on salmon trolling.

It is not, however, named for the weather or sea conditions found there, but rather for 15,320 foot Mt. Fairweather, that looms so dramatically 50 miles to the northeast.

This is fishing only for the hardy; when the wind comes, vessels face a difficult choice - travel 4 hours to Lituya Bay, and hope they can get in, or 7 hours to Graves or Dixon Harbor (near Cape Spencer) where they know they can get in.

Look for La Perouse Glacier at mile 1060. With its almost perpendicular 200-300' face, it's an outstanding outstanding landmark along this section of coast. It is unique along the North Pacific coast as the only glacier to reach the open ocean. (All other tidewater glaciers are in protected bays.) This is an active glacier: in some years, like 1997, advancing into the ocean, while just a year earlier receding enough to allow foot passage across the front at low tide.

The Fairweather Ground is is the Grand Prix of commercial salmon trolling - only the most seaworthy vessels need apply.

All the land from Lituya Bay south to Cape Spencer is still part of Glacier Bay National Park. Except for the rare

The Remarkable Survival Suit

It was at Astrolabe Bay, **mile 1052**, that a survival suit - a foam rubber overall style floatation and insulation outfit - first saved the life of an early user. Paul Stratton was traveling south on the 42' seiner *Marmot Cape* in October of 1978, when they ducked into this bay north of Cape Spencer to seek shelter from a gale. The storm got worse and things started happening pretty fast - waves capsized the seiner after her anchor line parted and Stratton washed up on the isolated, wilderness beach in his suit, the only survivor. It was four days before he was rescued, kept alive by the suit.

Remarkable tales such as this one spread quickly through the maritime community, and

Halloween? No - this is my crew during a regular safety drill, in their foam survival suits.

long before the Coast Guard required these suits to be aboard fishing vessels, most had purchased them. Some with limited space even have them tied to the mast! Many mariners are alive today thanks to these ungainly looking suits.

hiker, and occasional fishermen, it is little visited.

If the coast of British Columbia had been like this, the development of coastal Alaska would have been very different. The myriad harbors and sheltered passages of the Inside Passage allowed very small craft to travel to Alaska. Many would never have dared head north if their only route was outside, along a coast like this.

A Journey to West'ard

Joe's Log

"**March 3, 1971** - At dusk, Glacier Bay was to the north. The day faded until just the jagged raw peaks of the Fairweather Range glowed with that last pink light, and the icy wilderness below was all purple black. In hooded parkas and gloves we tightened and rechecked the lashings of the crab pots on deck. A thousand miles behind us, we still had that many to go, but from here on the journey would be along the open ocean with sometimes hundreds of miles between good harbors.

"The mood in the pilothouse after supper was subdued. Astern was the sweeping beam of the light at Cape Spencer, the entrance to sheltered, inside waters. Ahead was the Gulf of Alaska. The night was hazy, black, and cloudless. The bow rose and fell with the long Pacific swell, and there was neither star nor horizon to guide us.

"On my watch, I made out the shape of Lituya Bay on the radar screen. I stepped outside into the bitter air, peered intently to the east, trying to get some glimpse of the breakers in the dangerous entrance, of the glaciers, the snow and ice mountains that overhung the bay. But there was only black. Uninhabited, guarded by a treacherous bar, haunted by violent and recurring tidal waves, that invisible bay seemed somehow a taste of all that lay ahead of us."

As your ship angles intoward the shore, look for the flashing light of **Cape Spencer Lighthouse, mile 1035**. This marks the entrance to the sheltered waters of the Inside Passage. Many a traveler in small craft has breathed a huge sigh of relief to leave the 'big waters' of the Gulf of Alaska behind!

"Dawn Princess, Oct 11, 1997, 7 p.m*. - Tonight, after we rounded Cape Spencer, most passengers went below, for dinner, or for cocktails. But for the handful of us who remained on deck, nature put on a remarkable show, lighting up the vast Fairweather Range and the rugged coast below it with her long shadowed light. The glaciers and snowfields first grew yellow, then pink as the sky darkened, and finally the first stars winked out. The unfolding beauty of the scene stunned us into silence. And more - ahead, rising clearly from the ocean, was an island, where none should have been. Only in the morning did I understand what we had seen - a mirage of the 1400' peak of Kayak Island, 210 miles away!"

Dawn Princess
Evening, N. of Cape Spencer.

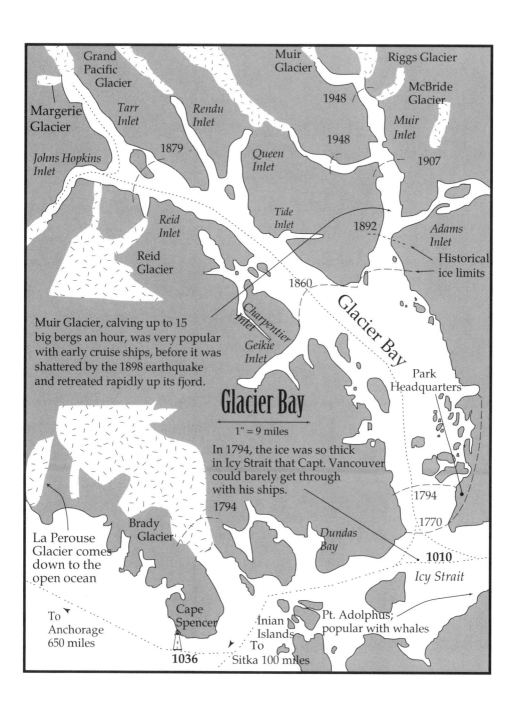

Grand Pacific Glacier

Muir Glacier

Riggs Glacier

McBride Glacier

Margerie Glacier

Tarr Inlet

Rendu Inlet

1948

Muir Inlet

Johns Hopkins Inlet

1879

Queen Inlet

1948

1907

Reid Inlet

Tide Inlet

1892

Adams Inlet

Historical ice limits

Reid Glacier

1860

Glacier Bay

Muir Glacier, calving up to 15 big bergs an hour, was very popular with early cruise ships, before it was shattered by the 1898 earthquake and retreated rapidly up its fjord.

Charpentier Inlet

Geikie Inlet

Park Headquarters

Glacier Bay

1" = 9 miles

In 1794, the ice was so thick in Icy Strait that Capt. Vancouver could barely get through with his ships.

1794

1794

1770

La Perouse Glacier comes down to the open ocean

Brady Glacier

1794

Dundas Bay

1010

Icy Strait

To Anchorage 650 miles

Cape Spencer

Inian Islands

Pt. Adolphus, popular with whales

To Sitka 100 miles

1036

CHAPTER 5

Into The Ice

CAPE SPENCER, MILE 1035 TO
GLACIER BAY AND ICY STRAIT, MILE 1000

*"Then setting sail, we were driven wildly up the fiord, as if the
storm wind were saying, 'Go then, if you will, into my icy chamber;
but you shall stay in until I am ready to let you out.' All this time
sleety rain was falling on the bay and snow on the mountains; but
soon after we landed the sky began to open. The camp was made on
a rocky bench beneath the front of the Pacific Glacier, and the
canoe was carried beyond the reach of the bergs and berg waves.
The bergs were now crowded in a dense pack against the discharging front, as if the storm wind had determined to make the glacier
take back her crystal offspring and keep them at home."*
—John Muir, *Travels in Alaska.*

Look ahead when you pass **Cape Spencer** to the
myriad islands and channels. These are the inside
waters that makes this part of Alaska such a special
place. On occasion, boats used to these sheltered waters
are called to go beyond the Cape, into the outside waters
of the Gulf of Alaska. Sometimes they aren't fully prepared:

"They shouldn't have been out there - they'd never been
outside in that boat... always worked inside waters. So, of
course, after dark the wind came up, and then Ed came over
the radio, just terrified: 'Bob, get over here, quick..Mary's
washed overboard!' It was a bad night to be looking for any-

Lighthouse

The high bluff is Cape Spencer; the actual lighthouse is sited on an island a mile offshore.

one, blowing maybe 30, with a big sea running, but we swung back and started scouting around with the spotlight, but I figured Mary was gone, washed overboard with no life jacket or anything..

"Then maybe ten minutes later Ed called saying he'd found her. Turns out a big cross sea busted out a galley window and the door, and Mary got knocked under the table, and buried under about 300 pounds of dog food that had split open from some bags they was freighting for somebody. But they never should have been out there..."

— Bob Holmstrand, fisherman

Small craft bound for Sitka and the outside coast usually take a short cut via Lisianski Strait, visible to the south here.

Look north at mile 1,029 to Taylor Bay and Brady Glacier. Glaciologist extraordinaire Muir was here the summer after his 1879 Glacier Bay trip, hiking with a dog over the flats and up to Brady Glacier on a cold and rainy August day. In the late afternoon, he had to take a running jump across a very wide crevasse. Fortunately the other side was lower, but even so he barely made it; a few minutes later he realized he and the dog had jumped onto a sort of island, surrounded by wide and deep crevasses. The only ways out were back across the wide crevasse that he had barely managed to jump over, or across a frighteningly precarious ice bridge: curved, drooping, knife-edged, eight feet down in the abyss of a crevasse from the surface of the glacier.

Muir chose the ice bridge, notching steps into the side of the crevasse, and sliding across, straddling the ice, chipping away the sharp-edged top as he went so that the dog could also use it. As he worked, the dog whimpered and cried, refusing to follow. See the picture on P.119

Only with difficulty did he get across. It began to get dark, and Muir could wait no longer. He moved away, calling to the dog that he could make it if he only tried.

"Finally, in despair, he hushed his cries, slid his little feet

slowly down into my footsteps out on the big sliver, walked slowly and cautiously along the sliver as if holding his breath, while the snow was flying and the wind was moaning and threatening to blow him off. When he arrived at the foot of the slope below me, I was kneeling on the brink ready to assist him in case he should be unable to reach the top. He looked up along the row of notched steps I had made, as if fixing them in his mind, then with a nervous spring he whizzed up and passed me out on to the level ice and ran and cried and rolled about fairly hysterical in the sudden revulsion from the depths of despair to triumphant joy. I tried to catch him and pet him and tell him how good and brave he was, but he would not be caught. He ran round and round, swirling like autumn leaves in an eddy, lay down and rolled head over heels."

—John Muir, *Travels in Alaska.*

How'd you like to have one of these bump into your anchored boat at night? On occasion stray icebergs drift into Inian Cove, a popular anchorage for fishing vessels.

Look for fishing boats coming out of the community of **Elfin Cove**, southeast of **mile 1,029**. This tiny settlement, with its boardwalk and its anchored fish buyers, is the center for the salmon trollers working this area.

Look southeast from **mile 1024** - you may be able to glimpse the cove between the Inian Islands, a favorite anchorage for purse seiners and tenders. Even in August, snow clings in the folds of the hills here, and occasional icebergs drift among the anchored fleet at night. I spent much of my 18th summer in this cove, buying fish from our native seiners. These were powered with big, straight 8 Chrysler Royal gas engines, and one of my jobs was to keep them tuned and running smoothly. In these 50-footers, the fo'c's'le was right in front of the engine, and as I worked, replacing spark plugs and filing points, I could hear the natives talking. Sometimes they spoke their native language, but other times it was English. They spoke of the fishing, but also of the legend of Lituya Bay, over and beyond the ice mountains to the north. I didn't understand all that was said, but they seemed to be speaking of an angry spirit that sometimes lashed out, creating great waves that washed away villages.

And once or twice that summer, ice drifted into the anchorage at night, a powerful, magic experience for me:

DAY THREE
MORNING

In July and August you may see open skiffs or hand trollers fishing in the Icy Straits area for silver or coho salmon.

Joe's Log

You may see whirlpools and tidal swirls in this vicinity as the tide rushes through the constricted passager between the islands.

"**August 17, 1965, Inian Cove**. Something woke me in the night, and I sat up in my bunk, wondering what it was. And then it came again, a faint but insistent scraping, as if another boat had drifted down on us in the night. I stumbled out on deck and, there, eerily lit by the three-quarter moon, was a big iceberg, moving gently down our port side, pushed by the tide. Its irregularly shaped top was even with my head; I reached out to touch it, to try and retrieve some of the gravel clearly visible within its pale, translucent flank. The gravel had been scraped off a canyon floor, hundreds of miles away, thousands of years before I was born. But the ice was hard, its contours softened by melting. My hand could find no purchase, and after a moment the berg moved away in the tide.

"Outside the point I saw a ghostly armada moving in the seven-knot current of North Inian Pass: eight or nine little bergs, maybe a thousand tons each, showing as big as medium-sized boats above the surface. In the moonlight they seemed to glow as if lit from within. I wanted to wake my shipmates, but then the tide pushed them around the corner and they were gone."

Aound dawn your ship will swing north at **mile 1010** and enter Glacier Bay. The great rivers of ice are still almost 50 miles away, but when Vancouver and his men passed this way in July of 1794, **Glacier Bay didn't exist!** Instead they found only a wide indentation in the shore, filled with a solid wall of ice, and so much floating ice in seven mile-wide Icy Strait that they could barely pick their way through! They named Icy Strait, continued their explorations to the south, and Glacier Bay disappeared into the mists of time for almost 75 years.

The next visitor was a C.S. Wood, traveling by canoe in 1877, just ten years after the U.S. had purchased Alaska from Russia. What he found was astonishing. Instead of the ice front pushing all the way out into Icy Strait, it had **receded almost forty miles**, or almost a half mile a year, an event almost unprecedented in geologic history. What caused such a great recession of the vast ice sheets during this period - some earlier version of global warming? No one really yet knows. But events in the late 1890's suggest substantial seismic activity in the Glacier Bay area. As these events were to prove, earthquakes seem to have

American Geographic Society, Univ. of Wisconsin - Milwaukee Library

the ability to shatter the ice in glaciers. Where such glaciers face the water, they will calve off immense amounts of ice after an earthquake, causing them to recede rapidly.

John Muir and Glacier Bay

In the middle of October, 1879, John Muir and his missionary companion, a Mr. Young, set out from Fort Wrangell by canoe. With a crew of native paddlers, they were bound for the ice mountains of the north that prospectors had told Muir about. As they traveled, the youngest native, Sitka Charley, told Muir he'd hunted seals as a boy in a bay full of ice and thought he could show Muir the way.

Muir was skeptical. Sitka Charley said the bay was without trees, that they'd need to bring their own firewood. The other paddlers, in all their lives throughout the region, had never seen a place without firewood.

They came to a bay cloaked in fog and storm. Sitka Charley became uneasy; the bay

Muir Glacier in 1893, from 1800' up the shoulder of Mt. Wright. Shortly after the earthquake of 1899, Muir Glacier began a rapid retreat up the inlet.

J.F. Moore, American Geographic Society, NY

Steamer Queen *at Muir Glacier, about 1890. This graceful liner was one of the first to regularly bring visitors to Glacier Bay.*

was much changed, he said, since he had seen it before. Even Vancouver's chart, a copy of which Muir so much relied upon, failed them, showing only a wide indentation in the shore.

Fortunately, they found a group of natives hunting seals and staying in a dark and crowded hut. One of the men agreed to guide them, and northward they paddled, off the chart and into that astonishing bay that had been birthed from the ice almost within their lifetimes.

The weather got worse, and Muir's paddlers wanted to turn around:

Icebergs don't always fall; sometimes they come from the underwater foot of the glacier, surfacing suddenly and unexpectedly.

"They seemed to be losing heart with every howl of the wind, and, fearing that they might fail me now that I was in the midst of so grand a congregation of glaciers, I made haste to reassure them that for ten years I had wandered alone among mountains and storms, and good luck always followed me, that with me, therefore, they need fear nothing. The storm would soon cease and the sun would shine to show us the way we should go, for God cares for us and guides us as long as we are trustful and brave, therefore all childish fear must be put away."

—John Muir, *Travels in Alaska.*

And so on they went, camping in rain, on snowy beaches, pushing farther and farther, only glimpsing the vastness and grandeur of the land.

California Historical Society FN26339

Finally Muir climbed the flanks of one of the mountains just as the clouds passed, and he gazed, stunned, at the grandeur and the size of the many-armed bay that was revealed below him.

When the party headed back, the lateness of the season was evident. Each morning before they reached Icy Strait, the ice was frozen a little thicker, and the men had to cut a lane for their canoe with an axe and tent poles.

Muir's description of the moment of their departure is a shining icon of Alaskan literature:

John Muir - few people have ever come to the area as prepared to explore and celebrate its beauty as this Scottish born conservationist.

"The green waters of the fiord were filled with sun spangles; the fleet of ice-bergs set forth on their voyages with the upspringing breeze; and on the innumerable mirrors and prisms of these bergs, and on those of the shattered crystal walls of the glaciers, common white light and rainbow light began to burn, while the mountains shone in their frosty jewelry, and loomed again in the thin azure in serene terrestrial majesty. We turned and sailed away, joining the outgoing bergs, while 'Gloria in excelsis' still seemed to be sounding over all the white landscape, and our burning hearts were ready for any fate, feeling that, whatever the future might have in store, the treasures we had gained this glorious morning would enrich our lives forever."
—John Muir, *Travels in Alaska*

DAY THREE

After Muir's discovery and powerful writings about what he'd seen, the bay became one of the premier sights of the Western hemisphere, becoming within a few years a regular stop for steamers such as the *Ancon*, the *Idaho*, and especially the *Queen*.

For many of the early steamer excursions, part of the trip was taking the ships boats to shore and if conditions permitted, taking groups to the top of the glacier itself to climb around amongst the crevasses!

The destination for most was Muir Glacier, the face of which was an ice cliff towering above the decks of the approaching steamers, and calving up to 12 icebergs an hour.

Dawn Princess at Johns Hopkins Glacier.

"The Muir presented a perpendicular ice front at least 200 feet in height, from which huge bergs were detached at frequent intervals. The sight and sound of one of these huge masses of ice falling from the cliff, or suddenly appearing from the submarine ice-foot, was something which once witnessed was not to be forgotten. It was grand and impressive beyond description."

—Fremont Morse, *National Geographic*, January, 1908.

Look for several lone spruce trees near the base of the spit in Reid Inlet. These were planted by gold miners Joe and Muz Ibach, around 1941, in soil they had carried from their homestead on Lemesurier Island, 48 miles away.

THE 1899 EARTHQUAKE - At midday on September 10, 1899, as he was waiting for lunch at his salmon saltery in Bartlett Cove, now site of Glacier Bay National Park headquarters, August Buschmann was surprised to see his trunk come sliding across the floor at him. Moments later, the cook's helper came running into the building, frightened. He had been up on the hill at the native cemetery as the ground started to heave around him, and he thought the dead were coming to life.

The earthquake shattered the front of Muir Glacier and others, and within 48 hours Glacier Bay was a mass of floating ice so thick that ships could not reach the saltery at Bartlett Cove for two weeks. Icy Strait filled with ice, making Dundas Bay, 10 miles to the west, inaccessible.

It wasn't until the following July that the steamer *Queen* ventured close enough to Muir Inlet to see what had happened. The bay was still full of ice; only by picking their way along the shore west of Willoughby Island could

they make any progress. The closest they could get to Muir Glacier was 10 miles; the rest was solid ice.

Hidden behind a fleet of icebergs, Muir Glacier commenced a rapid retreat up the inlet; today the face is 25 miles north of where Muir found it in 1879.

Lampugh Glacier pokes its icy snout into the salt water just south of the entrance to Johns Hopkins Inlet.

"Dawn Princess, **Glacier Bay, September 11, 1997**: Today the ice gods smiled and let our ship venture deep into their mighty kingdom. For Johns Hopkins Inlet is sometimes so choked with small bergs and drift ice that approaching the glacier is impossible. But today the inlet was mostly clear, and our captain eased our vessel close in to the front of Johns Hopkins Glacier and its icy breath lay cold and harsh amongst us. Closer still we moved, until the ice wall seemed to truly tower above our ship. For a long, long while we remained almost motionless, watching and listening. For of all the sounds of The North, this is the most haunting - the grinding and cracking as millions of tons of ice works its tortuous way down these winding canyons. Occasionally there would be a sharp crack louder than the others, and part of the glacier, several tons of ice, would fall, as if in slow motion, into the ice filled waters beneath. This is what we have all come for, the true magic of The North.

"A half an hour earlier we had passed Reid Inlet, and I had glimpsed the cabins that Joe and Muz Ibach, gold miners, had built on the spit in 1940, with Reid Glacier looming beyond. They lugged dirt all the way from their homestead on

DAY THREE

Four humpback whales cavorting near Pt. Adolphus, just south of the entrance to Glacier Bay.

Lemesurier Island in Icy Strait, planted a couple of spruces, and tended a bit of a garden. Each summer for almost 20 years the Ibachs would make a sort of pilgrimage to their Reid Inlet cabin. Their gold claims never amounted to much; one suspects instead that it was the immense and haunting beauty of the place that drew them back, year after year."

ROUTES IN GLACIER BAY - the bay is all part of Glacier Bay National Park and Preserve, administered by the US Park Service. In order to allow each visitor to have the richest experience of the park's unusual beauty, cruise ship visits are limited in number. Furthermore, the schedule and routes of the ships that are allowed into the Park are managed to try to allow each major ship to have one of the major glaciers/inlets to itself for a substantial viewing period. Johns Hopkins Inlet and Tarr Inlet are generally considered to offer the best opportunity for cruise ship visitors.

HUMPBACK WHALES IN GLACIER BAY - for reasons not fully understood, Glacier Bay seems also to attract a substantial population of these huge mammals, which generally summer here, and then travel, like many other Alaskans, to Hawaii for the winter! Part of the reasons for limiting the daily number of visiting vessels in Glacier Bay is to reduce the impact of this sort of activity upon the summer whale population.

Look for the familiar puff-of-smoke exhalation that marks a surfacing humpback.

BEARS AND MOUNTAIN GOATS - Get your binoculars and look sharp - mountain goats are frequently seen on mountainsides here, appearing like white dots, except that they are slowly moving. Likewise, it is not uncommon to see bears, especially on the beaches in places like Russel Island. So have those binoculars handy at all times!

In the late afternoon, your ship will make its way south of Glacier Bay, drop the Park Service naturalist to a small boat, and enter Icy Strait. If your captain has heard about humpback whales in the vicinity of **Point Adolphus, mile 1000**, he may investigate before continuing.

What's wrong with this picture? Answer: Boat is in danger. Icebergs can topple suddenly as melting changes their center of gravity.

Like Snow Pass, Stevens Passage, and Point Baker, this is one of those places where the big mammals like to regularly congregate, and there are regular whale watching tours from Gustavus to this particular area.

"*Dawn Princess*, **September 11, 1997**: After a truly stunning day in Glacier Bay, the best was saved for the last. While leaving the bay, Captain Warner saw the spout of a blowing humpback in the distance, and swung south, gingerly approaching to about a quarter mile from a pod of 9 or 10 humpback whales - very unusual for this late in the season. For a long time we idled close to the forested shore, watching the show as they alternately blew, blew, then lifted all their tales and sounded to disappear for 3-4 minutes. Then, marked by that little white vapor cloud, they'd appear again together, always surfacing within twenty or thirty feet of each other. Once we thought that they had sounded and disappeared for good, and the ship began to move away. Everyone on both sides of the ship, and especially on the promenade deck where I was, waited and waited. Some began to drift back inside, but then after about 5 minutes, the whales all came up right next to the ship - perhaps 30 yards away - a truly remarkable experience. They were so close I got a whiff of their noticeably bad breath and heard the trumpet-like sound they occasionally make as they exhale - what an amazing afternoon!"

DAY THREE
EVENING

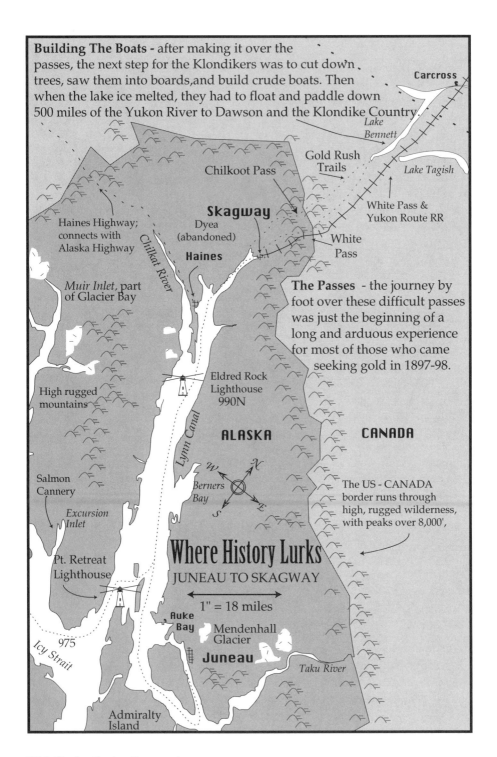

Building The Boats - after making it over the passes, the next step for the Klondikers was to cut down trees, saw them into boards, and build crude boats. Then when the lake ice melted, they had to float and paddle down 500 miles of the Yukon River to Dawson and the Klondike Country.

Carcross

Lake Bennett

Gold Rush Trails

Lake Tagish

Chilkoot Pass

White Pass & Yukon Route RR

Skagway

Dyea (abandoned)

White Pass

Haines Highway; connects with Alaska Highway

Chilkat River

Haines

Muir Inlet, part of Glacier Bay

The Passes - the journey by foot over these difficult passes was just the beginning of a long and arduous experience for most of those who came seeking gold in 1897-98.

High rugged mountains

Eldred Rock Lighthouse 990N

Lynn Canal

ALASKA

CANADA

Salmon Cannery

Berners Bay

The US - CANADA border runs through high, rugged wilderness, with peaks over 8,000',

Excursion Inlet

Pt. Retreat Lighthouse

Where History Lurks

JUNEAU TO SKAGWAY

1" = 18 miles

Auke Bay

Icy Strait

975

Mendenhall Glacier

Juneau

Taku River

Admiralty Island

CHAPTER 6

Where History Lurks

GLACIER BAY, MILE 1000 TO JUNEAU, MILE 930, VIA SKAGWAY

"We came to a place where the water was covered with boards and stuff. But there wasn't a soul left living to call to us for help. Seemed like, just standing at the rail and looking at little boards that had once been a ship and straining our eyes to see folks that weren't there no more, and then looking at them high mountains around Lynn Canal and thinking we had to go over them and on beyond before we even got to the gold country, quieted us all down. Somehow we didn't feel the same way we'd been feeling on the trip up. That country up there didn't look cordial. It made you feel like cutting out the horseplay and saying a prayer for the fellows who wasn't there no more, and for the rest of us who didn't know what was ahead, neither."
        —Margaret Ferguson Mckeown, The Trail Led North.

DAY THREE
LATE EVENING

Gustavus lies to the north at **mile 1,003.** This settlement is somewhat unusual in this part of Alaska - the land is flat and almost perfect for gardening. Farmers in the early part of the century grew vegetables here for the canneries at Excursion Inlet, Hawk Inlet, and other places. The Gustavus Inn offers lodging and family-style dining. Juneau residents sometimes take charter flights over for dinner. A road connects Gustavus with the Park Service headquarters for Glacier Bay at Bartlett Cove.

You're traveling through **Icy Strait** - when Vancouver's men explored here in July of 1794, they could barely get through Icy Strait because of the enor-

Look for northern lights if it's dark before you retire for the night.

mous amount of ice in the water: "The space between the shores on the northern and southern sides, seemed to be entirely occupied by one compact sheet of ice as far as the eye could distinguish."

Look for salmon seiners and trollers working these waters, as well as humpback whales. For many years Icy Strait has been the site of a strong run of silver (coho) salmon. Trollers usually fish them with small, pastel-colored trolling spoons. A good day might be 200 fish, worth a thousand bucks or so to the fisherman. When the fish are running here, there may be 50 or 60 boats, circling around that day's hot spot. Get your binoculars if you get close - when the "bite is on", the fish will be coming aboard hot and heavy. Look for the fisherman leaning over the side of the boat with a long gaff in hand. He or she must gaff the fish quickly and bring it aboard.

The big inlet to the south at **mile 988** is **Port Frederick**. Around the point at the eastern entrance is a disused cannery and the Tlingit village of **Hoonah**. On the Fourth of July, salmon seiners put in here for a boisterous celebration.

Fishing used to be the community's bread and butter, but today logging on tribal lands is the primary revenue source. Much of the timber goes to Japan. Accessible by floatplane or the smaller ships of the Alaska ferry system, lodging is available in Hoonah for the traveler who is seeking a quieter time than is possible in the larger towns, with their thousands of visitors a day.

The center of town is the L. Kane Store, founded in 1893, just 14 years after John Muir came to Glacier Bay. There is a new cultural center here, with a rich display of Tlingit art. Ask how to get there; there may not be signs.

Your ship makes a big swing to the west here, around Point Couverden and into Icy Strait

Packers or tenders serve as mother ships, buying fish and providing fuel and other supplies to fishing boats operating a long way from their home canneries.

It was near here that my first Alaska skipper would usually turn the steering wheel of the old salmon tender *Sidney over* to me on our night runs from Icy Strait down to the cannery at Metlakatla, on Annette Island, near Ketchikan.

It was always a totally magic time. The mate had bad eyes, the cook didn't steer, the insurance man's kid couldn't be trusted, and skipper liked his sleep. And so, after a long day of buying fish and attending to the mechanical problems of the Tsimshian seiners that fished for us, I'd get a late dinner, and then bring my coffee forward into the wheelhouse, let my eyes get accustomed to the dark. Skipper would do his routine of showing me exactly where we were on the chart, what to look out for, when to wake him, ask me if I was ready, and then retire.

The dark canyon of Chatham Strait opened ahead of me on the radar, and I'd fiddle with the old AM radio until I found a Seattle rock station, fading in and out.

House and airplane float at **Hoonah,** *south of mile 988.*

Sometimes there'd be the lights of another vessel, occasionally the wink of a navigational aid. But the land was always dark, and I was stunned by it: all that waterfront, and never a town, hardly even a house.

At **mile 975,** your ship takes a wide right angle turn to the north into Lynn Canal, a 60 mile long canyon of a fjord, at the head of which are the towns of Haines and Skagway. Look for the flashing white light, off to port, at **Naked Island,** beyond which is **Funter Bay,** site of an abandoned cannery and small settlement, accessible only by boat or floatplane.

Point Retreat, mile 960, is the lighthouse to starboard. It was named by Vancouver's Lieutenant Whidbey after being repulsed by armed natives each time his party tried to land for the night: "Where they drew up in battle array, with their spears couched, ready to receive our people on landing."

Lynn Canal, together with Chatham Strait to the south, form sort of a natural wind tunnel for the North Pacific lows and the Arctic highs that from in the interior. Particularly in the spring and fall, storms tend to march through here, one after another.

Moreover, there is something about this landscape

DAY FOUR
VERY EARLY

The mountains on either side of Lynn Canal form a natural wind tunnel.

Troller, Bridget Cove, mile 971N. The more austere landscape of Lynn Canal is evident here.

that humbles a person. Salmon fishermen bound north in their 30- to 40-foot gill-netters have a word for the vista north: "Looking up at the Big Lynn."

At mile 990N, your ship passes to the east of **Eldred Rock**, an unusual octagonal lighthouse, reminiscent of Russian architecture. Here, on a morning in 1908 the light keepers were astonished to find part of the hull of the *Clara Nevada* that had been lost with 100 souls on a winter night a decade earlier. The seaweed-draped hull, still containing the bones of many victims, had been lifted from the canal floor and deposited on the rock by the storm the night before.

Look for glaciers in the valleys on both sides here. Since Vancouver's time, these small rivers of ice have receded substantially.

Joe's Log

"**September 24, 1972, Twin Coves, Lynn Canal**. Beach picnic tonight, with four other gill-netter families in here, our boats laying in the cove before us, the glaciers seeming to hang, glowing over us in the high latitude dusk. In the stillness after supper as we sat around the fire, there was a noise like thunder, and we looked up and saw house-size pieces of ice tumbling from Rainbow Glacier into the trees below."

If there's daylight, look carefully at the vegetation along

the shores here. The spruce, cedar and hemlock are joined by deciduous trees as the effect of latitude and the cold mainland land mass that surrounds the canal makes itself felt. Like in Juneau, the climate here is much more severe, much less moderated by the sea, than in Ketchikan or Sitka.

Northwest of **Seduction Point at mile 1,002N**, (Vancouver named it after the natives had tried to lead his Lieutenant Whidbey into a trap,) is Chilkat Inlet, the last hurrah each season for salmon gill-netters. Into this narrow and steep-sided bay hundreds of thousands of chum salmon return each fall. As many as 450 vessels, each deploying a 900-foot-long net, will crowd into its barely six-square-mile area in a chaotic and competitive high-stakes frenzy. Along with the crowds, the fishermen have to fight the weather, for snow comes early to these northern fjords.

"It came on hard, snow and wind, while we were still fishing. They hadn't yet pulled the floats for the winter in Cannery Cove, and the storm broke them all up. The smart guys quit fishing right with the first of the snow and headed for Haines, but we stayed until the fishing period was over. By that time it must have been blowing seventy out in the canal, and the fish

Eldred Rock Light, mile 990N. Painting by Ann Upton, author's collection.

DAY FOUR
EARLY

Glacier Bay lies beyond the high mountains on the west side of the canal.

Huddled into Cannery Cove, with a wild Lynn Canal gale roaring by past the point, the Haines gillnet fleet waits for a chance to get out and fish.

Substantial salmon runs return to the Chilkat River each fall.

buyers were huddled with us in two little coves. We were the last boat at the *Emily Jane*, our fish buyer, and the cannery was calling on the radio telling him to head on down to Petersburg, storm or not. They weren't none too eager to go, and when they picked up the anchor and disappeared into the snow and the black, I wasn't sure I'd ever see him again."

—A Lynn Canal salmon fisherman.

Salmon that make it past the fishing fleet spawn each fall in the lower reaches of the Chilkat River, where thousands of bald eagles await their arrival. Look for eagles along the west side of the canal, especially in the fall. Possibly the largest concentration anywhere occurs around the shallow mouth of the Chilkat River, as the eagles feed on the carcasses of spawned-out chum salmon.

The Last Easy Miles

For the tens of thousands who came north during the Gold Rush years, upper Lynn Canal represented the last easy miles of their journey to the diggings.

As you enter Taiya Inlet at **mile 1,014N** from Seattle, imagine yourself at the crowded rail of a ship like the *Queen* or the *Victoria* in the fall of '97, jostling for your place with hundreds of other Klondikers, looking out through a snow squall, trying to get a glimpse of what lay ahead. There is but an hour or two before you must put on your pack, get the boxes and sacks of your "outfit" (a year's worth of supplies) ready to unload, and step out into the wind and the cold and whatever fate had in store for you.

Bella Coola mask representing Komokoa, the chief of the undersea world. AMNH 16/771

Northwest Native Art

"My wife's uncle told me this more than once. He told me that everything has a **yuk**, a spirit. He told me that he had seen them. He said that even a piece of wood that was split in half was half of a person. It was their life. Everything has a person."

—Paul John, Tooksook Bay, Alaska, quoted in *Agayuliyararput: The Living Tradition of Yup'ik Masks* by Ann Fienup-Riordan

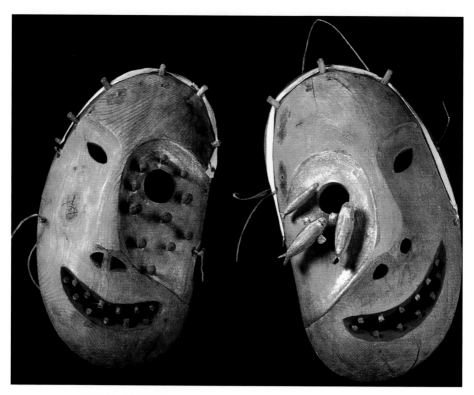

Masks were often made as pairs with asymmetrical features. These were col-lected near St. Michael on the Yukon River around 1900. Alaska State Museum, IIA1451 & IIA1452

Yup'ik is the name for the Native American tribes living in the Yukon - Kuskokwim delta area of Southwestern Alaska. They are members of the larger family of Inuit or Eskimo cultures that extends from Alaska, all the way across the top of North America to Labrador and Greenland.

Freeze-up marked the end of the fishing and berry gathering seasons and a time for celebrating. Traditionally masks were created for elaborate dance cere-monies, and most were destroyed afterwards in ritual cleansing ceremonies. Some survived to be traded for various goods, slowly making their way into the hands of collectors and museums,

Christian missionaries generally discouraged masked dancing, but begin-ning in the mid 20th century, there has been a revival in masks and masked dancing.

One of the best Alaska mask collections is in the Sheldon Jackson Museum in Sitka.

Some masks were so large as to be almost sculptures. This represents two birds flying side-by-side. Pairs of human hands are common features of masks coming from the central Yup'ik area. Collected by Ellis Allen at Goodnews Bay in 1912 **Burke Museum, Seattle, 4530**

*Blue killer-whale mask holding
small beluga whale or porpoise
in mouth. This mask was carved
for the 1946 Hooper Bay dances.
Initiated by the arrival of fil-
makers for the Disney film,*
Alaskan Eskimo, *the native
community was genuinely
excited by the opportunity to
make new masks and begin
dancing again.* Alaska State
Museum, Milotte Collection,
IIA5413

Human / Fox Ircit mask. Many masks represent the Yup'ik view of the dual nature of reality, with half human, half animal faces. Nunivak Islanders believed Ircit were extraordinary persons who were able to appear as humans, or as various animals including wolves and killer whales. Many of the contemporary masks found in galleries today have this round style.
Burke Museum, Seattle 2-2128

Tlingit dance headdress, wood, inlaid with abalone shell. It represents a fish and a man's face. Used during ceremonies at the feast after the fishing season. Collected at Angoon around 1890
AMNH E/1871

The tribes of Southeast Alaska and the British Columbia coast - Bella Coola, Haida, Kwakiutl, Tsimshian, Tlingits and others - are blessed with a much more temperate climate than their Yup'ik brothers.

Due to the availability of huge cedar trees they were able to create their well known totem poles. Masks were also an important part of their art and mythology. As with the Yup'iks, masks generally reflected the view that all creatures have spirits who must be honored.

Thunderbird mask, open and closed. The Kwakiutls, of lower coastal British Columbia, produced some particularly remarkable art. Some masks, like this one, were designed with moveable parts. Dancers would, by skillfully moving their heads, present themselves alternately as birds or humans. Collected by George Hunt in Hopetown, B.C., in 1901 AMNH 16/8532

Totems

One fair July day in 1981, when I was a young fish buyer waiting for our boats to come in, my wife and I rowed ashore to the long-abandoned site of a Tsimshian village near the southern border of Alaska. Mary Lou searched the fine white sand for glass trading beads, and I poked through the nearly impenetrable undergrowth for the remains of the village.

Detail, Kwakiutl Totem, Brockton Point, Stanley Park, Vancouver, British Columbia.

The beach yielded a dozen exquisite glass beads, some little larger than the grains of sand that hid them, yet all of bright color, little faded with the passing of centuries. In the forest was a single totem base, decayed from decades of rain and wind.

A century earlier, there would have been high-prowed canoes drawn up below the simple cedar plank-and-beam houses. In front would be art: carved cedar in its many forms, the most dramatic of which were the totems.

Totems were a highly visible sign of the success and wealth of the native cultures that evolved along the coast, whether Haida, Kwakiutl, Tlingit, or Tsimshian. Sheltered by a benevolent forest, blessed with a food-filled sea, the tribes could afford the luxury of permanent village sites and ornamental art. Their art celebrated legends, events, or simply the wealth and crest of the family for whom it was carved. The poles had no religious significance, but were records of the past in a society where there was no written language.

At first, the coming of the whites was the catalyst for a burst of creative energy among northwest tribes. Steel tools, and the cash from the fur

Detail, top of Haida style mortuary pole, Stanley Park. The Haidas of the Queen Charlotte Islands were the only tribe to built this unusual style of totem.

trade and native employment, led to an affluence celebrated in larger potlatches, more carvings, and
totems.

By the 1860s, the situation had changed radical-
ly. Epidemics had ravaged the coast, and missionaries and government worked to reform a way of life
they viewed as pagan and against the spirit of modern commerce.

At the beginning of the 20th century, travelers
remarked on the curious combination of the presence of sophisticated carved art and its apparent
abandonment. The reason was simple: so many
natives had died that villages were abandoned.

The result was that much native art disappeared,
either rotted into the forest, purchased by individuals, or, fortunately for us, collected by museums. But
in many villages, where the people struggled with
poverty and alcoholism, the tradition of art, as it was
practiced in the 19th century, essentially disappeared.

Fortunately the 1960s and '70s brought a rekin-
dling of the flame of carved art among northwest
coastal tribes. Today, intricate newly carved totems
fetch high prices and are in demand from Disney
World to corporate offices.

Totems have become cultural icons for the northwest coast. We shouldn't forget what they were
carved to celebrate: the centuries-old success of a
native culture that suffered badly with the coming of
the whites.

*Detail, Bishop totem,
Sitka NHP.*

*Haida village of Skidegate in the Queen
Charlotte Islands, British Columbia, circa
1881.*

AMNH Dossetter 42264

Alaska Cruise Companion 201

Bella Coola wooden sun mask, collected by George Hunt and Franz Boas in 1897. Ironically, while waiting for the steamer that was to take them further north, Boas ran into a competing collector from the Field Museum of Chicago. He was very annoyed to have competition!
AMNH 16/1507

Kwakiutl mask of Born-To-Be-Head-Of-The-World. Collected by George Hunt at Hopetown, B.C., in 1901. This mask opened to reveal another human face, with hands painted on the inside of the opening sections. AMNH 16/8410

Eskimo and musk-ox herd group, of carved ivory on a humpback whale vertebra. Musk-oxen tend to line up like this when confronted by a situation they are unfamiliar with. Very fine carvings such as this are still being produced by native carvers and are available throughout much of Alaska. Author's collection.

Northwest Artists Gallery

Marvin Oliver
Box of Daylight 1992

This carved and painted door represents Raven, releasing the sun. According to legend, Raven stole the box containing the sun, the moon and the stars, and placed them in the sky.

Marvin Oliver is an internationally recognized contemporary Native American artist. He is best known for combining a variety of materials: bronze, copper, steel, glass, wood and paper. Marvin merges the spirit of past traditions with those of the present, creating a unique and innovative style. His works can be found in private and public collections nationwide, and are on display at the Marvin Oliver Gallery in Seattle and the Alaska Eagle Arts Gallery at #5 Creek Street in Ketchikan, Alaska.

Northwest Artists Gallery

"WHALING CAMP", Rie Muñoz

Rie Muñoz

Whaling Camp, 1983

"A beluga whale has just been spotted and pandemonium breaks out. The villagers rush to the boats, taking oil, gas, floats, rifles, and outboard motors. This is another scene from the whaling camp at Sigik."

Juneau artist Rie Muñoz's cheerful watercolors are perhaps the most widely distributed Alaskan images from any contemporary artist. For some 40 years, she has been traveling the state, to the most rural and remote areas, to gather ideas for her remarkable pieces. Whaling Camp, like much of her work, celebrates village or native life.

Available from fine art galleries or Rie Muñoz Ltd., 2101 N. Jordan Ave., Juneau, Alaska, 99801, 907-789-7441.

Northwest Artists Gallery

Nancy Stonington

Detail from Cloudscapes

In the fjord country of Prince William Sound, the low-lying clouds lift for a moment, revealing the rugged, high, and glaciated mountains that ring the sound.

Each year artist Nancy Stonington divides her time between Alaska and Idaho, with stops up and down the northwest coast in between. Her particularly realistic watercolors of the northwest scene have become a regular presence in this region's homes and galleries.

Nancy's and other northwest artists' work is available at the Stonington Gallery in downtown Seattle, and galleries throughout Alaska.

Northwest Artists Gallery

John M. Horton, C.S.M.A., F.C.A.   Detail from Close Quarters

The historic tug *Ivanhoe* tows a log raft into Vancouver Harbor, circa 1910. As she comes up on the Moodyville Mill, she passes a big three-masted sailing ship, deck-loaded with freshly cut lumber and being pushed downstream with the tide by another tug.

Canadian artist John M. Horton is well known for the accurate detail of his historic marine paintings. Presently he lives and paints in Steveston, British Columbia, where as a volunteer he is also active in marine search and rescue.

Available from Gulf of Georgia Galleries, #5-3500 Moncton Street, Steveston, British Columbia, Canada, V7E 3A2. 604-271-3883.

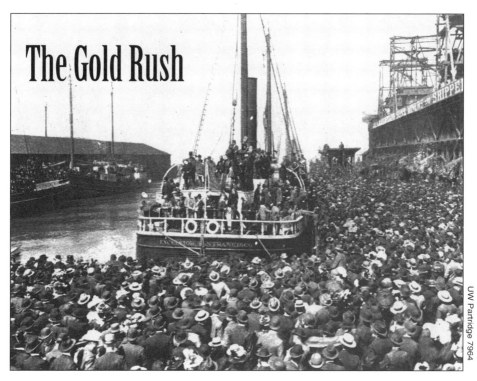

The Gold Rush

UW Partridge 7964

Much of the United States was gripped in a depression at that time. Perhaps you were a farmer from the Dakotas; you had left your family to try for fortune in the North. You had bought your outfit in Seattle and steamer passage to Skagway, with little more knowledge than that somewhere beyond those mountains men like yourself were staking out gold claims and getting rich.

The snow clears, and a cold and cheerless sun shines on as bleak and unfriendly a landscape as you've seen on this trip. The mountains rise vertically out of the water; there doesn't even seem to be a beach. The chatter of the crowd fades as all look at the mountains and what lies ahead.

If you were very lucky, your steamer tied to a wharf, but for those in the first wave in 1897, there were no wharves. Most gold seekers unloaded their outfits from steamers onto lighters, shallow-draft barges. If the tide was up, the lighters took you right in to shore. If it wasn't, the lighter got as far as the flats and you had to cross 200 or 300 yards of sand and mud to get to shore.

Many had brought animals and staked them out with their piles of boxes and gear while they made the first trips

The Grand Adventure begins - the Excelsior *departs San Francisco, loaded with gold seekers, 1897.*

DAY FOUR
EARLY

UW Thwaites 0394-1286

Ready for the North. Klondikers aboard ship, 1897.

All manner of ships of questionable seaworthiness were pressed into Gold Rush service. It is remarkable that so few sank!

across the flats to shore.

Some weren't familiar with the big tides in the northern fjords of Alaska. They rested, perhaps, after lugging their first load up the beach, and visited with others about what they might expect in the rough hewn town, visible through the snow, and hiked back to find their outfit underwater, their animals drowned. Few were really prepared for the rigors of that journey, or the true nature of the gold country.

The steamers didn't wait; their owners wanted them back in Vancouver or Seattle as soon as possible, "To get another load of suckers," as one bitter Klondiker put it.

For most of the hundred thousand or so who came north in 1897 and 1898, their Gold Rush experience had three phases. The first was often the hardest: the passes. The high mountain wall that lay between the salt water of upper Lynn Canal and the edge of the Yukon had but two routes over it: Chilkoot Pass and White Pass. Most of the men who came that first winter used Chilkoot Pass.

The most powerful image from '97 and '98 is the long line of climbers, each bent with his load, on the steps cut into the ice on Chilkoot Pass. At the top lay the Canadian

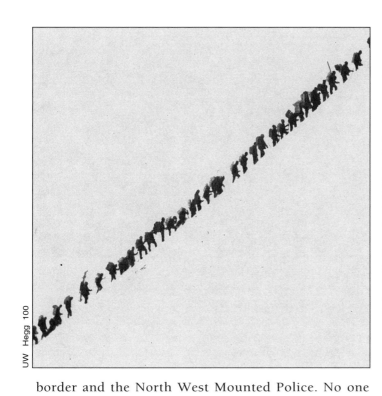

UW Hegg 100

The Golden Staircase - Chilkoot Pass, in the winter of 1897-8. To be allowed into Canada, where the gold lay, you had to have approximately 1,000 pounds of supplies. If you had money you could hire native porters to carry it.

If you stepped out of line to rest, it might be a long time before you could find a place to step in again.

DAY FOUR

border and the North West Mounted Police. No one could pass without a year's supplies, about 1,000 lbs.

Wealthy men hired porters, but most just carried it all up themselves, load by backbreaking load, caching it at the top and hoping no one would rob them before they got back. A solid stream of upward bound men filled the steps. If you wanted to rest, you stepped off to the side, but when you wanted to get back in, you had to wait for a gap in the line; it was that crowded. By 1898 cable tramways could carry your gear over the pass for a fee, but the men in the first wave had only their feet.

Down the other side from the summit was Lake Bennett, and after that it was the boats and the rivers. They were 50 miles from salt water, but there was another 500 to the gold country. Arriving in winter, the men camped on the shore, cut down the trees, whipsawed them into planks and built boats, and waited for the ice to melt to launch their boats and begin the journey:

"Some leaked, some didn't steer. They had lots of things wrong with them. But a lot of the boats, made of whipsawed lumber, had beautiful lines and sailed as pretty as anything I

The first of the rapids: Once over the passes, the Klondikers cut trees, built boats, and faced 500 miles of rivers and rapids.

ever did see on the Columbia. Yes, sir, that was an expedition, that fleet of boats getting ready to set out from Lake Bennett, come spring of '98."

—Margaret Ferguson Mckeown, *The Trail Led North.*

The trip became a journey of true epic proportions. Down the canyons and through the rapids they came, some capsizing or breaking up, the survivors trying to hitch a ride with the next boat that had room. The

The Lucky Few

With no convenient banks, many miners simply brought their gold south with them. One woman, hearing that her husband might be coming home on the steamer, brought their children to meet it, hoping he'd have enough money to buy them groceries (he'd been gone six

Alaska gold at Scandanavian American Bank, Seattle, 1897.

months and they were out of money). He staggered down the gangplank under the weight of his duffle and its 116 *pounds* of gold.

wealthier switched to Yukon steamers as soon as the river got wide enough, but all were heading for Dawson and the last phase of their epic sagas: the diggings.

The best claims were staked before most of the gold seekers arrived. Many who started north gave up before they got to the Yukon. Only half who made it staked a claim. Just a very few struck it rich. Most found some kind of work in Dawson City or in the diggings, made a little money, and moved on.

Yet their adventure transcends time. All experienced the powerful drama of **The North**. Those who returned to the lower 48, even penniless, brought back stories and memories to entertain generations of breathless children and grandchildren.

Haines and Port Chilkoot

The spot that looks like a New England village at mile 1012N is Fort William H. Seward, sometimes known as Port Chilkoot. Decommissioned after World War II, it was purchased sight unseen by five veterans and their families to pursue their dream of a planned community. Now part of the city of Haines, just to the north, the fort offers a variety of cultural activities.

Haines, until a highway was recently completed out of Skagway, was the only place in southeastern Alaska with a road that went anywhere (it connected to the Alaska Highway). Today it is rich with Tlingit culture and is especially known for the dramatic fall migration of bald eagles that feed on Chilkat River salmon.

Totem poles under construction at Port Chilkoot.

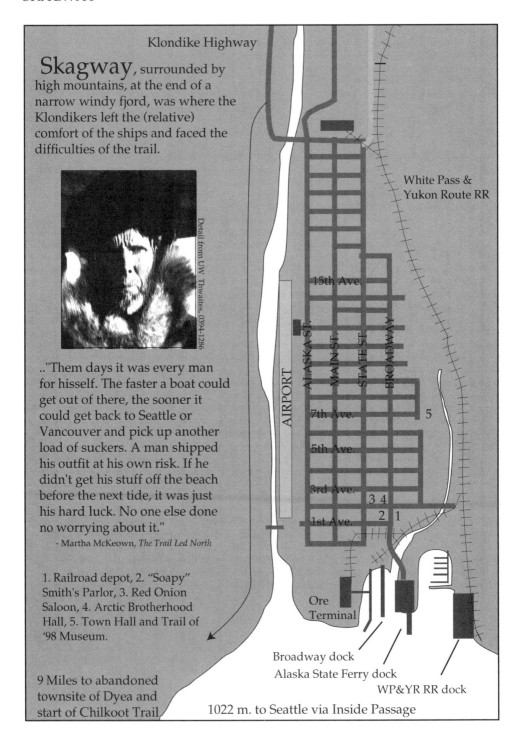

Klondike Highway

Skagway, surrounded by

high mountains, at the end of a
narrow windy fjord, was where the
Klondikers left the (relative)
comfort of the ships and faced the
difficulties of the trail.

Detail from UW Thwaites, 0394-1286

White Pass &
Yukon Route RR

15th Ave.

AIRPORT

ALASKA ST.

MAIN ST.

STATE ST.

BROADWAY

7th Ave.

5

5th Ave.

3rd Ave.

3 4

2 1

1st Ave.

.."Them days it was every man
for hisself. The faster a boat could
get out of there, the sooner it
could get back to Seattle or
Vancouver and pick up another
load of suckers. A man shipped
his outfit at his own risk. If he
didn't get his stuff off the beach
before the next tide, it was just
his hard luck. No one else done
no worrying about it."

- Martha McKeown, *The Trail Led North*

1. Railroad depot, 2. "Soapy"
Smith's Parlor, 3. Red Onion
Saloon, 4. Arctic Brotherhood
Hall, 5. Town Hall and Trail of
'98 Museum.

9 Miles to abandoned
townsite of Dyea and
start of Chilkoot Trail.

Ore
Terminal

Broadway dock
Alaska State Ferry dock
WP&YR RR dock

1022 m. to Seattle via Inside Passage

Skagway

It is the drama of '97 and '98 that fills this town. Skagway blossomed for but a few years, lawless and rough, then almost disappeared.

The gaunt-faced men have passed through to whatever fate the North had in store for them. But the town the boom built at the jumping-off place for the Klondike remains, looking much as it did in 1897 and 1898, when some 80 saloons and many professional women were anxious to serve the lonely men on the trail north.

Today, Skagway offers a unique experience to visitors. Even the vegetation is different from the rest of Southeast Alaska, as the town is under the influence of the harsher temperature extremes of the interior instead of the milder, cloudier maritime climate elsewhere in the region. Some of the native craftwork available here, especially of ivory, is unsurpassed in Alaska.

The White Pass & Yukon Route RR train pulls right onto the dock next to the Regal Princess. *The train ride, along the route followed by many headed to the Yukon during the Gold Rush, is one of the most popular excursions in Alaska.*

*This steam powered rotary snowplow, recently restored to operating condition, kept the passes open. The black cab houses the locomotive engine that was used **just to turn the plow!** Another steam engine, coupled behind, did the pushing!*

Skagway entrepreneur Dennis Corrington used to be an ivory trader along the Yukon River. His museum houses some of his excellent collection, along with some unusual items for sale. Don't miss it!

Sam's Tour; "Ever since my dad showed me some old photos of the Goldrush, I've always wanted to see Chilkoot Pass—not by chopper or plane, but to see it, even maybe hike the whole route. It's a tough hike for my old bones, and I didn't have the time this trip — the guidebooks say allow for 3 to 5 days of strenuous going — but I just wanted to get a taste of it. So I rented a bike, checked in with the Park Service for trail conditions, and had a great six mile ride to the trailhead. Then I parked my bike and just started, with a lunch pack, and an extra sweater. What a gorgeous trail—winding along the riverbank, but all I could think about was those who went before—you know, left their families behind, to make it in The North! I only went a couple hours in, ate and hiked out, but I made a vow: someday, I'll get in shape and do the whole thing! And that beer back at Moe's Frontier Bar, back in town, went down pretty smooth, too!"

Elsie's Tour: "What a train ride, what views - It was super! I had thought that once the gold rush guys got over the pass, they were there! No way—turns out they still had another 500 miles to go—not only that, but most of them went over in winter and had to chop down trees, and handsaw planks to build boats to go down the rivers, after the ice melted - those guys were tough!

I loved Skagway—I like the way they've got all those old buildings fixed up. I found this beautiful carved ivory cribbage board, with whaling ships and scenes all over it, almost like stuff you see in museums!"

Note: Only ivory harvested by Native carvers in accordance with federal regulations may be legally sold. Make sure you get a export/transit permit if you buy ivory and plan to go into Canada on your way home. You'll need it to bring the ivory back into the US.

Skagway Excursions

Bald Eagle Preserve Jetboat Excursion – 6 hours.
Chilkoot Lake Fresh Water Fishing – 5.5 hours.
Chilkoot Trail & Glacier Helicopter Tour – 1.5 hours.
Dyea Bicycle Tour – 2 hours.
Eagle Preserve Float & Glacier Flight – 5.5 hours.
Glacier Country Flightseeing – 1.25 hours.
Historical Skagway by motorcoach. – 2 hours.
Horseback Riding Adventure – 3.5 hours.
Klondike Bicycle Tour – 2 hours.
Klondike Summit Van Tour – 1.5 hours.
Pilot's Choice Helicopter Odyssey – 1.75 hours.
Skagway by Streetcar – 2 hours.
Skagway Sportsfishing – 3.5 hours.
Skagway Trailcamp and Salmon Bake – 3 hours.
Summit & Trail Camp Exploration – 3.5 hours.
Valley of The Eagles Nature Tour & Glacier
    Flightseeing – 4 hours.
White Pass Heli-Hiking and Train Ride – 5 hours.
White Pass Scenic Railway – 3 hours.
Yukon Territory Adventure (motorcoach) – 5-6 hours.
Yukon Expedition & White Pass Scenic RR – 6.5 hrs.
See your ship excursion desk for more information.

Downtown Skagway with Island Princess in background. Note the steepness of the mountainside behind the ship.

DAY FOUR

Skagway entrepreneurs wasted no time when the Klondikers came to town - this curio store opened in 1897.

MOHAI

Princess May, on Sentinel Island, mile 966N, in 1910. She was lucky— there were no injuries, and she was refloated with little damage.

There is a major sea lion rookery on Benjamin Island, east of mile 967N.

Leaving Skagway, you'll be retracing your steps to lower Lynn Canal. The bottom is littered here with the pieces of two of the finest steamers to travel north, both belonging to the Canadian Pacific Railroad. First was the *Princess Sophia*. At around 1 AM on October 24, 1918, the gold miners and the crews from the 10 Yukon River paddle-wheelers aboard the *Sophia* were probably still celebrating. They'd left Skagway a few hours earlier, the rivers freezing up, their season over, the bright lights ahead.

Upstairs in the pilothouse, the atmosphere was more subdued, the captain anxious. He'd seen Eldred Rock Light, **mile 994**, at midnight through the snow but navigation on such a night relied on something called "time and compass." The skipper would calculate from the engine revolutions how fast his vessel was traveling. Taking his course line from the chart and making allowances for the wind and the tidal currents, he would steer until his time ran out, that is, when he should be at the next point of reference.

On that bitter night in 1918, with blowing snow and limited visibility, the next checkpoint after Eldred Rock was Sentinel Island Light, 28 miles away. Over such a distance, a steering error of one degree would put the vessel a half-mile off course.

Sometime around 2 AM, as her skipper was groping through the snow and trying to see the Sentinel Island Light, the *Sophia* drove her whole length ashore on Vanderbilt Reef. Fortunately the rocks cradled her, and there was no need to try and launch lifeboats on such a rotten night.

By first light a rescue fleet was standing by: the *Cedar, King and Winge, Estebeth, Elsinore*, and others. But as the *Sophia* seemed to be resting securely on the rock, it was decided to wait until better weather to evacuate the passengers and crew.

It proved to be a tragic mistake. In the late afternoon, the northerly began to blow with renewed fury, and the rescue fleet was forced to seek shelter in a nearby harbor. Darkness came with driving snow and bitter wind, and the vessels had to set anchor watches to make sure they weren't dragging.

Roaring down the canal, the wind caught the *Sophia*'s high exposed stern, driving her off the reef, ripping open her bottom, and sending her into the deep water beyond. There was time for one desperate radio call: "For God's sake come! We are sinking." In the morning only her masts were above water, her 343 passengers and crew drowned in the northwest coast's worst maritime disaster.

Alaska's Bermuda Triangle? A lot of ships have come to grief in this area.

Thirty-four years later, miscalculation of a course change drove the graceful *Princess Kathleen* ashore at Lena Point, **mile 956**. Her passengers were more fortunate. They climbed down ladders to the rocky beach and watched the favorite of all the Alaska-run steamers slide off the rocks and disappear into deep water.

To the east at Lena Point is **Auke Bay**, a community connected by highway to Juneau, about fifteen miles away. The road system here, like those in most Southeast Alaska communities, isn't connected to the 'outside'. However, it is the longest, running from Juneau all the way up to **Berners Bay, mile 970N**.

Juneau is at the head of 10 mile long Gastineau Channel. Surrounded by land, and tucked into the mainland shore, winters here are a lot colder than Ketchikan or Sitka.

Had the settlement of Alaska proceeded at the same time as, say, Boston, or Philadelphia, five thousand miles to the east and south, it is unlikely that anyone would have chosen Juneau for a town site. According to Vancouver, Gastineau Channel was impassable because of the ice, and his men passed through in August.

Juneau, right, and Douglas, left, from the Mt. Roberts Tramway Station. Mendenhall Glacier is just out of sight at upper right. The waterway is Gastineau Channel. Almost dry at low tide in its upper reaches, it is used as a small craft shortcut to Auke Bay and points north.

Juneau

"The Glory Hole" was the nickname for the cavernous entrance to the gold mine across Gastineau Channel from Juneau. In those days, at the turn of the century, men were cheap and safety regulations were few. Sometimes a miner a week went to glory—in a cave-in or an accident in the pit and the miles of tunnels that led off it.

Just as it did for the territory, gold put Juneau on the map. But the fine gold in the creeks that Joe Juneau and Richard Harris found in 1880 played out, to be replaced by a very different enterprise: industrial-style hard-rock mining.

The gold at Juneau was embedded in rock, which had to be drilled, blasted, and transported to one of the noisiest contraptions of the industrial age: the stamp mill. This crude device crushed the ore-bearing rock into pieces small enough for chemical removal of the gold to be effective. The Treadwell mill at Juneau was the largest in the world, with 960 stamp machines crushing 5,000 tons of ore a day.

Today, the mines are gone and city, state, and federal governments now provide half the jobs in Juneau. Cosmopolitan, yet surrounded by wilderness, Juneau is a town where you can come out of an espresso shop and encounter a bear rummaging through a garbage can.

There are many things to do around town; these are some of the editor's choices:

•GO SEE THE ICEFIELDS: In the mountains behind town is the dramatic Juneau Icefield and nearby Mendenhall Glacier. To see the glaciers by air is a remarkable experience, allowing the traveler to comprehend more easily the geology and the dynamics that produce the region's glaciers. If small airplanes are not for you, take the coach tour to Mendenhall Glacier, 14 miles from downtown; the visitors' center at the glacier has a comprehensive display on glaciology.

•RAFT THE MENDENHALL RIVER: Mendenhall River raft excursions begin on Mendenhall Lake, with great views of the glacier, and follow the Mendenhall

River, with a snack of smoked salmon, reindeer sausage, cheese and a beverage along the way. The guides provide rain gear, life jackets and boots. Total trip time, including travel to and from downtown, is three and a half hours.

•TAKE THE TRAM - Just completed in 1997, this cable car runs from the docks to near the top of Mt. Roberts. Visitors may hike, shop, have a meal, and watch a film presentation on Tlingit culture. Terrific views!

•FLY-IN TO A SALMON BAKE: The Taku Glacier Lodge, built in 1929 on the Taku River 17 miles northeast of Juneau, offers a unique tour. Floatplanes pick up guests downtown for a flight over the glaciers and up the Taku River valley to the lodge for a baked salmon lunch.

•WALK AROUND THE TOWN: Like most Southeast Alaska towns, Juneau is small enough to know quickly: just grab a walking-tour map and hit the trail. The neo-colonial place with a totem pole out front is the governor's mansion. Don't pass a stop at the Alaska State Museum. And make time for shopping for crafts and gifts around Seward and South Franklin streets.

The new Mt. Roberts Tramway station is close to the docks.

Juneau Land Excursions:
Authentic Alaskan Salmon Bake - 2 hrs.
Deluxe Mendenhall Glacier and City Tour - 3.25 hrs.
Douglas Island Nature Walk - 3 hrs.
Juneau Mountain Bike Tour - 4 hrs.
Mendenhall Glacier and Gastineau Hatchery Tour - 2.75 hrs.
Mount Roberts Tramway - 1.5 hrs.
Mount Roberts Tramway and Guided Nature Walk - 1.5 hrs.
Naa Kahidi Theatre & The SeaAlaska Cultural Arts Park - 1.5 hrs.
Sea Excursions:
Auke Bay Sea Kayaking - 3.5 hrs.
Juneau Sportsfishing Adventure - 5 hrs.
Mendenhall Glacier Float Trip - 3.5 hrs.
Taku Glacier & Scenic Wilderness Cruise - 3.5 hrs.
Wildlife Sightseeing Cruise - 3.25 - hrs.
Air Excursions:
A Trip to Taku Lodge - 3 hrs.
Glacier Helicopter Expedition - 2 hrs.
Juneau Icefield Floatplane Sightseeing - 1 hr.
Mendenhall Glacier Helicopter Tour - 2.25
"The Pilot's Choice" Glacier Explorer Helicopter Tour - 2.5 hrs.
For more information visit your ship's excursion desk.

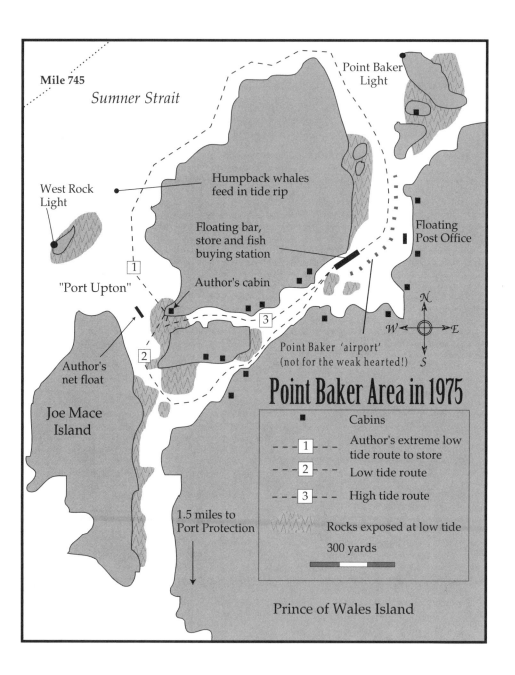

Mile 745

Sumner Strait

Point Baker Light

West Rock Light

Humpback whales feed in tide rip

Floating bar, store and fish buying station

Floating Post Office

"Port Upton"

Author's cabin

Author's net float

Point Baker 'airport' (not for the weak hearted!)

N
W E
S

Joe Mace Island

Point Baker Area in 1975

■	Cabins
- - 1 - -	Author's extreme low tide route to store
- - 2 - -	Low tide route
- - 3 - -	High tide route
〰〰	Rocks exposed at low tide

300 yards

1.5 miles to Port Protection

Prince of Wales Island

CHAPTER 7

Life in a Roadless Community

I magine, cheap waterfront land and good fishing close at hand. This was the situation at the remote and road-less communities of Point Baker and nearby Port Protection (south of **mile 745**) in the early 1970s . A person could get an acre-sized waterfront lot on a shel-tered cove, with the right to harvest 10,000 board feet of timber a year from the adjacent forest for personal use. You could build a cabin out of the trees on your land and make enough cash fishing from an outboard skiff to sup-port a family.

A floating store/bar/fish buyer at Point Baker served the needs of the hundred or so souls settled around these two coves on the edge of the vast woods. The mail and freight boat came once a week, supplemented by the occa-sional floatplane. Families with gill-netters or trollers tried to make a trip to town — Wrangell or Petersburg, each about 40 miles away, a long day's round trip — every few months to stock up on supplies a little cheaper.

Puddle jumper near Point Baker, 1974.

Point Baker from the air: with limited takeoff space and tide rips at the harbor entrance, it was a particular challenge for floatplane pilots.

Strangers should use these narrow channels on a rising tide.

Behind the shore was the forest, thick, almost impenetrable. For the most part walking was so difficult everyone traveled by outboard skiffs or "puddle jumpers." At Point Baker especially, one's traveling decisions were dictated by the tide. Have a whiskey warmup some snowy winter afternoon with your groceries at the store? Stay too late and the trip home might be a nightmare: wading along the shallow channel, towing your skiff behind you, lifting, scraping it over the thin places, picking your way with the flashlight through the snow, and hoping your batteries last until you make it home.

When I arrived here with my wife on our 32-foot gillnetter in the spring of 1972, the flavor of the place was compelling. The older residents welcomed younger blood, and the salmon fishing in Sumner Strait was great. We found part of an island, on a private cove, with a gorgeous western exposure and view, for $17,000, 10 percent down and 10 years to pay.

After the season, in our houseboat on Seattle's Lake Union, we set to making plans for a cabin on our newly purchased land in Point Baker. As our money dwindled, so did the size of our new-home-to-be until whatever roof we could get over our heads for fifteen hundred bucks would have to be it. We settled on a 16-by-20-foot box with a

Retired salmon troller, living aboard boat at Point Baker dock.

half loft, 480 square feet, total, tiny.

With tight-fisted determination, we scoured garage sales and discount building suppliers. At a second-hand store we found a big diesel oil range for $35; at another, all our windows and doors for $175. In my tiny floating shop I prefabbed a Formica kitchen counter top, complete with sink and drawers. We got plywood, nails, and shingles, all on deep discount, and purchased a 16-foot cedar skiff with a 10-horsepower 1958 Evinrude outboard. Tool by tool, fitting by fitting, we packed all the supplies and extras aboard my 32-foot gill-net vessel and skiff to tow north.

The weather gods granted us an easy trip, and shortly after arriving in Point Baker, the mail boat arrived with our pickup truck-sized bundle of lumber from the sawmill in Wrangell, and our first major problem.

The plan was to tow the tightly strapped bundle of lumber through the narrow back channel to our secluded cove and house site. But when the mail boat's crane lowered the bundle of lumber into the water, it kept right on going. The wood was so green and dense it wouldn't float. It was what the locals called, "pond dried."

We had to set it temporarily on the dock and then haul it in our skiff, load by load, to our cove.

Our front window, 1975.

This was our Alaska dream - to have a waterfront place with our fishing boat out front. It was a truly satisfying experience.

In the two weeks before the salmon season began we struggled: the wood was so wet it splashed when your hammer missed the nail. My one and only hand saw bent on the first beam we cut. It rained every day; every night we would take the skiff back to our boat at the Point Baker dock, heat up something quick, and fall, exhausted, shivering, into our sleeping bags.

And we created something exquisite: out every window was the water. As we ate at the driftwood table, we could see eagles swooping low over the cove. There were curious seals, and most marvelous of all, a pair of humpbacks that hung out in the tide rips by West Rock, off the mouth of our cove. On still nights, we could hear the sigh-like breathing of the whales as they surfaced and exchanged fresh air for stale. When the first snow came

Getting in the Firewood, Southeast Alaska Style

At Point Baker on a breezy winter morning, the CB radios crackle from cabin to cabin: good firewood logs have been spotted in the ebbing tide pouring around the tip of the island. Within minutes a handful of skiffs and small fishing craft set out across the mile or so of crooked water between the harbor and the logs. As each arrives, they stop alongside the closest large log, hammer in a big steel staple, attach a tow line, and begin the long, slow tow back to the harbor. The first to arrive latch onto really huge logs, 60 feet long by four feet in diameter, *four cords of firewood in a single log*. Hauled up on the beach at high tide, such a find would be enough for most of the winter for the smaller cabins.

Evening at "Port Upton".

one November evening, the fire in the wood stove crack-led cheerily, our kerosene lamp shone out on the vast and wild world beyond the windows, and it was magic.

Many of the new young people who arrived in the 1970s couldn't afford the price of an outboard and fell back on the traditional puddle jumper, whose origins were in the 1930s and '40s, when so-called hand trollers (they didn't have engine-operated equipment to haul in the lines) were spread all over Southeast Alaska.

The power plant in the 1970s-vintage Port Protection-to-Point Baker puddle jumper was usually an air-cooled Briggs & Stratton one-cylinder gasoline engine, turning a propeller through a homemade reduction gear of belts and pulleys. Such engines could be ordered through the Sears catalog and delivered by the mailboat.

With such a craft, sporting two fresh-cut-from-the-woods trolling poles, a young fisherman or woman could catch perhaps $6,000 to $8,000 worth of fish in the summer, with very little overhead.

A young entrepreneur brought in a portable sawmill and the building boom was on.

Point Baker Scrapbook

Clockwise from upper left: Hand trolling family; heading for Port Protection through the back channel; view out our kitchen window, Point Baker, Dec. 1973; homesteader, Port

Protection, 1972; building a float with salvaged beach logs and store-bought lumber; winter-time, Port Protection.

THANKSGIVING AT PORT PROTECTION: In the fall of 1973, a good fishing season behind us and excited to be in our new, if small, cabin, we went by outboard to one of the three or four Thanksgiving dinners being held around the cove at Port Protection.

We arrived to a Norman Rockwell scene: the harbor was still, the daylight was dying, snow was falling, and kerosene lamps burned cheerily in homes along the water's edge. Tying our skiff to a big moored firewood log, we walked up the beach and went inside a big three-room cabin with attached shop. My wife went in to help the other women, and I stayed in the shop with the men. The wood stove was hot, the rum was flowing and we talked about the hunting and the fishing.

But when we were all called in to sit down, my wife and I learned a new Thanksgiving tradition. It was a big group and a small table, but it wasn't a problem. The men sat down side by side at the table, decorated for the occasion and heaped high with food. The women just sat wherever they could: on the sofas or cross-legged on the floor.

In summer, with daylight that lasted from four in the morning until after eleven at night, the focus was fishing: making enough to make it through the long winter. But when the season was over and the days got shorter, there was time for the kind of relaxed visiting that is a highlight

Heard at the Point Baker Bar

Being a rough-and-tumble sort of place, the Point Baker Bar didn't offer the wide selection of drinks some of the newcomers in town were used to. Once in 1972 two gill-net vessels freshly arrived from Seattle tied up to the bar to celebrate their trip.

Bartender: "What'll it be, fellas?"

Newly arrived fishermen to wife: "What d'ya think, honey, you wanna Manhattan?"

Bartender: "Hey guys, we got whiskey and water, whiskey and Coke, and whiskey and Tang. What's it gonna be?"

The Point Baker Bar

of life in such places.

The center for much of the activity in these two communities was the floating bar and store in the harbor at Point Baker. Built on a raft of logs, one of the most tedious problems for fishermen drinking in Alaska's harbor towns was avoided: *The Ramp.*

The tides in the region are huge: in a six-hour period the water level might vary 20 feet. Imagine: you come in tired from a fishing trip at high tide, tie up your boat at one of Ketchikan's many marina-style floats, walk across the nearly horizontal ramp to the shore to, say, the Fo'c's'le Bar.

Troller's home, Port Protection.

There, surrounded by acquaintances, you relive and celebrate many fishing experiences. Six hours later, your vision blurred and equilibrium unsteady, you head back, only to discover that the tide is way down, and the ramp is almost vertical.

At Point Baker you could tie your boat right up to the bar, with no ramp to negotiate. Not only that, it was less than half a mile from the fishing grounds, and it sold groceries and hardware and bought fish.

Seeking greener pastures for salmon fishing, I sold my cabin at Point Baker in the mid-1980's and built a new boat for the remote salmon fishery in Bristol Bay, Alaska, 1,000 miles west. Bleak, austere, remote, with violent tidal currents and few good harbors, it was the opposite of Southeast Alaska. The fishing was a competitive frenzy I'd never experienced before, but there were friends to guide me and the shorter season allowed us more time at home with our families and children.

Yet to a man (Alaska law allows salmon fishermen to only fish a single region), we all missed the wooded waterways and the secluded harbors we'd left behind.

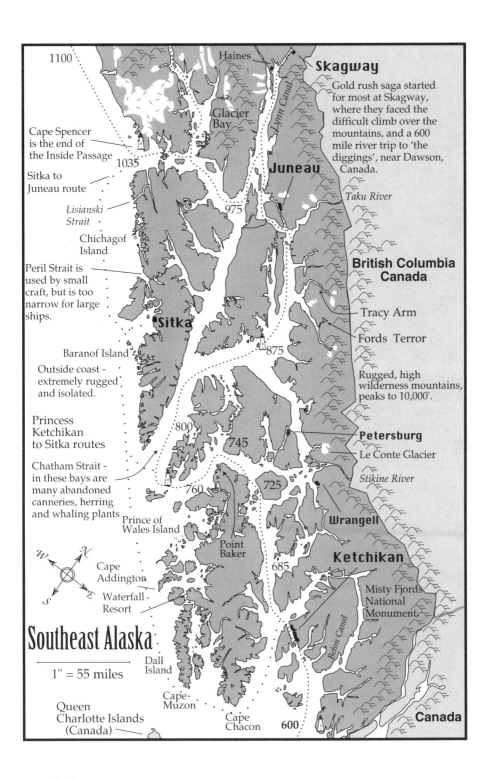

1100

Haines

Skagway

Gold rush saga started for most at Skagway, where they faced the difficult climb over the mountains, and a 600 mile river trip to 'the diggings', near Dawson, Canada.

Cape Spencer is the end of the Inside Passage

1035

Glacier Bay

Juneau

Sitka to Juneau route

Lisianski Strait

975

Taku River

Chichagof Island

British Columbia Canada

Peril Strait is used by small craft, but is too narrow for large ships.

Sitka

Tracy Arm

Baranof Island

875

Fords Terror

Outside coast - extremely rugged and isolated.

Rugged, high wilderness mountains, peaks to 10,000'.

Princess Ketchikan to Sitka routes

800

745

Petersburg

Le Conte Glacier

Chatham Strait - in these bays are many abandoned canneries, herring and whaling plants

760

725

Stikine River

Prince of Wales Island

Wrangell

Point Baker

685

Ketchikan

Cape Addington

Misty Fjords National Monument

Waterfall Resort

Southeast Alaska

1" = 55 miles

Dall Island

Behm Canal

Cape Muzon

Queen Charlotte Islands (Canada)

Cape Chacon

600

Canada

N
W E
S

CHAPTER 8

Islands Without Number

JUNEAU, MILE 930 TO
ALASKA BORDER, MILE 600

*"So we came to Alaska, on a wild and lost afternoon, caught in
a tide race off a nameless point, in failing light, far from any help.
The heavy westerly swell, the dirty southwest chop, and the push of
the tide on top made it all I could do just to keep way on the boat,
throttling over the big ones and then diving deep into the troughs.
The seas came from all directions, and even at dead slow, waves
slapped at the windows, sagging-in the thick glass".*

—Joe Upton, *Alaska Blues*

Taku Inlet is the wide channel leading northeast
at **mile 929**; it is the mouth of the Taku River.
Vancouver's Lieutenant Whidbey and his party
faced sleet, rain and thick ice as they traced the continental
boundary here in early August, 1794; they went only 13
miles before being stopped by the ice.

DAY FIVE
EVENING

All the land to the west here, for almost the next hundred miles, is **Admiralty Island**. Much of the island is
part of the Admiralty Island National Monument. This
island is the only one in Southeast Alaska where one is apt
to encounter brown bears.

The inlet to the east at **mile 914** is **Port
Snettisham**, at the head of which is a dam supplying
power to Juneau. The sides of the inlet are so steep the
power lines had to be strung by helicopter.

The Southeast Alaska mainland here is narrow, with
only 14 miles separating the head of Port Snettisham and
the Canadian border.

Tracy Arm: Traveling up Tracy Arm (the entrance is

five miles northeast of **mile 900**) is like going back through geologic history. The fjord's dramatic walls lose their vegetation until they become bare shining rock, shaped and ground smooth by the ice. There is no shore to speak of, the mountains plunging vertically into the water, which in many places is more than a thousand feet deep.

Tips for mariners: Use care here; some of the bergs calving off these glaciers weigh thousands of tons and create waves up to 25 feet high as they fall into the water. Large bergs may roll over or break up without warning, also creating large and unexpected waves.

Muir was genuinely moved by the power and the beauty of the glaciers, and he was able to communicate some of this enthusiasm to his companions. Once, when they had paddled most of an afternoon up Tracy Arm, frustrated with the narrow and ice-choked channel, they turned yet another corner and found what he had come to seek, the glacier itself. While Muir stood in the canoe, sketching the glacier, several huge icebergs calved off, thundering into the water of the narrow fjord. "The ice mountain is well disposed toward you," one of the native paddlers said to Muir, "He is firing his big guns to welcome you."

The Arm is a popular excursion from Juneau, as vessels do not need a difficult to obtain Park Service permit, required in Glacier Bay. If you take a excursion to Tracy Arm, be sure to move up to the bow of the vessel, away from the engine noises as you approach the glacier face itself. For one of the most impressive things about glaciers is the noise. You have millions of tons of ice being pushed forward through a frequently twisting channel, and it is an impressively noisy process.

On the shore of **Harbor Island**, which guards the entrance to Tracy Arm, west of **mile 900**, is an abandoned homestead and fox farm These were common on small Southeastern Alaska islands in the 1940s and 1950s. Typically fed salmon, the foxes were a problem to feed when the fish weren't running.

"When we were low on fox food, Dad would send my brother and me over to Point Astley, where there were lots of seals and sea lions. We'd shoot those big sea lions, and then we had to cut the carcasses into pieces with a two-man saw to load into the skiff. God, it was a mess."

—A fox farmer.

Hood Bay Cannery room number 12 waits for workers who will never return.

Look for humpback whales throughout Frederick Sound and Stephens Passage. Much larger than orcas, up to 50 feet long, humpbacks sometimes breach—leap completely clear of the water—a good trick for a 30-ton creature. No one knows for sure why whales breach; one theory is that they are trying to shake parasites that sometimes cling to them.

John Muir passed this way by canoe on his way to discover Tracy Arm::

"Around noon we rounded Cape Fanshaw, scudding swiftly before a fine breeze, to the delight of our Indians, who had now only to steer and chat. Here we overtook two Hoona Indians and their families on their way home from Fort Wrangell. They had exchanged five sea otter skins, worth about a hundred dollars apiece, and a considerable number of fur-seal, land-otter, martin, beaver, and other furs and skins, $800 worth, for a new canoe valued at 80 dollars, some flour, tobacco, blankets, and a few barrels of molasses for the manufacture of whiskey. The blankets were not to wear, but to keep as money, for the almighty dollar of these tribes is a Hudson's Bay Blanket."

—John Muir, Travels in Alaska.

DAY FIVE
EVENING

Be alert for the white spouts indicating the presence of whales. If the water is calm, they may be seen for quite a distance.

Victrola in abandoned fox farm, Harbor Is., east of mile 900.

Admiralty Is.

Stephens Passage

Taku Hbr.

910

900

Tracy Arm

Sumdum Glacier

Windham Bay

Endicott

Fords Terror

Map - to the east of your ships course are several deep inlets that wind far back into the mountainous interior.

A little later the two canoes began to race each other, continuing until after dark. The water was "firing" that night: exhibiting phosphorescence, showing each stroke of oar or paddle and the wakes of the canoes as shining tracks in the black. The group was heading for a well-known salmon stream to camp for the night. As they approached, they could see the schools of fish glowing in the water. Muir and his traveling companion set up their tent against the steady rain. The Hoona natives, two families, simply took their rest on the wet ground: "Our Hoona neighbors were asleep in the morning at sunrise, lying in a row, wet and limp like dead salmon."

Ford's Terror is a remote inlet with an extremely narrow entrance - see sidebar on opposite page. The only place to anchor inside is near the mouth of a creek on the northeast corner of the inlet. As is usually the case in such places the bottom comes quite suddenly out of very deep water into the shallow creek delta. An eighty foot charter vessel had a close call here:

"The relief skipper was on that trip. If I'd known he was going to try Ford's Terror, I'd have nixed the idea. He got in O.K., but then he wasn't watching the sounder when he went into anchor and slid up onto the sand bar before he could back off. Of course the tide was going, so they were stuck there for the night. He had to get all the passengers onto the beach because the boat laid way over onto her side. So they built a big bonfire and just slept around it.

Some of the [8] passengers were pissed and wanted a partial refund, but for about half of them, they thought it was the most exciting part of the whole and wouldn't have traded it for anything. The boat floated off fine when the tide came up. "

—a friend

Start looking for ice at Turnabout Island, mile 856. This is the southern limit of drift ice from the glaciers in **Tracy Arm**, east of **mile 900**, and Le Conte Glacier, east of Petersburg. On occasion Le Conte Glacier puts out

Fords Terror Journal

My salmon boat seems dwarfed by the brooding steep walls of Fords Terror.

About 20 miles southeast of **mile 900,** hidden in a fold in the hills, is the remote and little visited inlet called Fords Terror. We explored it one weekend between fishing periods in 1973. The memory is etched in my mind still today:

"September 5, 1973: Just at one, traveling dead slow, with little water under us, we passed the rapids in the creek-like entrance to Fords Terror. Hardly spoke a word for the next mile, so overpowering was the scenery. The channel was barely a hundred feet wide. To the north a sheer rock wall rose out of the water a thousand feet before sloping back out of sight. We passed a waterfall, with at least a hundred foot clear drop into the trees. The gorge opened up to a basin perhaps one mile by three, and we dropped the anchor, rowed ashore, and walked, until our boat was just a dot on the far shore.

"The sun went over the mountain at 4:30, and the evening came early and chill. At dusk, flight after flight of ducks came in low and fast, to settle on the water near the shore with a rush of many wings and soft callings.

"The night was chilly, with northern lights again. Stood out on deck and watched, until the cold drove us in. Yesterday and today, the places we visited make us feel tiny indeed.

"September 6, 1973: First frost! The stove went out in the night, and we woke to find the dog nestled in between us. To go out onto the frosty deck on such a morning, with the still glassy basin around, and the dark forests and frozen hills above - words can't tell it, pictures can't show it.

"Our cup seems pretty full just now."

tremendous amounts of ice, some of which may find its way into Wrangell Narrows.

Five Finger Light, at **mile 870**, was the first manned lighthouse in Alaska and the last one automated, in 1983. Compared to other coastal areas, Alaska has relatively few lighthouses because of the difficulty of building and supplying such structures in remote areas. Wherever possible the Coast Guard relies on buoys and untended lights for navigational aids.

*If you see the lights of a village to the south near **mile 845**, it will be the native village of Kake.*

The village visible to the southeast from **mile 845** is **Kake**, a Tlingit village supported by a cannery and logging on native land. Locals use narrow Rocky Pass (see P. 239) frequently as a short cut to Sumner Strait. According to one story Kake residents were astounded a few years back, to see a tug towing a big barge emerging from the constricted passage. No one could remember such a vessel or barge coming through the pass before. The skipper of the tug came out of the pilothouse and hailed those on shore.

"Say," the rough-looking man said, waving a hand back toward Rocky Pass, "that Wrangell Narrows ain't nothing like the chart." He stopped and looked over at the village on the shore, "And I thought Petersburg was larger than this." He was 40 miles west of where he thought he was!

Unusual places

Kootznahoo Inlet, north of the Tlingit village of Angoon on the western side of Admiralty Island, is a narrow channel leading tortuously east to 10,000 acres of intricate channels, lagoons and bays.

On a large tide, the current boils in through the entrance, swirling at up to 10 knots. Some of the passages to the inner waters appear more like creeks in the forest, through which the water

Humpback whale blowing in the extremely narrow entrance to Kootznahoo Inlet.

seems to tumble downhill into the basins and lagoons beyond. At slack water, humpback whales have entered as far as the native village, feeding on herring. Considering their size, the current, and the constricted passage, it seems remarkable that none have stranded.

Look southeast from around **mile 845** to the head of the island-choked bay and to Rocky Pass, the narrow back channel to Sumner Strait. It was this narrow channel ("we paddled on through the midst of the innumerable islands") from which John Muir, an evangelist companion and a group of native paddlers emerged on the morning of October 19, 1879. The natives dreaded the crossing of Frederick Sound to Point Gardner at the southern tip of Admiralty Island:

In calm waters, vessels may tie together for more convivial traveling.

DAY FIVE
AROUND MIDNIGHT

"Toyatte said he had not slept a single night thinking of it, and after we rounded Cape Gardner and the comparatively smooth Chatham Strait, they all rejoiced, laughing and chatting like frolicsome children." — John Muir, *Travels in Alaska.*

I passed this way as well, after a week long king salmon trolling trip in Chatham Strait:

"**June 5, 1974**: Underway at 5 from Kake, on yet another gem of a morning. Across the channel, looming eerily over the trees and water, pink in the rosy dawn, towered Baranof Island, 30 miles away. Then we were in Rocky Pass, weaving in and out of the flats and rocks, in the very shadow of the trees - twice my trolling poles knocked branches down on deck. There was a warm smell to the air, the alders and birch bright green on the shore. We even saw Mr. Bear today, clamming on a beach, scooping up a pawful, and smacking one big paw down to smash the clam, then putting the whole mess up to his mouth.

"The day was so fair we stopped at a long deserted cabin in a small sheltered bight on Sumner Island for lunch. We lay on a grassy knoll and got pleasingly sunburned for the first time in two years, with the wind in the trees, and the cries of the gulls in our ears. When the sun grew cool and dropped in the sky, we were on our way to cover the last miles to Point

Joe's Log

Baker, where we tied up after five weeks away.

"On the flats behind our cabin, the grass was green, the garden had sprouted, and the flowers were all out. With the gill-net season opening here in two weeks, a float to build, and a net to hang, we'll just stay here.

"So ended our Chatham Straits troll trip. We fished a lot of country; we hardly made a dime. Yet I'd do it again in a minute. That lonely canyon cast a spell on us. We fished for days, went in and out of a dozen bays, and in all that time, hardly saw another boat."

Abandoned equipment, Pillar Bay.

Before the old fish plants deteriorated too badly, young fishermen working out of small, open craft would sometimes live in the old residences.

For much of this century, **Chatham Strait** was a beehive of activity. Between the salmon plants, the herring plants, and the whaling stations, almost every bay in this canyon-like region was home to some sort of commercial activity. Then the herring and the whales disappeared, and refrigerated tenders allowed consolidation of the salmon canneries into towns like Petersburg and Ketchikan.

For many of the plant operators, who were headquartered in Seattle, the decision to close a plant came in the wintertime, when just a caretaker remained in the remote Chatham Strait bay. Sometimes it was easier to abandon the plant than to send up a vessel and a crew to bring out the supplies. The plants were in reality whole little towns, with well-built houses for the managers and their families, bunkhouses and mess halls, warehouses, workshops, powerhouses, and so forth. When they were no longer needed, the owners just walked away, leaving the warehouses full of supplies. Word that the company in a particular bay had "jerked their watchman" was notice that it was free pickings, and the region's fishermen and trappers were quick to make sure nothing was wasted.

For the small craft traveler, it is almost spooky to travel in Chatham Strait, to anchor and go ashore and wander through the ruins, rarely encountering another traveler.

Bay of Pillars, east of mile 813, and **Washington Bay**, east of mile 820, both contained substantial herring or salmon processing plants in their day. In a visit to Wash-

ington Bay in 1975, the buildings were intact, but the forest was growing up around them.

To the west at **mile 800 is Port Walter**, the wettest place on the United States mainland, with 240 inches of rain a year. Hidden at the head of the bay is the narrow entrance to **Big Port Walter**, an unusually steep-sided basin containing the village-like ruins of a herring plant.

One wonders about the spirits of the winter caretaker, with the sun gone over the mountain on October 15, not to appear again for four or five months, and the inner basin frozen eight to ten feet thick.

Likewise, Tyee, now abandoned, at the southern tip of Admiralty Island, was a major salmon cannery in the 1940s, the brightest lights for miles around.

At **Port Conclusion**, three miles north of Port Alexander, Vancouver anxiously awaited the four overdue cutters and yawl boats that were filling in the last blank places on his chart in August, 1794. Finally the boats hove safely into sight during a rainstorm on the 19th.

Then with grog for all hands, and cheers ringing from ship to ship in a remote cove halfway around the world from England, there ended one of the most remarkable feats of navigation and exploration in modern times. In three summers of exploring and charting this unknown coast, through persistent fogs, swift currents and occasional thick ice— losing just one man to bad shellfish— Vancouver had disproved the ages-old notion of a Northwest Passage back to

Sperm whale, Port Armstrong, circa 1940. Today protected by law, several species of whales frequent Alaskan waters..

DAY SIX
VERY EARLY

Captain Vancouver finished his three seasons of searching for the Northwest Passage at Port Conclusion, west of **mile 800** in 1794.

the Atlantic. In doing so, he charted, explored, described and named much of the Northwest coast. It was nothing less than a stunning achievement. He was 38 years old.

In a cove on Baranof Island, west of **mile 792, is Port Alexander**. With a good harbor, a settlement, a fish buyer and a store, and good fishing at Cape Ommaney (west of mile 786), it's a popular spot in summer. In its heyday, the 1920s and 1930s, it was Alaska with a capital A, as the *Maggie Murphy* boys noted:

> "It became the number one trolling port in the territory, a wide open, carefree, money-kissed little place that old-timers still recall with nostalgia."
>
> —John Joseph Ryan, *The Maggie Murphy*.

When they walked into town, they were halted by an elderly man who told them, "Boys, it's illegal to walk on the streets of Port Alexander sober."

In those days, many trollers worked out of open boats, some without motors, rowing as they towed their lines through the water. A little tent city sprang up south of the

A Hand-troller's Life

"Port Alexander, June 1975: Visited Amy and Scott in their little cabin on the upper lagoon today. With a garden in back and his beautiful 14-foot hand-trolling skiff in front, they've come a long ways since the last time I heard about them.

"That was last year, and she was very pregnant. They were squatting at a tumbledown cannery in Pillar Bay and trying to make a living hand-trolling from his small open boat. The fishing was poor, so they moved south to Port Malmesbury and camped on the beach. There was a fish buyer there, but when he needed medicine or groceries the fish buyer didn't have, he'd take that little skiff of his all the way across Chatham Strait to Port Alexander. Those are big waters for an open boat, and he told me once that old engine pounding away was the only thing between him and a pretty cold and wild sea.

Scott's hand troller at the Port Alexander float

"Now, with a fat baby nursing, a garden planted, a pile of firewood outside, good fishing here, and friends all around, it looks as if he's about got 'er licked."

dock each summer. By the late 1940s the party was over, the great runs rapidly diminishing as the newly built dams on the Columbia River, 1,200 miles south, prevented the big kings from reaching their spawning grounds.

25 miles after passing Port Alexander, your ship will swing east, pass the lighthouse at **Cape Decision, mile 775**. Today the lighthouse, like all in Alaska, is unmanned, but up to about 1975, the lightkeepers had a pretty lonely existance there.

Coronation Island is on the right here. On its south side is **Helm Point**, the most conspicuous headland in Southeast Alaska. Rising sheer from the sea to a thousand feet, it is the nesting place for thousands of sea birds.

The bays of Coronation Island have a bad reputation among fishermen for williwaws: violent, unpredictable gusts of wind.

Port Alexander is another popular spot for hand trollers or skiff fishermen.

DAY SIX
EARLY

"Fishermen are not certain what causes the williwaws. They only know that on peaceful summer evenings, when the sea is calm and boats are resting at anchor, a dull roaring noise is sometimes heard in the harbors of Coronation Island. The noise gains steadily in volume, and suddenly, with terrifying force and swiftness, a blast of wind sweeps down off the rocky hills, scattering boats like bowling pins."

—John Joseph Ryan, *The Maggie Murphy.*

UW Thwaites 0098-1

Getting in the winter's meat, Southeast Alaska style.

A pair of humpbacks make Point Baker their regular summer stomping grounds. The place to look is right in close to the shore, near the small island with a light on it, just west of the entrance to Point Baker harbor.

Hole in the Wall, east of **mile 751**, is one of Southeast Alaska's special places. A channel, so narrow that trollers must use care if their poles are down, leads to a tranquil and lake-like basin where deer and bear may be seen along the shore.

To the north here is Rocky Pass, See P. 239. It was there in in August, 1794, Lieutenant Johnstone, exploring in Vancouver's small boats, was approached by several canoes, with natives who apparently wanted to trade:

"One of the canoes now advanced before the rest, in which a chief stood in the middle of it, plucking the white feathers from the rump of an eagle and blowing them into the air, accompanied by songs and other expressions, which were received as tokens of peace and friendship."
—Capt. Geo.Vancouver, *A Voyage of Discovery*

However, ever since the near-disastrous struggle with natives at Traitors Cove the previous summer, Vancouver's men were wary of situations in which they were outnumbered. So they wisely declined the invitation to stop and kept on rowing.

Watch for humpback whales at Point Baker, mile 745, usually in close to the shore, west of the point. Typically a pair remains here for most of the summer, feeding on herring in the tide rips. In the 1960s, a particular whale got to be known as Ma Baker. Local lore has it that she once surfaced under one of the puddle jumpers, or small fishing skiffs, lifting the surprised fishermen and his boat completely clear of the water for a moment.

Point Baker and the nearby community of Port Protection are two roadless fishing communities. It was here that we built our little island homestead. See Chapter 7.

This bay was the site of one of Vancouver's closest calls. Late on the afternoon of September 8, 1793, while exploring and charting Sumner Strait, a storm was seen approaching the area. It was at last light that Lieutenant Broughton in the *Chatham* saw the entrance to what looked like a cove and signalled Vancouver to follow him into the bay, south of **mile 745**. It was just in time:

Look for small fishing skiffs fishing near Point Baker.

View from the window over the kitchen sink at our Point Baker cabin, 1974. The cabin may be glimpsed, partially hidden by the trees in the cove behind the little island with the light, just west of Point Baker.

"We had scarcely furled the sails, when the wind shifting to the S.E., the threatened storm from that quarter began to blow, and continued with increasing violence during the whole night; we had, however, very providentially reached an anchorage that completely sheltered us from its fury, and most probably from imminent danger, if not from total destruction. Grateful for such an asylum, I named it Port Protection."

— Captain George Vancouver, *A Voyage of Discovery.*

DAY SIX
EARLY

If your ship slows and seems to zig zag after passing Point Baker, the skipper might be avoiding the nets of the **Sumner Strait salmon gill-net fleet** from **mile 740** to about **mile 743**. Typically they will fish from Sunday noon to Thursday noon. The fish come from the west here, and the trick is to set your net back from the district boundary at Point Baker, so that the ebbing current carries you to the line, then stops, just as the tide turns. This gives you a front row seat, with no room for another boat to set legally between you and the incoming fish.

Gillnetters, distinguished by the net reel on the stern, work these waters for salmon.

It was this strongly flowing tidal current that caused Captain Johnny O'Brien's luck to run out in the black of a November night in 1917. The *Mariposa* was one of the

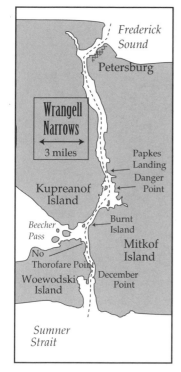

Frederick Sound

Petersburg

Wrangell Narrows

← 3 miles →

Papkes Landing

Danger Point

Kupreanof Island

Beecher Pass

Burnt Island

Mitkof Island

No Thorofare Point

Woewodski Island

December Point

Sumner Strait

finest steamers on the Alaska run, but while Dynamite Johnny caught a nap in his stateroom as a pilot steered, the strong current set her off course and onto Mariposa Reef, **mile 745**, where parts of her still remain.

About 90 minutes after Point Baker, your ship will swing south into Snow Pass. If you see ship lights to the north near here, it might be a work boat, entering **Wrangell Narrows, 10 miles north of mile 725**. All Vancouver found was a muddy slough in September of 1793; but industrious fishermen and loggers, aided by Coast Guard and Corps of Engineers dredges, have dug out the thin spots and put in 65 buoys and markers to create a 20-mile short-cut between Sumner Strait and Frederick Sound. The scenery is dramatic, like a river through the woods, and the route knocks 90 miles off the run to Juneau, but it's too narrow for large ships.

The Alaska state ferries also take this route, generally going through when the tide is high. At night or in fog, their skippers are doubly challenged, as not only does the tidal current run hard, but in places it runs obliquely across the dredged channel.

Consider this foggy meeting between a big ferry and a 70-foot fish packer:

Busy with fishing boat traffic, 22 mile long **Wrangell Narrows** is just big enough for Alaska ferries, but way too shallow and con-stricted for larger cruise ships.

"I hate to go through them narrows in the black and the fog, but the cannery wanted the fish, so we had to go. Then right in the narrowest place, the radio blasts in my ear: 'This is the Alaska ferry *Matanuska*, southbound at marker 16. Northbound traffic please advise.' The *Matanuska*? Just a mile ahead, and him with the tide pushing him on? I called him right back, and mister, I could hear the tension in that man's voice. '*Matanuska* back.

Petersburg

Also known as Little Norway for the heritage of its residents and spectacular setting, this is a town that fishing built. Originally shipping their fish south with ice from nearby LeConte Glacier, Petersburg fishermen have created a waterfront with three canneries and several custom processing facilities. In recent years these fishermen have expanded their operations into the crab and salmon fisheries of the Bering Sea and western Alaska.

Yeah... I see you on my radar... but you'd better pull over and let us by... it's pretty damn tight here.' We were right below Burnt Island Reef, and I could see his target on the radar getting bigger and bigger all the time, and I knew it was time to get the hell out of the way. So I just slowed down and pulled over into the shallows. I'd rather put 'er ashore on a mud bank than get T-boned by a 400-foot ferry!

Petersburg's cannery row with mountains rising to 10,000' behind.

DAY SIX
AROUND DAWN

"I slowed right down until I was just idling into the current, and looked out into the black, trying to see him. You know how it is with that radar: when something gets really close, it just disappears into the sea clutter in the middle of the screen and you can't really tell exactly where it is. Well, the ferry did that, he was that close. I was just bracing myself to hit either the shore or him, when I saw him—just a glimpse of a row of portholes rushing by fast in the night, the big tide pushing him on, and then he was gone. Man, I don't know how them fellows do it, but I know I wouldn't have liked to been him that night."

—An Alaskan tender skipper.

You can imagine how rapidly the tide runs through a narrow channel like this. At Petersburg, a fishing community at the north end of the narrows, the tide can rush past the wharves at up to 6 mph! When you make a landing with a boat, the trick is to get the lines all tied to the dock before you take the engine out of gear. Landing a big fish packer

Tricks of the old time fish buyers

The great thing about the Icicle Seafoods cannery in Petsrsburg is that it's right next to the grocery store. When you get your groceries, usually two or three carts worth, you just roll the carts right out onto the dock, over to the big boom mounted electric hoist, and then *lower the whole full shopping cart right down to the deck of your boat!* It sure beats carrying them one bag at a time all the way down a 30 foot steel ladder dripping with slimy fish guts.

Tight quarters in Wrangell Narrows - note how the tug has shortened the tow-line so the barge is right behind him. When these boys come through, you want to give them plenty of room!

loaded with several hundred thousand pounds of fish into a berth with no room on either side can be a real challenge with the tide running — once you're committed, there's no second chance!

Once, when I was the young skipper of a 60' fish buying vessel, we approached our Petersburg cannery after a 20 hour run down from the Chilkat Inlet fishing grounds. It was just break time on a glorious August afternoon and the entire cannery crew was out, sitting on the railing at the top of the dock, having coffee as we swung in toward them. I could see the superintendant there too. It was my first job as skipper of a cannery tender and I really wanted to impress him with my boat handling skills.

Unfortunately the engine died just as I put it into reverse and we hit the pilings a mighty glancing blow, scattering workers and their coffee cups far and wide!

Off the Beaten Track - the village of **Wrangell** is 24 miles east of Snow Pass. The muddy water sometimes seen near here is from the **Stikine River**, six miles north of town. Before 1900, eager hordes from three different gold rushes ebbed and flowed through this town to board steamboats headed up-river. The Stikine Strike occurred in 1861, followed by the Cassiar Strike in 1873, and the Yukon Strike in 1897; for a while Wrangell was the busiest spot in the new Alaska territory. But when John Muir arrived by steamer from Portland in 1879, the town was between rushes and it was life in the slow lane:

John Muir in Alaska

This well known naturalist came to Alaska during a limbo period in the place's history. He arrived in 1879, just 12 years after the territory was purchased from Russia, but 18 years before the gold strike that kicked off its modern history.

Few have come as prepared. With a powerful writing style that reflected a boyhood spent memorizing Bible verses in Scotland and decades of hiking the California Sierra Nevada behind him, he was the preeminent naturalist of his time.

Muir didn't have Gore-Tex waterproof clothing, nylon tents, Kevlar canoes or Coleman camp stoves. Yet in his five trips to Alaska, he made journey after journey that many of today's outdoors people wouldn't attempt. And he wrote—glorious prose, some of the best ever written about Alaska.

"Of all the thousands of camp-fires I have elsewhere built none was just like this one, rejoicing in triumphant strength and beauty in the heart of the rain laden gale. It was wonderful—the illumined rain and clouds mingled together and the trees glowing against the jet background, the colors of the mossy, lichened trunks with sparkling streams pouring down the furrowed bark, and the grey bearded old patriarchs bowing low and chanting in passionate worship."

— John Muir, *Travels in Alaska.*

"The most inhospitable place at first sight I had ever seen. The little steamer that had been my home in the wonderful trip through the archipelago, after taking the mail, departed on her return to Portland, and as I watched her gliding out of sight in the dismal blurring rain, I felt strangely lonesome... There was nothing like a tavern or lodging-house in the village, nor could I find any place in the stumpy, rocky, boggy, ground about it that looked dry enough to camp on until I could find a way into the wilderness to begin my studies."

— John Muir, *Travels in Alaska.*

Owl totem from Kah Shakes Island, Wrangell Harbor.

Visited by few cruise ships, **Wrangell** has a slower pace. Visitors can expect to be greeted by children selling garnets (a dark-purple stone) gleaned from a ledge in the **Stikine River**, five miles north of town. A half-mile walk south of the dock in Wrangell Harbor is Shakes Island, with impressive totems and a replica Tlingit lodge.

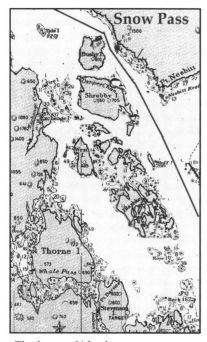

The dozens of islands and miles of intricate waterways around Snow Pass are popular with kayakers.

The narrow passage your ship transits around **mile 720 is Snow Pass**.

Look for humpback whales feeding in this area. These 40- to 50-foot mammals seem especially to like the tide rips in Snow Passage.

If you're really fortunate and have strong binoculars, you may be able to observe bubble net feeding, a method used by humpback whales to herd fish into compact, easy-to-eat schools. Several whales circle beneath the herring, exhaling slowly from their blow holes. The circle of bubbles serves to contain or herd the fish, and the humpbacks then surface in the middle, with their mouths open. See P. 114

"*Dawn Princess*, **Snow Pass, September 8, 1997**: Just a few of us are up on the bow as we slide through the oily-looking tidal swirls. To port the mist seems entwined in the trees of Shrubby Island. When I used to take my old fish tender through here, Mary Lou and I would always get our crew to steer, and we'd go up to the very bow to watch the dolphins riding the pressure wave right in front of our bow. They would swim to just in front of the stem, and let the pressure wave push them forward, their pleasure evident. It was obvious they were doing it just for the thrill of it.

"Any place the tides swirl strongly around a point seems to attract humpback whales as well. Today was no different. I looked for a long time, and finally saw a pair, working the rips about a mile north of the pass. I felt the ship slow, waited for the Captain to make an announcement, but the whales sounded and didn't come up within eyesight, and after a bit we speeded up again."

Whale stories: Do orcas (killer whales) take revenge? In British Columbia they tell the story of a logger who, sighting an orca below him as he was falling a tree, dropped it on the whale for sport. Onlookers said the whale appeared to be hurt but swam away. Later that day, the logger got in a small boat to motor across the inlet.

Halfway across, a killer whale struck and capsized the boat, and the logger drowned.

Eskimos on Alaska's North Slope tell a similar tale. A whaler harpooned an orca instead of his usual quarry, the much larger bowhead. After that, whenever he would go down to his skin boat, orcas would be waiting for him, and he was afraid to go out. He finally had to give up fishing and whaling.

Handtrollers or skiff fishermen can make a good living out of small craft.

Float Home Tales

Land to buy is so scarce in this region that some enterprising folks build their houses on floating log rafts. Of course, living like this entails a few wrinkles that wouldn't occur to land dwellers. For one family with growing kids, sometimes the house just doesn't seem big enough. So when the kids have cabin fever, this mother just sends them out to fish in the outhouse!

Another time, the husband noticed one of his big hundred pound propane bottles was leaking, and he was unable to fix it. Concerned that the leaking gas would be ignited by the nearby fish smoker, he disconnected and rolled it into the cove, thinking he'd let it drift out a bit with the tide, and shoot a hole in it so as to let it sink harmlessly to the bottom. But, by accident, his first shot instead knocked the valve off , and, propelled by the escaping gas, the propane bottle began moving rapidly like a torpedo in a circle back toward the float home.

Now the man really had a problem — as his horrified wife and children watched, the propane bottle gathered speed and straightened its course into a beeline right for them.

Letting his rifle rest on the porthole opening in the door to steady his aim, he tried to get a bead on the speeding bottle, but each time he was ready to shoot, the propane bottle would submerge and travel along just under the surface, impossible to hit with the rifle! Finally, when it was about 20 yards away, it surfaced just long enough for him to get a clear shot, blowing a hole in its side and it quickly sank!

UW 12141

In the north woods - before chain saws, loggers used spring boards to stand on while they worked their two man saws.

The Wards Cove Packing Company salmon cannery is located on the right side of the cove.

The deeply indented land to the west that you've been parallelling since early this morning is **Prince of Wales Island**, the third largest island in the United States. From these shores and others like it come the fish and the logs that are the mainstays of the region's economy.

The wide channel to the northeast as you approach the Ketchikan area is **Behm Canal**. It narrows to less than a half-mile wide at Behm Narrows and continues east and south, putting Ketchikan on an island.

Sixteen miles up the canal is **Traitors Cove**, where Vancouver had his closest brush with death. Low on food, circumnavigating Revillagigedo Island in the launch and the yawl boat, his boat was nearly overwhelmed by the natives before the other boat could get close enough to aid them. Vancouver attributed their behavior to bitter trading experiences with other Europeans, the natives exchanging the best they had for goods that turned out to be shoddily made of inferior materials.

Look east for the big pulp mill in **Wards Cove at mile 654**. This is the Ketchikan Pulp Company, the engine that has driven the local and regional economy since it was built in 1954. Trees cut throughout lower southeastern Alaska were towed here to become "dissolving pulp," a product used in the manufacture of cellulose-based products such as rayon and cellophane. In recent years concerns about the impact of logging on salmon steams reduced the amount of timber available for harvest and the mill closed in 1997.

Look for brooms tied in the upper rigging of purse seine salmon vessels. A sign of very good fishing, a broom means a vessel has caught at least 100,000 fish. When prices were good in the late 1980s—50 cents a pound for pink salmon—that translated to $200,000 or more, but when the price plummeted a few years later to 10 or 15 cents, a one-broom season meant barely breaking even.

Fish Pirates and Crick Robbers

If there was one burr under Alaskans' saddles, spurring the push for statehood (1959), it was the fish traps. Made of netting and hung from big, floating log frames or from piles driven in shallow water, the traps caught salmon and held them alive until a trap tender could take them to a cannery. Alaskans resented that Seattle companies owned most traps and canneries.

Each trap had a watchman. Trap robbers or fish pirates would approach the trap at night and threaten or, more

Brailing a fish trap, circa 1940. Such devices, mostly owned by Seattle fishing companies, were banned shortly after Alaska became a state in 1959. Tongass Historical Society.

commonly, pay off the watchman and make off with whatever fish they could load. Few Alaskans frowned on this, feeling that the Seattle-owned canneries were stealing their resource to start with. It depended on the watchman, though:

"The cannery told me it wasn't worth getting shot over a few fish, so if pirates came, I was to let them have what they wanted. But I decided no pirate was taking fish when I was watching, so the first one that came, sneaking around in a big boat with no lights on one night, I got my rifle and shot out his pilothouse windows, and I didn't have no trouble after that."
—*A fish trap watchman.*

"Crick robbing" is the practice of fishing in closed areas, typically the mouths of creeks or rivers where spawning fish congregate. Today, to deter such robbing, "Fish cops" patrol in float-planes, and seasonal workers camp on some creeks and count fish.

Ketchikan was known as the Salmon Capital of the World, from the 1930s and '40s when 11 canneries operated here and in nearby inlets. Today, two big canneries and several small freezer plants operate in town and the resource is strong again after a prolonged slump in the 1970s. You may have heard that salmon are scarce, even in danger of extinction, in northwest states. Not in Alaska. The 1994 statewide catch of 194 million salmon was the largest in Alaska's history. So please, eat plenty!

On a weekend, perhaps a hundred of the graceful 58-foot "limit seiners" (Alaska limits the length of salmon seiners to 58 feet) might be tied up along the wharves of Ketchikan, the young crews "uptown" for whatever entertainment they might find. On Sunday they'll leave, dispersed to hundreds of coves and bays to fish.

Kayakers below Creek St. boardwalk.

Ketchikan

A Saturday afternoon in summer, 1951: the steam whistle at The Great Atlantic and Pacific Tea Company's Sunny Point salmon cannery echoes across Tongass Narrows as hundreds of workers stretch their tired muscles, start to clean up, and fan out to the bars and eateries that line the waterfront. Out in the channel floatplanes start to land, big twin-engine Grumman Geese, and the slow, lumbering Stinsons, bringing in loggers from Prince of Wales Island and Tsimshian Indians from the village of Metlakatla. As the sun slants toward the northwest, the fish boats begin arriving from the outer districts, Dixon Entrance in the south and Clarence Strait to the north: big 60- and 80-footers loaded with salmon for canning and fishermen in for a night on the town.

At Big Dolly Arthur's and the other brothels along the boardwalk at Creek Street, the ladies finish their makeup and wait for their first customers. At the police station downtown, the boys in blue check their nightsticks and their pistols before heading out; Saturday night is always busy.

Almost half a century later, Ketchikan is still *ALASKA* in capital letters: all the rough-and-tumble elements that make this region what it is still ebb and flow through the streets and harbors of this town.

Second largest of only nine towns in an area larger than many states, Ketchikan is the economic center of lower Southeast Alaska. A narrow strip of a town along the steep western side of Revillagigedo Island, its few miles of roads aren't connected to anywhere else.

WHAT TO DO: The historical sights celebrate, in some fashion, Tsimshian and Tlingit culture, logging, or fishing. At the minimum, take the walking tour around downtown, and make the trip to one of the totem centers. The Creek Street Historical District, the Tongass Historical Museum, and the Thomas Basin Boat Harbor, as well as good shopping, are all within an easy walk of each other.

Just to the right of where your ship docks is Thomas Basin, a boat harbor. A stroll here is a good chance to see some of the Alaska fishing fleet up close.

A particularly good hike is up the Deer Mountain Trail that starts just a mile from downtown. At the top of the three-mile ascent is a dramatic view of the waterways and islands around Ketchikan.

FISHING: If catching a salmon is high on your list of things to do on your Alaska cruise, Ketchikan might be a good bet. Strong hatchery silver, and abundant pink and king salmon runs make for good fishing. If you really want to go after those big halibut, probably Sitka, being right on the ocean would be better. Remember — as well as a fishing trip it's also a chance to cruise along a real working waterfront and see some of Alaska's sea and bird life up close. Bring your camera.

DAY SIX

Tip: If you go out sportsfishing, consider having your catch smoked at one of the local smokeries like Silver Lining Seafoods. Most will smoke, hold, and ship your fish to you after you return home.

If it seems like everyone in town must have a plane, it's because Ketchikan is the main supply point for most of the remote communities of lower southeast Alaska, and most of the freight moves by plane. This is the ubiquitious Cessna 180, the most popular small plane in Alaska.

Ketchikan Excursions:
Alaska Wilderness Fly-In Fishing - 3.5 hrs.
Heritage Town & Country Tour - 3.25 hrs.
Historical Waterfront Cruise - 2 hrs.
Ketchikan by Kayak - 2.5 hrs.
Ketchikan Mountain Bike Tour - 3 hrs.
Ketchikan Sportsfishing Expedition - 4 to 5 hrs.
Misty Fjords Seaplane Exploration - 2 hr
Mountain Lake Canoeing - 3.5 hrs.
Orca Beach Nature Hike - 3.5 hrs.
Saxman Native Village Tour - 2.5 hrs.
Salmon Falls Jetboat Excursion - 4.5 hrs.
Totem & Town Tour - 2.5 hrs.
Visit your ship's excursion desk for more information

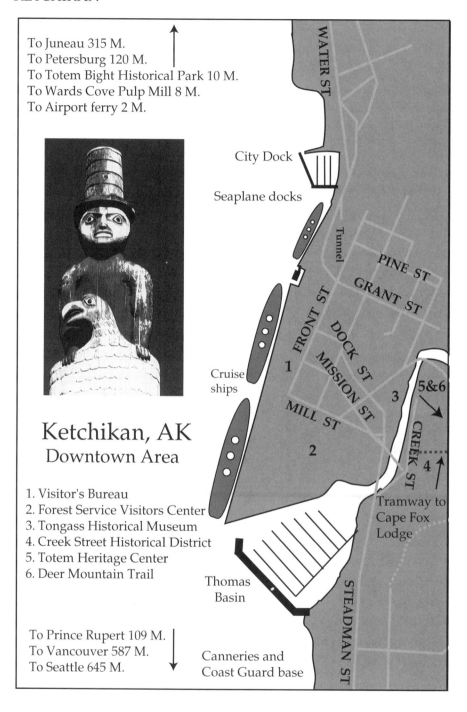

To Juneau 315 M.
To Petersburg 120 M.
To Totem Bight Historical Park 10 M.
To Wards Cove Pulp Mill 8 M.
To Airport ferry 2 M.

City Dock

Seaplane docks

PINE ST
GRANT ST
Tunnel
FRONT ST
DOCK ST
MISSION ST

Cruise
ships

1

3

5&6

4

MILL ST

2

CREEK ST

Ketchikan, AK
Downtown Area

1. Visitor's Bureau
2. Forest Service Visitors Center
3. Tongass Historical Museum
4. Creek Street Historical District
5. Totem Heritage Center
6. Deer Mountain Trail

Tramway to
Cape Fox
Lodge

Thomas
Basin

STEADMAN ST

To Prince Rupert 109 M.
To Vancouver 587 M.
To Seattle 645 M.

Canneries and
Coast Guard base

Don't Miss Creek St.

An easy walk from the cruise ship docks is the Creek Street Historical District, a unique over the water boardwalk setting for shops, restaurants and sightseeing. In Ketchikan's not so long ago rough and tumble days, this is the place where the men and the fish came to spawn. Off the main drag and out of sight, but convenient to visiting fishermen, loggers and natives, this was a busy brothel community.

'Cleaned up' n the 1950's, the flavor of the place remains unique in the region.

A sampling of the many interesting shops:

Poker Creek Gold - this is a jewelry shop and mini gold mining museum all rolled into one. High marks for creativity and visitor friendly environment.

Soho Coho Gallery - Ray Troll's eclectic art has become a northwest regional icon. This gallery is a must stop. From T-shirts to sculpture, from Ray and other artists, it's all here.

Parnassus Books - great books and gifts - grab a chair and browse while you enjoy the view from her upstairs location.

Hungry? - downstairs are the Star Cafe and the Good Fortune Restaurant (Mandarin, Chinese, and Szechuan) to sit and enjoy something hot.

A free tramway operates from Creek to the Cape Fox Lodge, located on a bluff with great views.

Bigger than life sized sculpture of the legendary humpalope, a cross between a salmon and an antelope, in Ray Troll's Soho Coho Gallery on Creek St.

DAY SIX

Downtown Ketchikan in 1965. These old navy patrol bombers, converted for passenger use, took travelers to the old airport on Annette Island, 20 miles south. The seams leaked, and sometimes when they took off, you had to lift your feet because of the water running down the aisles!

Pennock Island is on the right across from down-town. Take your binoculars and inspect the homes along the shore. These are essentially little Alaska homesteads, very popular with fishermen. Without roads, most Pennock residents do their shopping by outboard skiff.

More salmon canneries are just south of town at **mile 649.** The big containers, or vans, stacked on the dock are filled with frozen or canned salmon during the season.

Look for totem poles and a big native lodge, partially hidden by trees, on the left, near **mile 647.** This is the native village of **Saxman.**

Entrepreneurial blood flows through the veins of many Alaskans. Before Southeast Alaska had weekly barge service from Seattle, people like Captain Niels Thomsen, who had a small freight boat running regularly from Seattle to Ketchikan and other Alaskan towns, kept groceries on the store shelves. You met Niels a little earlier as skipper of the Aleutian Mailboat, see P. 90, putting up singles bulletin boards on his vessel! Thomsen started his freight business here on a shoestring with the help of Ketchikan investors:

> "Most of my stockholders lived by Mountain Point, and I really wanted to impress them, so I'd made a dummy radar antenna out of wood, with a pipe coming down into the pilot-house. Every time I came past Mountain Point, I had my son cranking on that pipe to make the antenna go around. This was back in the early 1950s when radar was really expensive. 'Boy,' those guys must have thought, 'Radar! Well, old Cap Thomsen must really be doing well.'"

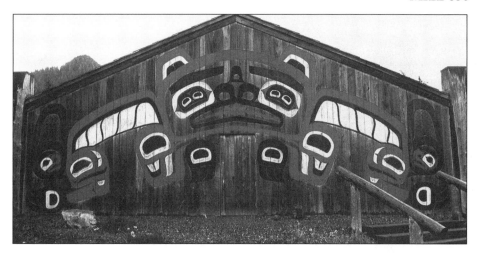

The large island to the west, from **mile 628** to **mile 645, is Annette Island, a reservation for the Tsimshian tribe**. Most of the Tsimshians originally lived in Metlakatla, Canada, across from Prince Rupert, where they thrived under the supervision of their pastor, a Mr. William Duncan. A dispute with authorities in 1887 led Mr. Duncan, along with most of the tribe, to move across to their prsent home on Annette Island, where they built a village, also named Metlakatla.

Today Metlakatla, supported by its own sawmill and salmon cannery, is a tidy and successful native community. It was to this cannery that I came as a lad of 19, engineer aboard a fish-packing vessel.

Before the Ketchikan airport was built across from town on Gravina Island in the 1970's the airport was near Metlakatla. Travelers flew in and out of Ketchikan in converted navy patrol bombers or PBYs. Taking off from Tongass Narrows in front of Ketchikan, they flew 20 miles to Annette Island, lowered their wheels and landed to meet their connections.

The southernmost part of the Alaska mainland is part of the Misty Fjords National Monument, the centerpiece of which is the canyonlike Boca de Quadra area, to the east at **mile 625**. Also dramatically beautiful are Rudyerd Bay and Walker Cove, 30 miles farther north.

Several excursions from Ketchikan visit Misty Fjords.

The Boca is 50 miles of steep-sided fjords and side channels, whose sides quickly rise to two and three thousand-foot peaks. Aside from the ubiquitous cannery ruins and a lodge on the shore of Mink Bay, the land is wilder-

Native lodge at Saxman Village, mile 647. There are excursions to this village from Ketchikan.

DAY SIX
AFTERNOON

Misty Fjords has some stunning scenery - I hope you got a chance to visit on an excursion.

A small excursion vessel noses slowly into Punchbowl Cove, in Misty Fjords National Monument.

ness, visited mostly in summer by people seeking its natural beauty and in winter by shrimp and crab fishermen.

The Boca is also the proposed site for the largest open-pit molybdenum mine in the world.

"Here?" you ask, "here in this gorgeous National Monument, an open-pit mine?"

The same question was asked by hundreds of fishermen who were concerned about the effects of toxic mine tailings on nearby salmon and crab stocks.

The original plan was to discharge the toxic mining tailings directly into the pristine waters of the Boca de Quadra. It was later amended to build two big tailings ponds back in the hills, but toxic material would, in all likliehood, still leach into streams and eventually the rich waters of the Boca.

In the late 1970s, when Southeast Alaska's two key industries, forest products and fishing, were in a cyclic

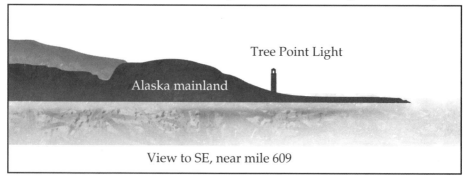

Tree Point Light

Alaska mainland

View to SE, near mile 609

downturn, the mine promised employment to the region. Eventually, to the astonishment of most of its opponents, it received all the necessary permits for construction.

Then, to the surprise of almost all, the project faded away without being built, the victim, apparently, of the end of the cold war. (Molybdenum is a key ingredient in steel alloys, particularly those used in aircraft and missile parts.) Today, all that is left of the grand plans so widely proclaimed is a dock on Smeaton Bay and a road that is slowly being taken over by the forest.

The two-mile-wide channel extending to the northeast at around **mile 630** is **Behm Canal**, named by Vancouver and charted by his small-boat crews, rowing into and out of each inlet and bay. Halfway up the canal he remarked on a rock that from a distance looked like the sail of a ship.

New Eddystone Rock springs from the deep waters of Behm Canal to rise 234 feet into the air. Look for it if you take a Misty Fjords excursion.

"On the base of this singular rock, which, from its resemblance to the lighthouse rock off Plymouth, I called the New Eddystone [Rock], we stopped to breakfast, and whilst were thus engaged, three small canoes, with about a dozen of the natives, landed and approached us unarmed, and with the utmost good humor, accepted such presents as were offered to them."

—George Vancouver, *A Voyage of Discovery.*

Day Six
Afteroon

If you traveled through here in April, you'd be right in the middle of one of Alaska's stranger activities — the herring sac roe fishery, occasionally known as "Kazunoko madness" (kazunoko is the Japanese name for salted herring roe).

Fishermen use strange craft called herring skiffs (which may be 35' long and carry 60,000 pounds of herring) to gill-net for herring about to spawn. Many times the fishermen will wait, anchored up, while the authorities and fish buyers monitor the 'ripeness' of the herring, which should be harvested just before they are ready to spawn. Sometimes the waiting can go on for weeks...

Many commercial salmon fishing vessels work these waters. Can you tell the difference between a salmon seiner and a gill-netter?

Dusty going in a tide rip near Cape Fox, mile 604.

Tree Point Light at **mile 607** is the first in Alaskan waters. Before it was automated in the 1970s, the crews lived in four beautifully crafted houses set in the woods near the cove south of the light. One house was barged to Ketchikan after the families left.

"***Dawn Princess*, 3 a.m., September 8, 1997**: Oh the treats that lay in wait for us night owls! The warm coat, the top deck forward, and the magic show envelopes our ship and her sleeping souls. For the night was cloudless — rare for this place. In the southeast a faint glow from Prince Rupert, B.C., in the northeast the luminous snow cover on the mountains of Alaska. But above was only stars as we sliced almost silently across Dixon Entrance.

"Hidden in the darkness to the east was Garnet Point where my wife and I had spent two summers buying fish with the old *Emily Jane*, a tired 80 footer. Our boats didn't come in from the grounds until dusk, and so we spent the days beach-combing, fishing, and crabbing. On a beach below totem poles rotting in the forest, we'd found glass trading beads, cast into the waters as gifts to the gods when the Indians paddled away on trading or hunting voyages.

"And when the sea was very still we ventured to Lord Islands, and saw a truly dramatic sight — fifteen foot orcas chasing four-foot seal pups through the shallows, almost beaching themselves in their frenzy!"

Look for salmon gill-netters, typically fishing Sunday noon through Wednesday noon. If the weather is calm, you may also see fish packers (they're larger) making their rounds among the fleet, buying fish. Many vessels

remain the summer here, remote from any town or cannery, getting water, groceries, fuel, and supplies from the
tenders, or fish packers, that service the fleet. The nets
they use here are 1,800 feet long by 30 feet deep; a good
day might be 2,000 pounds (400 fish) of red salmon or
10,000 pounds (2500 fish) of pink salmon.

*The dramatic short
herring fishery at
Kah Shakes Cove
near mile 620.*

The United States border is at **mile 599**. There are
no flags, nor duty free shopping here. The border runs
across windy Dixon Entrance, a place where small craft
hurry to cross. It's not as wide as Queen Charlotte Sound,
but the tidal currents pouring out of all those deep inlets,
when opposed by the southwest breeze, can get ugly. The
passage, "So we came to Alaska," which opens this chapter, describes a crossing of the tide rips near the border.

DAY SIX
LATE EVENING

Look for the high ridge of snow-covered peaks to the
east. They effectively seal off Southeast Alaska from any
land connection, except in the very north at Haines and
Skagway, and tiny Hyder, far up Portland Canal.

Study the map carefully here. This region to the east,
with many winding inlets that all had to be explored, was
very difficult for Vancouver and his men.

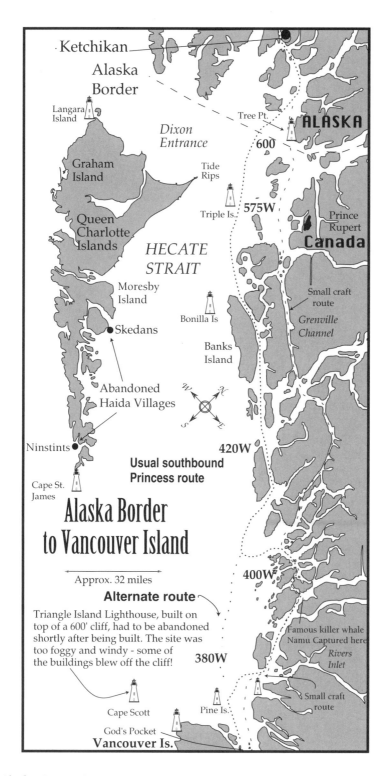

·Ketchikan

Alaska
Border

Langara
Island

Dixon
Entrance

Tree Pt.

ALASKA

600

Graham
Island

Tide
Rips

Triple Is.

575W

Prince
Rupert

Canada

Queen
Charlotte
Islands

*HECATE
STRAIT*

Moresby
Island

Small craft
route

*Grenville
Channel*

Bonilla Is

•Skedans

Banks
Island

Abandoned
Haida Villages

Ninstints •

420W

**Usual southbound
Princess route**

Cape St.
James

Alaska Border
to Vancouver Island

Approx. 32 miles

Alternate route

Triangle Island Lighthouse, built on
top of a 600' cliff, had to be abandoned
shortly after being built. The site was
too foggy and windy - some of
the buildings blew off the cliff!

400W

380W

Famous killer whale
Namu Captured here

*Rivers
Inlet*

Small craft
route

Cape Scott

Pine Is.

God's Pocket

Vancouver Is.

CHAPTER 9

The Winding Way South

ALASKA BORDER, MILE 575W TO
VANCOUVER, MILE 95

*"The little steamer, seeming hardly larger than a duck, turning into
some passage not visible until the moment of entering it, glided into a
wide expanse – a sound filled with islands, sprinkled and clustered in
forms and compositions such as nature alone can invent; some of them
so small the trees growing on them seem like little handfuls culled from
the neighboring woods and set into the water to keep them fresh"*
—John Muir, Travels in Alaska

DAY SIX
LATE EVENING

NOTE: THESE TIMES
ARE APPROXIMATE, AS
YOUR CAPTAIN WILL
HAVE TO ADJUST THE
SCHEDULE TO ARRIVE
AT SEYMOUR
NARROWS, MILE 205,
JUST AT SLACK WATER,
THE TIME OF WHICH
CHANGES DAILY.
TIP - SEYMOUR IS AN
EXCITING PLACE - STAY
UP FOR IT!

I f you feel your ship slowing around midnight, and look
out to see the flash of a lighthouse nearby, you'll be at
lonely Triple Island, where your Canadian pilot will
board the ship to help your Captain through the narrower
passages of the Canadian Inside Passage.

For the next 12 hours or so you'll be traveling along one
of the most remote sections of the British Coast. There is a
single town, **Prince Rupert**, on the mainland at **mile
570**, but there are few settlements between 'Rupert' and
Alert bay, mile 279. A rail line winds down the Skeena River
canyon to Prince Rupert, and many trains loaded with wheat
from the vast Canadian prairies come to Prince Rupert to
load Asia bound freighters.

If it was daylight and very clear, you might be able to see
the **Queen Charlotte Islands** on the western horizon: five
large islands and many smaller ones separated by intricate
waterways. They were settled by Haida Indians, who suffered
the same ravages of disease and alcoholism as their coastal
brothers. Logging and fishing employs most island residents.

Kayakers, campers, and travelers seeking a quieter vacation
pace have found it in the Charlottes. Boating guides stress the

You may see the
glow of lights in the
east from Prince
Rupert. It's the only
town for many miles.

There are many abandoned Haida villages among the Queen Charlotte Islands. The largest and most well known are Skedans and Ninstints. Both are World Heritage Sites.

remoteness of the coast and the importance of carrying adequate survival equipment and leaving a travel plan with a friend ashore.

From 1910 to 1941, a whaling station operated at Rose Inlet, about 35 miles west of **mile 420W**, taking hundreds of the blue, sperm, finback, and humpback whales each year. These boats operated in one of the most rugged parts of the northwest coast, in all sorts of weather, without the navigational electronics we take for granted today. (See P. 268)

Thirty miles west of **mile 480W** is Skedans, the site of a large Haida village, now abandoned, but with many remaining totems and other artifacts. The Haida watchmen guide visitors who come by boat from Sandspit or Moresby Camp.

It was near here, on a wintry march afternoon in 1971 that we had a very close call in our brand new steel 104' crab boat. We were running before a strong southerly gale, unaware that in certain winter conditions, the entire north end of Hecate Strait could become a tidal malestrom in which no small or medium sized vessel could live:

A Close Call

Joe's Log

"**March 2, 1971:** At around 3, alone in the wheelhouse on my afternoon watch I noticed an odd, blotchy looking target on our radar screen. There was supposed to be no land where it showed *something*, and after I had fiddled with the controls to make sure that it was really there, I woke our skipper.

He quickly scanned the chart and radar, pulled the throttle back to an idle, then stepped to the intercom, "Johnny, flood both crab tanks..quick as you can." We had been running with our huge crab tanks, or holds, empty. Filling them lowered our center of gravity, increasing our stability in heavy seas.

Sensing something was happening, the rest of the crew filed into the big pilot-house, peering foward into the early and snowy dusk.

For a long while there was nothing but the march of the big, grey-bearded seas past in the thickly falling snow. But then there was a lightening in the snow ahead and we all peered forward intently, trying to get a glimpse of whatever it was that the radar was seeing ahead of us.

Then, just for the briefest moment we saw it, glimpsed through the gloom and as quickly gone —heavy breakers, covering the entire area ahead of us.

"Shit..hang on, guys." Our skipper swiveled to look behind us, throttled up to a third, and pushed the steering lever all the way to starboard. As we swung into our turn, our boat dropped suddenly, at the same time rolling sickeningly to port for what seemed like a very long moment as a huge sea plowed into us. Time seemed to stand still. I heard dishes crashing, a strident alarm bell ranging, and then only slowly did we come around, and tilt back to an even keel, and finally the alarm stopped ringing.

The combination of a southerly gale and a strong tide from the north created seas in which even our stout steel 106 footer would not live.

Our skipper stood at the chart, shaking his head.

"Lookit this..breaking here, in a hundred feet of water..breaking, fer crissake..I heard about it once, but I didn't really believe it until just now..."

The combination of the heavy southerly gale and a flooding tide from the north was producing breaking seas in deep water, seas that we'd be foolish to risk, even in our brand new and very rugged 106 footer.

For an hour, in that wild wasteland of snow and white water, we sought a way through, for the little gully of deeper water that might not be breaking. But if it was there, we couldn't find it. With the coming of the dark, the wind came on stronger still, and it was no place to be.

We headed east, to find a way to the sheltered waterways of the Inside Passage, through a maze of islands.

We had no detailed chart, only the hazy memory of the mate, from a trip through several decades earlier.

Snow and black enveloped us. Our radar could barely penetrate it. Three false starts led only to dead ends with the sea beating violently on three sided narrowing cul-de-sacs. Once there was not even room to turn around and we had to back out, ever so carefully, and no one spoke and the tension in the pilothouse was very thick.

Finally, the fourth channel we attempted stayed deep, opened up to another, and that to yet another. The heavy sea died away, the channel widened, and long after midnight, we found our way into the calm waters of the Inside Passage.

A Whaler's Tale

The shores of the rugged Queen Charlotte Islands, are exposed to the full force of the gales that sweep in off the North Pacific Ocean. One whaler who worked those waters put his experience candidly:

"The entire area is a sailor's nightmare, offering unexpected, conditional shelter to the knowing, and anxious, if not disastrous, moments to the ignorant.

"Those damn willies [williwaws, violent winds that sweep down unexpectedly off the mountains] would spring up in the middle of the night and shake you loose. Then we'd have to heave up the anchor, stow the chain, and then steam around in the pitch darkness to find a place out of the wind to try it again. Anthony Island, off the west coast, had good holding ground, but it was only a lee for a southerly wind; if she backed up to the west, we had to get the hell out of there, too."

—William Haglund, in *Raincoast Chronicles: Forgotten Villages of the British Columbia Coast*, edited by Howard White.

South of **Triple Island**, your vessel will enter the narrower waters of Principe Channel and pass between Banks and Pitt Islands. These are wild and uninhabited islands, visited in summer by fishermen, loggers, and the occasional passing yacht. In winter, except for the few hardy souls trying to create a fishing lodge out of the old cannery at **Butedale, mile 473**, they are totally deserted.

Routes:
Hecate Strait or Inside?

Mariners need to be self sufficient in these waters, remote from any help or source of fuel or supplies.

The right angle turn and blind corner at Boat Bluff , **mile 439** is very difficult for large cruise ships to negotiate, and so most large ships take a somewhat more westerly route via the scenic, narrower waters of Laredo Sound, Caamano Sound, Principe Channel and and then into Heate Strait before entering more sheltred waters behind Vancouver island. (See map on right.)

The other problem at Boat Bluff is other boats - it's a blind corner where encountering another vessel in the wrong spot could be awkward, if not dangerous. Today, with all large ships monitoring VHF radio channel 16, vessels routinely announce their position as they enter constricted passages: "Alaska ferry *Columbia* approaching Boat Bluff light southbound. Northbound traffic please advise".

Small craft, however, need to take the narrowest and most protected channels, many of which would be too restricted or narrow for cruise ships. Many times these little fishing or pleasure boats will stay in the wider channels as long as the weather is good, but duck into much narrower and creek-like side channels when the wind blows.

Distance saved? Actually, it doesn't matter much. The distance from Pine Island to Tree Point (the first lighthouse in Southeast Alaska) is almost exactly the same whether you follow the narrowest passages of the traditional Inside Passage, or go straight up Hecate Strait.

The whole east side of Hecate Strait is a maze of islands, channels, and rock piles with hardly any permanent settlements, and is frequented mostly by Canadian salmon trollers.

Look for commercial and sports salmon trollers near mile 380W at Hakai Passage. You may also see the larger vessels that carry and house sport fishermen in this area. These are essentially **floating sports-fishing lodges**, allowing sportsfishermen access to good fishing, without the expense of maintaining a shore based lodge. This way, when the fish move, the whole lodge can move with them.

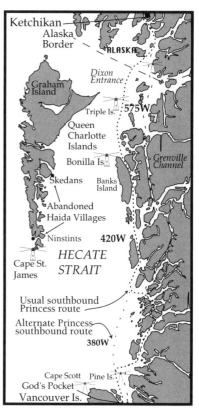

Some of the very best fishing requires threading your way, towing hooks and lures, through a maze of underwater peaks and valleys. It is challenging; being off course by 50 feet can mean having your fishing gear torn off on the rocks. The successful fishermen know the shapes of the underwater landscape by heart. When the fish are running, when you're flying the trolling gear just off the walls of some unseen canyon below you, and your poles vibrate with the hits of the big kings—it's an exhilarating experience.

New York writer Edith Iglauer came to this coast when she married Canadian fisherman John Daly in 1974. It was a different life than any she had known before:.

"We trolled back and forth in a half circle, with the sounder plunging to sixty fathoms and leaping up to twenty, then dropping to thirty and then—hold your breath—rising to ten for a single flash before the (engine) roared as John revved up and swiftly moved away from jagged underwater peaks…

DAY SEVEN
EARLY

Cruise ships may take one of several routes in these waters.

Alaska Cruise Companion 269

There are lots of sheltered routes for small craft, but there is no protected route around the open waters of Queen Charlotte Sound.

There are some strange critters in these waters. This is a blackfish, or pilot whale, at a north coast cannery, circa 1910. Notice all the sail and oar powered fishing boats.

"I alternately looked ahead and watched John maneuver in and out among the rocks and pull in fish, in a sunset that threw a glow across the mountains, across the water, across John's face, setting off a fiery gleam from his sunglasses. He…gave me a radiant smile…and grabbed the wheel to turn into the pounding waves.

"I leaned over and shouted, 'Don't you ever get scared?' " 'I love it!' he shouted back. 'I've been steering this edge for thirty-five years and I love every minute of it!' "

—Excerpt from FISHING WITH JOHN by Edith Iglauer © 1988 by Edith Iglauer. Reprinted by permission of Farrar, Straus & Giroux, Inc.

At mile **475W**, somewhere around 6 A.M. if your Princess ship is right on schedule, you'll pass from between Princess Royal and Aristazabal Islands, and enter into the water waters of Laredo and Queen Charlotte Sounds. It'll be a breeze in your big stable ship, but for small craft traveling up or down the coast, they always had to cross Queen Charlotte, and sometimes it's a rough ride.

Consider the names along this route: God's Pocket, Storm Islands, Cape Caution, Safety Cove– they tell a lot about mariners' experiences here. The worst part about this crossing is it is so exposed to winds from any direction. The tides flowing out of the inlets, the bottom con-

Caught in a Salmon net. River's Inlet.

tours, and other features create tide rips far from land. If you are in a small boat, leave early. The fellow at Alert Bay in 1938 who said that had it right: mariners set their alarms for 3 o'clock, get up, sniff the weather, and if "it's a chance," start across. Most who cross Queen Charlotte Sound have stories to tell.

Soaking away the cares of a long season at the remote Bishop Bay Hot Springs, east of mile 484. That's your author soaping himself up in the ouside pool while the crew looks on from the big inside hot springs.

The *Maggie Murphy* boys squeaked across (the wind came up, but not until they were almost at Safety Cove), but they had other problems:

"Since leaving Tacoma we hadn't managed to warm even a can of soup on our camp stove. Each morning it dribbled gasoline all over its chin, then burst into flames two feet high when the match was applied. This called for vigorous action with the fire extinguisher. When we did succeed in starting it, the contraption would give off almost as many fumes as the engine, but nowhere near as much heat. The stove finally drove us to discovering the only convenient means of cooking on the boat. When the engine was running, we merely placed a can of beans on the exhaust manifold, and within an hour, the meal was piping hot and ready to serve."

— John Joseph Ryan, *The Maggie Murphy.*

DAY SEVEN
EARLY MORNING

Lighthouse Tales

Egg Island, **mile 337**. Words such as bleak, isolated, and lonely take on new meanings in places like this. Several lighthouse keepers nearly starved here when the twice-yearly supply vessel was delayed. Two died fishing for food when supplies were low. Another shot himself from loneliness and desperation.

And then there was the sea: it always seemed to have a grudge against Egg Island. After years of breaking windows and washing away outbuildings, it tried for a knockout blow late on the evening of November 2, 1948. Fleeing to higher ground as their home disappeared into a roaring sea, the lighthouse keeper and his family were near dead from hypothermia and lack of food when rescued five days later.

On The Queen's Pond

Joe's Log

"October 24, 1975, **Lucan Islands, B.C.,** : Started out at 4 A.M. at Bella Bella, on as peaceful and still a morning as you could ask for and ended up in the black of a windy night with violent squalls and lashing rains battering the boat in a tiny and constricted anchorage.

Slipped away at four and ran those dark channels until daylight. Queen Charlotte Sound started out as flat as I had ever seen it, but by lonely and windswept Egg Island, we were alone, bucking into a light SE chop and the other boats were lost in the murk ahead and behind.

An hour later we were in the thick of it - the wind a steady 35, and the sea a dirty 8' chop, and every now and then I'd have to chop the throttle and let a big one slide by. Found a piece of sheltered water about the size of a house lot in the lee of Storm Islands, to lay for a few minutes while I pumped the bilge, tightened the lashings on the deck cargo, and checked things in the engine room. Just then channel 16 came on with an emergency storm warning for the north coast: SE winds to 60 knots: thanks guys... Then there was nothing for it but cross our fingers and head out for the dirtiest kind of afternoon. Once in a tide rip, about all we could do for half an hour was idle and let the seas slide under, pitching heavily.

Lightly loaded as we were, I couldn't lay the course to Pine Island, without putting us in the trough of the waves, so we had to quarter up [run at an angle to the seas], find a moment between waves to make our turn, and then run down again. Pine Island at 3 p.m. and didn't the lights in the lightkeeper's house look cozy with the sea ripping up and the wild night coming on! Made the turn and then it was right on the nose for 12 long miles. Reduced to two thirds speed and still had to slow for the big ones to not break out a window! Even at Scarlett Point it was blowing so bad we couldn't make the turn, but had to run way over into the lee of the shore and then quarter back up to God's Pocket, and glad to be in, you bet!

But it wasn't over - for the anchorage was crowded with no more room. Just then my steering wheel went loose on my shaft but we were able to tie alongside a Canadian troller to make emergency repairs. Too much swell to stay long - chewed through a 3/4 inch bow line in just a few minutes.

The Canadian introduced himself, "Nelson" - maybe 50, heavy set with wool pants and shirt. As we were tying up, he asked my girlfriend if it was just the two of us, and when she said yes, he shook his head and said we were braver than he was. Said the best anchorage was right around the corner - just snuggle right up into the trees. Fixed at last and away, the light failing fast, the whole bay feather white and the wind blowing the tops off of everything. The anchorage was tiny and the wind howled through the trees, but there was no sea and we had a candlelit dinner with the wild world outside. That was a close one and we were glad to get through it.

The wind came on even harder after dark. Three other boats came in, one with plywood covering a busted-out pilothouse window, another with a broken trolling pole.

Then the storm started in earnest accompanied with driving rain and the blackest kind of night. Time and time I'd get up and shine the spotlight on the bar tight anchor wire to see that we weren't dragging. Just as I was finally drifting into a fitful sleep, WHAM! Jumped up to find 40' *Martha Maria* had dragged down on top of us, dislodging our own anchor in the process. So, suited up in oilskins and outside to get him clear and re-

anchor, and all the time it felt like someone had a fire hose aimed right at me the rain was so fierce. Through the rain I could make out the lights of two other boats re-anchoring in the squall. From then until five A.M. the wind shook the boat and the rain drove with such force it sounded like hail."

Just... how... bad does it get out there? In late November of 1993, the Canadian Coast Guard measured the highest sea ever recorded off the British Columbia coast. Fifty miles west of God's Pocket near Triangle Island, the sea was 93 feet high—nine stories tall.

But don't worry; that was in November - your ship will be in the Caribbean then. Besides - a twenty -five knot breeze that might have me thinking about turning around, wouldn't be noticed on a big cruise ship. Most of the tales that I include here were from trips taken in the early spring or late fall. Your trip across is more apt to be like the one I took one glorious September in the brand new *Dawn Princess:*

"*Dawn Princess*, **Queen Charlotte Sound, B.C., September 7, 1997**: In the hot tub, going across the Queen's Pond! The day cloudless, the sea glassy – so very, very different from the angry waters we struggled across – if only my old fishing buddies could see me now! To the west was Hurst Island and God's Pocket, to the North was Pine and Storm islands, all those places we'd clawed our way past, our hearts in our throats each time our engine missed a beat, or a big sea pushed heavily against the windows. In this graceful ship, all these miles seem so easy, but I'm not fooled; I know that when fall comes and the big North Pacific lows start tracking up the coast, even the big ferries will travel with caution."

DAY SEVEN
MORNING

Look for Scarlett Point Lighthouse, to the west, at around **mile 310**. God's Pocket is in a cove just south and east of the light.

Why they call it God's Pocket - Most Inside Passage travelers have a tale or two about Queen Charlotte Sound.

For small craft, the trick to crossing 'The Queen's Pond' is to start early - set the alarm for 3 a.m., sniff the weather, and if it's a 'chance', get going!

Your big Princess ship operates on a schedule, rarely affected by weather. Small craft, however, cross open passages like 'The Queens Pond' only when the weather Gods appear to smile for a few brief hours.

Two harbors, **Safety Cove, 354**, and **God's Pocket, mile 309** are the traditional places for small craft to wait for a window of good weather before crossing the sound. See map on P. 280. The wait at God's Pocket is an annual tradition for many fishermen:

God's Pocket, any afternoon in late May or early June—the boats start arriving and keep coming until well after the northern latitude dusk. They are Canadian fish boats bound for the northern fisheries and American salmon seiners and gill-netters. Some are friends who perhaps haven't seen each other since the previous season. The anchorage is small, vessels raft up and the crews visit their neighbors as they put their boats in order, tie down loose gear, and get ready for the trip across.

This small harbor, which is on the west side of Hurst Island in Christie Passage, is the traditional jumping-off place for the 40 breezy miles across Queen Charlotte Sound. On fall evenings the scene is apt to be different. Boats get beat up at that time of year, and the ones that slide in as the early dusk falls might have antennas snapped off, perhaps a window broken.

It is also the site of God's Pocket Resort, established in 1986 after its owners, who were cruising the area by sailboat, noticed its gorgeous location and good fishing. Don't want to cook after a breezy trip across The Queen's Pond? Tie up and stop in for a nice steak or halibut dinner. It wasn't like this in the old days!

TIPS FOR MARINERS: Harbor too full to anchor? Try going across to the narrow gut east of the Lucan Islands. The bottom's hard and a southeast wind will whistle through it, but there's no chop, and it's a lot better than being outside in the windy black.

You may see smoke from the sawmills at Port Hardy, on Vancouver Island.

Seventeen miles west, exposed to the full fury of storms sweeping off the North Pacific, Nahwitti Bar guards the passage to the west coast of Vancouver Island.

The high land to the west here is 200 mile long Vancouver Island. It shelters the lower British Columbia mainland from the cold and windy North Pacific Ocean and creates an inland sea with miles of protected channels and passages, through which you will be traveling.

The very north end of the island, however, is more exposed, and if you look carefully, you'll see that trees on shore are bent and twisted, conveying a clear sense of the power of the winter storms.

Mile 297: The native village of Fort Rupert lies on the south side of the cove on Vancouver Island. A Hudson's Bay Company trading post, established her in the 1880s attracted Indians from as far away as Alaska, who would come in their large canoes, to visit and trade, sometimes staying for weeks.

DAY SEVEN
MID DAY

Your ship may take several routes here, depending on fog, the time of slack water at Seymour Narrows, etc. If conditions allow, you'll pass to the west of the lighthouse at **Pultney Point**, **mile 287**, and enter **Broughton Strait**. If time or weather require, you'll continue down Queen Charlotte Strait.

If your ship takes the Broughton Strait route, look for the village of **Sointula**, on Malcolm Island, north of **mile 282**, a very different sort of settlement. The island was settled in the early 1900s by the Kalevan Kansa Colonization Company, a Finnish immigrant group seeking to establish an agrarian utopian community. Unfortunately, with few nearby markets for their produce, their dreams died and many settlers moved away. Today Sointula is a tidy village of Finnish farmers and fishermen.

Alert Bay, at **mile 279**, is one of the centers of the Kwakiutl tribe. The town used to be across the channel at the mouth of the Nimpkish River, where the salmon were plentiful. The tribe moved to its present site when the whites opened a cannery there in 1870. The crew of the Maggie Murphy stopped there for gas in the

Medium sized (40-80') fishing vessels here are apt to be drum seiners, recognized by the large net reel on the back deck. These vessels fish for salmon, typically setting their net in a circle around a school or fish, or setting it off a point, to catch migrating fish.

spring of 1938; the town wasn't what they expected:

> "That night we stopped at the Indian village of Alert Bay at the southwest approach to dangerous Queen Charlotte Sound. This village was a distinct disappointment to us, for the Indians were walking the plank main street in business suits, the shops were modern, and there wasn't a tepee in sight. The only touch of native color was a prominent burial ground where each grave was marked with a totem pole, but the poles were just cedar boards on which faces had been painted, rather than carved."

They did, however, get good advice about crossing Queen Charlotte Sound from the guy at the gas dock:

> "Remember this one thing. Get across before noon. In the morning the sound is usually calm, but in the afternoon the northwest wind comes up and it gets too bumpy for a little boat out there."

—John Joseph Ryan, The Maggie Murphy.

Your vessel may take a slow pass by **Alert Bay** - get your binoculars and go out on your balcony, or up on deck. Those really tall things behind town that look like overgrown phone poles are actually really tall totem poles - Alert Bay claims the world's tallest!

Kwakiutl Culture

This part of the coast was the center for one of the most powerful and influential native tribes in British Columbia, the Kwakiutls. (Sometimes the name *Kwakiutl* is rendered in English as *Kwagiulth*)

Like most northwest coast Indians, they enjoyed a high standard of living and culture before the Europeans arrived with the diseases that were to devastate native society.

The key to their success as a people was the abundant natural resources that surrounded them and the mild climate. While Indians of the interior, like the Cree and the Athabascans, had to face bitter winters and an often nomadic existence, the coastal tribes lived in a sheltering forest fronted by a sea rich in food, available year round.

Coastal villages were typcally a number of permanent large multi family houses built on the shore of a protected cove.

The forest and the sea provided well. Salmon, halibut, whales, berries, were all to be had for the taking. The cedar tree not only provided reasonably easily worked wood for shelter, but also for canoes, totem poles, and the bark even provided the raw material for items of clothing.

Photo by Edward Dossetter, AMNH 42298

In the terms and values of their times, these were wealthy and successful peoples. Their society afford them the luxury of permament villages, and elaborate ceremonial art.

Their villages were full of art - masks, carved totems and house poles, and much more. This art reflected the wealth and success of all these coastal tribesd.

Unfortunately, the first Europeans brought small pox and other diseases for which the Indians had no immunities. Like a plague in the middle ages, they swept up and down the coast, even to the most distant villages. The effect was catastrophic, according to some accounts, the coastal native population collapsed in the later part of the 1800s. By the turn of the century, many villages had been abandoned, and much valuable art was left out to rot and disappear into the forest:

"People-who-live-in-big-houses" was the way natives from the interior referred to coastal tribes. This is the Kwakiutl village at Hope Island, in 1881. Note use of what appear to be sawn planks, only available after the first white-operated sawmills came to the coast.

DAY SEVEN
AFTERNOON

"There was not a soul there today. The large totem that I took a photo of a year or two ago is now lying on the ground and the Hoh Hoh totem that I photographed last year has now only one wing. So it goes, til at last they rot."
   —Beth Hill, *Upcoast Summers.*

The Collectors

In a sense, it was fortuitous that collectors such as Franz Boas from the American Museum of Natural History and Johan Jacobsen from the Royal Berlin Ethnological Museum happened along in the late 1800s when the quality and availability of Northwest Indian art were at their peaks. After about 1920, many of the villages experienced the sort of decline witnessed by Blanchet and others, and it is possible much of the art would have been lost.

Those early collectors were tough. Jacobsen, for example, who bought artifacts on the West Coast of Vancouver Island and hired native paddlers to take him by canoe to Victoria, traveled in mid-November over the nastiest patches of water on the coast:

AMNH 2A 18983

Ghost masks from Kingcome Inlet, collected by George Hunt, 1901

"We tried to steer away from the wind, but lost control of the canoe. I must confess that this experience did not increase my respect for the local gods as we drifted like a piece of wreckage in a canoe half full of water until about three miles below Hesquiat we were tossed ashore by a thunderous wave, fortunately on a sandy beach, and lay there filled with salt water." —Johan Adrian Jacobsen, *Alaskan Voyage, 1881-1883*.

They also got *a lot* of art. So much disappeared to collectors and museums that decades later, when the Kwakiutls and other tribes wished to set up their own museums, many of the artifacts available to them were inferior to those on display elsewhere. Museums have become aware only recently that pieces in their collections are valuable parts of the tribes' cultural heritage, and some pieces are being returned.

GEORGE HUNT—A FOOT IN BOTH WORLDS: Both Jacobsen and Boas (See sidebar above) relied on George Hunt, an unusual man, to guide them through the intricacies of Kwakiutl culture and the logistics of traveling and collecting in the days when there was little scheduled transportation.

Born in 1854 at Fort Rupert (south of **mile 298**) to an English father and a Tlingit noblewoman (a tribe from northern British

Photo by J.B.Scott, AMNH 32734

Columbia and southern Alaska), Hunt was raised in the Kwakiutl culture. He learned much about customs from his wife:

> "Some times while we are sleeping my wife would start up and sing her PExEla (shaman) songs. Then while she stop singing she would talk to the spirit and she seems to get answer back. Next time spirit comes to her I will write what she say to it." —*Chiefly Feasts: The Enduring Kwakiutl Potlatch,* edited by Aldona Jonaitis.

Living at Fort Rutpert, which was a major cultural center, Hunt had an opportunity to meet members of many different coastal tribes. It was natural that the first collectors would come to Fort Rupert, and to Hunt for assistance in traveling to the remote native villages. In the process, Hunt became fascinated by the wealth of native art and became a collector himself, organizing the Kwakiutl display at the 1893 World's Fair in Chicago, with 17 tribesmen demonstrating their crafts. Many Kwakiutl artifacts in museums throughout the world were collected by Hunt.

George Hunt and wife Francine at Fort Rupert, 1930. Hunt, brought up surrounded by Kwakiutl culture, was responsible for the collection of much of the Kwakiutl art found in museums around the world.

DAY SEVEN
AFTERNOON

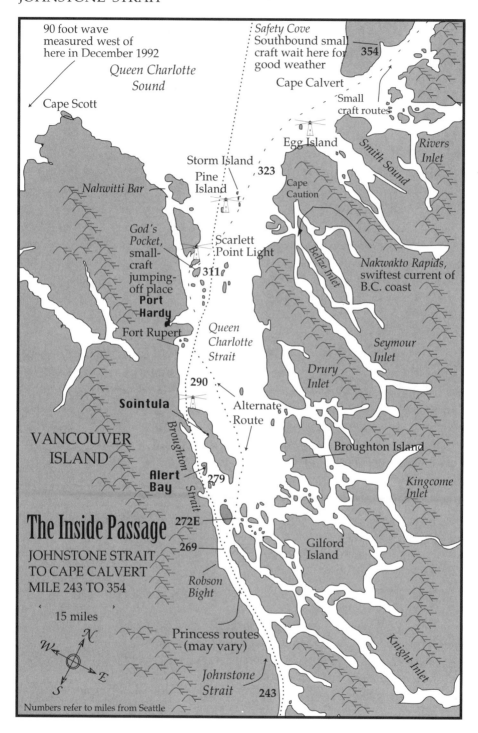

90 foot wave
measured west of
here in December 1992

*Queen Charlotte
Sound*

Cape Scott

Safety Cove
Southbound small
craft wait here for
good weather

354

Cape Calvert

Small
craft routes

*Rivers
Inlet*

Egg Island

Smith Sound

Storm Island

323

Pine
Island

Cape
Caution

Nahwitti Bar

God's
Pocket,
small-
craft
jumping-
off place

Scarlett
Point Light

311

Belize Inlet

Nakwakto Rapids,
swiftest current of
B.C. coast

**Port
Hardy**

Fort Rupert

*Queen
Charlotte
Strait*

*Seymour
Inlet*

*Drury
Inlet*

290

Sointula

Alternate
Route

VANCOUVER
ISLAND

Broughton Strait

Broughton Island

**Alert
Bay**

279

*Kingcome
Inlet*

The Inside Passage

272E

JOHNSTONE STRAIT
TO CAPE CALVERT
MILE 243 TO 354

269

Gilford
Island

*Robson
Bight*

15 miles

N
W *E*
S

Princess routes
(may vary)

*Johnstone
Strait*

243

Knight Inlet

Numbers refer to miles from Seattle

Editor's Choice: *The Curve of Time,* by M. Wylie Blanchet, published by Whitecap Books, is an unusually simple but powerful account of travel along the British Columbia coast in the 1920's and '30s. A widow with five children whose summer home was the 26-foot cruiser *Caprice,* Mrs. Blanchet cruised the north coast in the days when yachts were rare. Her account of an age less busy reminds us of the grace in simple lives:

DAY SEVEN
AFTERNOON

"They waited until they had each caught a shiner [a small fish easily caught by children]. 'Squeeze them,' finally ordered Jan. They squeezed them.... From the vent of each shiner came a perfectly formed silver baby. They were slim and narrow, not deep and round like their mothers. The second they were put in the water they darted to the bottom, to the weeds and safety. John kept on squeezing his, and his fish went on borning babies just as he had said. But each next baby was more transparent than the last; and they began to look like vague little ghosts with all their inner workings showing through."

Look northeast from **mile 268**: It was amongst these islands that Blanchet sought out deserted Indian villages, to "try to recapture something of a past that will soon be gone forever." We are fortunate she took those trips when she did. Although the decline and abandonment of the Kwakiutl villages had begun, the sites still were mostly intact, and they were rich with dramatic native art:

Middens, or shell heaps still mark many of the old village sites in this area.

"We lifted the long bar from the great door of a community house, and stood hesitating to enter. In the old days a chief would have greeted us when we stepped inside—a sea otter robe over his shoulder, his head sprinkled with white bird down, the peace sign. He would have led us across the upper platform between the house posts, down the steps into the center well of the house. Then he would have sung us a little song to let us know we were welcome.

"Sunlight and darkness; heat and cold; in and out we wandered. All the houses were the same size, the same plan, only the house posts distinguished them. Some were without wall boards, some were without roof boards—all were slowly rotting, slowly disintegrating, the remains of a stone age slowly dying."

—M. Wylie Blanchet, *The Curve of Time.*

There's probably no better place to look for orcas, or killer whales, than the Johnstone Strait area.

The wide cove to the south at **mile 264** is **Robson Bight**, an ecological preserve where orcas come to rub themselves against smooth rocks along the shore in the summer, for reasons not fully understood.

Orcas: The so-called killer whales (actually, all they're doing is feeding, like the rest of us) are frequently seen in this area. Before 1964, when the first killer whale was captured near Saturna Island by accident—they had been trying to kill one to use as a sculptor's model—killer whales were thought to be aggressive and dangerous. In captivity, however, the whale they named Moby Doll showed himself to be tame and docile. Unfortunately, injured in the catching, he became sick and died three months later. Since then, many orcas have been captured and sold to aquariums. The public's exposure to these gentle mammals changed our perception of their manner and intelligence. As a result, Puget Sound has become a sanctuary for orcas, and in British Columbia capturing them has been severely restricted. Today it is very difficult for aquariums to obtain orcas.

Did you know? Whale watchers listening with underwater microphones near **mile 235** heard what sounded like killer whales singing the tune, "It's raining, it's pouring." Researchers in other parts of Canada have reported the same experience.

Life in the Remote Inlets

The mainland shore north of Vancouver is a complex of islands and winding inlets. Half a century ago, logging camps, homesteads, Indian villages and small settlements dotted this coast, served by small steamers. Settlers in the most remote places such as Kingcome Inlet might row for days to the nearest store for supplies and back again.

In December of 1895, for instance, Ernest Halliday rowed his pregnant wife from their Kingcome Inlet homestead to give birth at the nearest doctor, at Comox, south of Seymour Narrows, almost 120 miles away. He couldn't leave their two small children behind, so they all piled into a rowboat, along with their dog and supplies. The trip took 14 days, although much of the time was spent waiting out storms in Indian villages. The baby was fine, but Mrs. Halliday had them at home after that.

At the head of **Kingcome Inlet,** and two miles up the Kingcome River, past the Halliday Ranch, is the Kwakiutl village of Kingcome and the setting for a novel.

Editor's choice: *I Heard the Owl Call My Name,* by Margaret Craven, published by Doubleday, is a haunting and powerful tale of a young Catholic priest working with the Kwakiutl people. Few books describe the mystery and power of native life as well. It has become a classic book of the British Columbia coast.

George Hunt collected some stunning pieces of Kwakiutl art from Kingcome Village at the turn of the century.

"The snow lay thick on the shoulders of the Cedar-man; the limbs of the young spruce bent beneath its weight. He saw the lights of the houses go out, one by one, and the lanterns begin to flicker as the tribe came slowly, single file along the path to the church. How many times had they traveled thus through the mountain passes down from the Bering Sea?

"He went to the door and opened it, and he stepped out into the soft white night, the snow whispering now under the footfalls. For the first time he knew them for what they were, the people of his hand and the sheep of his pasture, and he knew how deep was his commitment to them. When the first of the tribe reached the steps, he held out his hand to greet each by name. But first he spoke to himself and he said, 'Yes, my Lord.' "

The waterways that lead off to the north— Havannah Channel at **mile 253,** and Blackney and Baronet Passage at **mile 269,** open up to a whole world of islands, passages, inlets and tiny and secluded harbors, and all generally off the beaten path, without road or ferry access. This is the British Columbia north coast, where many harbors may see months pass without a visitor.

You may see trollers working these waters, seeking to catch salmon bound mostly for the Fraser River, near Vancouver.

Latitude is starting to make a difference in the climate once you get north of Seymour Narrows. Even though you're only 200 miles north and west of Seattle, the weather is noticeably moister and cloudier.

The normally conservative British Columbia Pilot, a detailed book of information on aids to navigation, harbors, sea conditions and much more, uses some unusually descriptive language (for them) to describe this country:

"Connected to the strait are several extensive inlets, the shores of which rise in almost sheer precipices to stupendous peaks, clad in perpetual snow. The inlets are very dreary and

Many of the logs processed by mills in the Vancouver area come from inlets off Johnstone Strait and the adjoining waters.

gloomy, due to their being overshadowed by the heights of the mountains and the frequent mist and rain."

—*British Columbia Pilot*, Volume I, 1965 ed.

Johnstone Strait, which begins at mile 218, is the Route 1 of the Inside Passage. Small craft may stay in sheltered channels for a while, but at **mile 242**, they have to emerge from the back channels if they're headed north.

TIPS FOR MARINERS: Get an early start! The wind will come up around midday and really boom in the afternoon; expect northwest or southeast wind as the mountains channel the wind. Use the tide: stand well out into the channel when the current is with you; go in closer to shore when it's against you.

Look for:

• The salmon fleet: (see guide P. 104). You'll see gillnetters and seiners operating in these waters. Many of the fish are headed for the Fraser River, near Vancouver, but some are headed for Puget Sound in United States waters.

• Log barges: On inside waters logs are towed in flat rafts. To make a flat raft, you tie long, straight logs together, perhaps 60 feet long, with short lengths of chain into a rectangular perimeter, which you then fill with parallel rows of logs, strapped or bundled into groups of a half dozen or so. A tug tows the whole works to a sawmill, very slowly. These rafts are O.K. for flat water, but more open waters can get rough enough to break up flat rafts. The roughly cigar shaped Davis raft, with thousands of log bundles chained together into a single towable mass, was developed for these rougher waters. Today, for longer passages across open waters, the logs are moved in self-loading or self-dumping barges. The latter have ballast tanks. At the destination, the tanks on one side are filled, the barge tilts, and the logs slide off.

Self-loading log barge. Note small push boat on barge below base of crane. It will be lowered into water at destination, to push logs into position for loading.

• Floating logging camps: Look into coves where you see logging activity, and you may see one of the floating camps, long a feature of life on the north coast. Whole communities were built on log rafts, sometimes with a store, a school, and gardens, and the camps were towed from place to place as the logging work moved.

"*Dawn Princess*, Johnstone Strait, B.C. Sept 7, 1997 - Seek and ye shall find - Up early to get a coffee and bring it down to my balcony, to just sit with binoculars, wait and watch. Two hours ahead is Robson Bight, the famous place where orcas come to rub against the rocks on shore, but anywhere along here is a good place to see them. Researchers have spent entire summers here, their nights camped on tiny islands, their days in their small boats, listening and watching, for it is only relatively recently that the orca has been perceived to be a surprisingly intelligent and friendly creature. The morning air was cool, the sun on the other side of the ship, but just as the dampness was driving me inside, I saw them - a 'pod' - of perhaps 8-10 individuals, maybe a half mile away. They seemed to be traveling today and not feeding, but another time I've seen a big male eating a seal, throwing pieces high in the air."

Tugs with log booms, near Loughborough Inlet, British Columbia, 1975. The tug's skipper had to work his awkward tow through Yuculta Rapids to get to the Powell River mill.

DAY SEVEN
EVENING

NOTE: THE TIME OF YOUR TRANSIT OF THESE NARROWS DEPENDS ON THE TIME OF SLACK WATER WHICH CHANGES DAILY.

Seymour Narrows Area Mile 195-208

"The pilot told me that an English man-of-war started through and the tide caught him. Some fellows over on the mainland claimed they seen the boat when it first got caught in the whirl. He went around faster and faster, until he was sucked down clean out of sight. Yes, sir, they never even seen so much as a

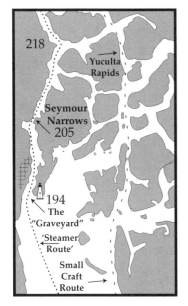

218

Yuculta Rapids

Seymour Narrows 205

194 The "Graveyard"

'Steamer Route'

Small Craft Route

For large ships, the challenge of Seymour Narrows is twofold. You have to make almost a right angle turn but do it at slack water - a 30 minute period that only comes every six hours.

Don't let your packing get in the way of being on deck when you pass through Seymour Narrows!

draw bucket come floating to the surface. Even the masts went down in that hole. It was just the end for every soul on board. Well, after he got done telling me about it, we waited a while, then we got the signal, and we run slow bell right through them narrows, and we never had a mite of trouble neither."

—Martha Mckeown, *The Trail Led North.*

This is really worth seeing. Set your alarm, or don't go to bed if your ship goes through here at night.

You'll start seeing current swirls and small whirlpools as you approach **mile 205, Seymour Narrows.**

"We're going through there?" There is no other route north (except the ocean) for ships of any size. This is a famous place. The tidal currents race through this canyon at speeds up to 15 knots (16.5 miles per hour), and safe passage is possible only at slack water, a brief period every six hours. It used to be worse.

Before 1958, Ripple Rock, a stone pinnacle beneath the surface, destroyed a ship a year. Besides the hazard the rock itself presented, its position created whirlpools and eddies strong enough to capsize small boats and shove passenger liners into the rocky shore.

Mile 200 to 204: Look for vessels waiting for slack water along the eastern side of the channel. During the Gold Rush years, from 1897 to about 1910, settlers on the Quadra Island shore would sometimes hear sled dogs barking on the ships waiting for the tide. If conditions allowed, they might row out for a visit and get the news from up north.

Mile 197, Campbell River and Discovery Pier. The big dock, with flags and banners, was built for sports fishermen to take advantage of the area's abundant salmon runs.

The village of **Quathiaski Cove**, on the eastern side of the channel at **mile 198**, is the site of the Kwagiulth Museum and its collection of native art.

Mile 193. Perhaps a third of the tide in the Strait of Georgia tries to fit within the confines of Discovery Passage. The current floods from the north here, and when a big flood

BCARS 19613

is opposed here by a southerly booming up the strait, small craft better watch out. The locals call this spot **The Graveyard**. The steam tug *Petrel* disappeared here on a winter night in 1952, overwhelmed by the tide rips so quickly there wasn't even time for a radio call.

Mile 194, Cape Mudge. Quadra Island settlers had a special present in December 1927, when the Alaska-bound steamer *Northwestern* ran ashore loaded with Christmas goods. The ship was abandoned without loss of life, and the local people made sure the cargo wasn't wasted. The hardy old ship was salvaged and put back to work.

Taming Seymour Narrows, Attempt Number 2, circa 1944. Drill barge moored to thick steel cables hung across narrows. Effort abandoned as too slow and dangerous after nine workers were lost from a capsized work skiff.

"*Dawn Princess*, **Seymour Narrows, B.C. Sept 7, 1997** - Put on my warmest coat, and walked up to the Sun Deck, went forward, letting my eyes get accustomed to the dark. Very black and windy - found a nook where there was a little shelter and just peered ahead. I sensed the trees very close on either side. Beneath me was the pilothouse, dimly lit with the pale eerie glow from the radars. It was here, more than anywhere else on the whole coast, that the British Columbia pilot earned his keep, sensing the canyon walls around him, feeling the push of the current, even at slack water, speaking quietly, commanding movements of the rudders, the thrusters in the bow, to nudge us carefully around the turn, and into the wider channels beyond.

"Even though there was almost no visibility, there was the powerful feeling of our great ship, plunging, almost silently into the vast darkness of The North."

DAY SEVEN
EVENING

Although the removal of Ripple Rock also stopped the worst of the whirlpools, the tide rips here are still fearsome and able to overwhelm sizeable vessels, should they misread their tide book.

The challenge of blasting a rock out from beneath some of the most violent tidal rapids on earth delayed efforts until 1943, when work was attempted from a barge held in place with 250-ton anchors. Before the anchor cables parted from the strain, they vibrated so badly as to make work almost impossible. Anchoring the barge to bolts drilled into the shore was no better; the bolts sheared off from the strain. Next came huge cables across the narrows, but these too failed to hold the barge steady and it was given up.

A decade later, 3,000 feet of vertical and horizontal tunnels were blasted through from Maud Island. Three million pounds of dynamite were loaded into Ripple Rock, and on April 7, 1958, the largest nonnuclear blast in history turned Ripple Rock into Ripple Shoal, deep enough for almost any ship to pass over safely.

These waters are challenging enough for us in our diesel powered craft with all the navigational gadgets modern electronics can provide, but consider Vancouver's men in their small and frail sailing ships, or rowing up small waterways in

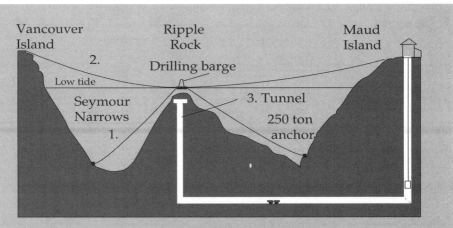

The Struggle to Blast Ripple Rock

1. 1943—Drilling attempted from barge anchored with 250-ton anchors. Soon abandoned—current caused too much motion.
2. 1944—Barge moored with cables to shore; barge motion still too much.
3. 1953—Test drilling reveals feasibility of tunneling under Seymour Narrows from Maud Island. Miners excavate 3600 feet of tunnels and shafts to place almost 3 million pounds of Nitramex 2-H dynamite. Adios Ripple Rock!

longboats, without chart, engine, or tide book. They were seamen of the humblest origins; most could neither read nor write. One wonders what they thought, rowing past these islands, through these channels, wondering if the next bend in the channel would be the entrance to the Northwest Passage or a tidal maelstrom.

DAY EIGHT
VERY EARLY

South of Seymour Narrows you enter the wide Strait of Georgia, which stretches from the cities in the south to wilderness in the north. To the east across the strait is the lower British Columbia mainland. Look for:

• The milky-colored water that enters the strait to the south. It is glacial flow from the Fraser River.

• Log and chip barges: British Columbia is a legendary producer of forest products. Wood chips are moved in big high-sided barges so full they seem almost submerged.

• Log booms: The rectangular rafts of logs towed slowly behind tugs are hard to see at night, because frequently they are marked only by dim and flickering kerosene lamps.

• Alaska-bound tugs and barges from Puget Sound, stacked high with container vans, with large items, such as boats, strapped on top.

The steep mountains made roadbuilding impossible along the mainland shore north of mile 188E.

Gateways to The North.

The land and waterways north of Seymour Narrows and Yuculta Rapids (see following page) are very different from those to the south. Gone are the frieze of settlements along the shore, the necklace of lights at night. Air and water are cooler, there are fewer pleasure craft, the land seems much wilder. This is *The North*.

Hole-in-the-Wall, near mile 208E.

No one traveling from the Strait of Georgia north to the cooler and lonelier country beyond can forget these narrow passes where the tide runs like rapids in a river. At the very place where the busy south coast ends and the wilderness begins, nature has set an obstacle, as if to warn the traveler of what lies beyond.

The winding way north — sometimes fishing boats and other small craft seek the narrowest channels to stay out of rough weather.

Along the Fisherman's Way

While ferries and cruise ships generally take the wider deeper channels, there are a number of alternate routes available for small craft. While your ship, for example, must transit Seymour Narrows, many small craft will travel north along a much more narrow and winding route, further east, via Yuculta Rapids, Greene Point Rapids and Whirlpool Rapids, rejoining the 'Steamer Route' near mile 241. A few highlights:

"Slack.... in the Yucultas? Nossir, don't be expecting no slack in that place. You get all that water up in Bute Inlet, see, especially after it's been raining inland, and it's too much for 'er, she just comes pouring out of there one way, and pow, she just turns around and runs hard the other way, she jes' ain't got no time for slack, see now?"
— A local logger.

"It was thick o'fog, when we were waiting below the Yucultas fer slack, and we kept hearing something, like it was blowing, then they came up all around us - this pack o'killer whales - Jesus, there musta' been ten or twelve of them, with them big fins. Wellsir, I want to tell ya', they waited and waited just like us, and then when that tide stopped running, they timed it just right and went through along with us.."
— A Friend.

There are a lot of winding and inter-secting channels in this vicinity and navigation can get a little tricky.

From my own journals:

"**May 30, 1981, Wellbore Channel, B.C**: My crew and my wife and I had worked for weeks to get our fish buying vessel ready for a long season. We'd left Seattle with a deckload of cargo to stow and a two-page list of jobs still to do. We'd gotten under-way early, traveled late, caught slack water at Yuculta Rapids at midnight, tied to a deserted wharf at Thurlow, B.C., an hour later.

West Thurlow Island   **Bulkely Island**   **Hardwick Island**

D'Arcy Point

To Desolation Sound via Yuculta Rapids

We just needed to rest, to sleep for a few sweet hours, before going on: to Whirlpool and Greene Point Rapids, on and on, until we got to our cannery in Alaska, 600 miles north.

In the hour before dawn, I got up quietly, stretched my legs in the starlight, making dark footprints on the frost covered dock, past the abandoned lodge, the rusting farm equipment. As I slipped back aboard, first light was coming to the sky above the dark hills, and the wild land all around.

The big Caterpillar engine rumbled into life. I threw the lines off the empty dock, got a coffee, and took it up to the flying bridge. We moved out into the channel; there was just the whistle of the turbo, the rush of the tide, the green smell of the woods and the rich smell of the sea."

And from a month long, difficult trip in the fall of 1975, with storms the whole length of the coast and two days of waiting, it seemed, for every one of traveling:

Somewhere in the Inside Passage the cook on a workboat empties the potato peelings over the side. A small boat, traveling just daylight hours, might take a week or more to travel the 640 miles from Seattle to Ketchikan, Alaska. A bigger boat, traveling day and night could do it in a weekend.

"Oct 26, 1975, **Stuart Island B.C**: Tied 5 p.m. to the dock at this closed fishing resort after difficult day. SE 30 in Johnstone Strait - right on the nose, with every third or fourth one coming right over the bow and slapping hard at the windows. Glad to finally turn off into the side channels and have the narrow slot of Whirlpool Rapids open up in the trees, leading into those winding waterways where the wind barely reached.

"Finally Yuculta Rapids with a big whirlpool spinning us around twice and this quiet dock where the kindly caretaker came down and opened up the showers for us - unlimited hot water - a true luxury and we soaked and let the cares of a long season in The North fade away. In the early dusk we looked out and saw the dim shapes of the islands and passages of Desolation Sound opening to the south. Tomorrow we'd be amongst the bustle of the busy south coast; the day after, Seattle and our winter lives.

"It's been a five and a half month season; you'd think we'd be glad to get off the boat. Yet the closer we get to the end, the slower we seem to go. Outside, the roar of Yuculta Rapids filled the night and the spell of The North was very strong; we were reluctant to let it go."

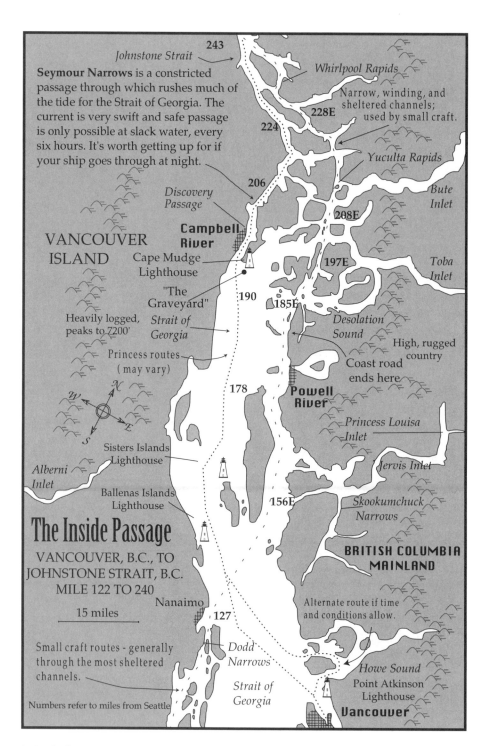

243

Johnstone Strait

Seymour Narrows is a constricted passage through which rushes much of the tide for the Strait of Georgia. The current is very swift and safe passage is only possible at slack water, every six hours. It's worth getting up for if your ship goes through at night.

Whirlpool Rapids

Narrow, winding, and sheltered channels; used by small craft.

228E

224

Yuculta Rapids

206

Discovery Passage

Bute Inlet

Campbell River

208E

VANCOUVER
ISLAND

Cape Mudge Lighthouse

197E

Toba Inlet

"The Graveyard"

190

185E

Heavily logged, peaks to 7200'

Strait of Georgia

Desolation Sound

High, rugged country

Coast road ends here

Princess routes (may vary)

178

Powell River

Princess Louisa Inlet

N
W
E
S

Sisters Islands Lighthouse

Jervis Inlet

Alberni Inlet

Ballenas Islands Lighthouse

156E

Skookumchuck Narrows

The Inside Passage

VANCOUVER, B.C., TO
JOHNSTONE STRAIT, B.C.
MILE 122 TO 240

BRITISH COLUMBIA MAINLAND

Alternate route if time and conditions allow.

Nanaimo

127

15 miles

Small craft routes - generally through the most sheltered channels.

Dodd Narrows

Howe Sound

Point Atkinson Lighthouse

Strait of Georgia

Numbers refer to miles from Seattle

Vancouver

• **Orcas, or killer whales**: Puget Sound and lower British Columbia, especially Johnstone Strait and the Strait of Georgia, are home to 200 to 300 of these intriguing mammals. Attaining an adult length of 20 feet or more and a weight of three to four tons, these handsome black and white whales are easily recognized by their tall dorsal fins as they travel on the surface. They travel in groups, called pods.

The winding way north - much of the north coast consists of lonely waterways with few if any settlements.

• Ferries: The British Columbia coast is served by a large fleet of ferries. Biggest are the 560 foot S-Class vessels such as the *Spirit of British Columbia*, which feature escalators between decks

B.C. Ferries S-class, 560'
Spirit of British Columbia, and *Spirit of Vancouver Island.*

Off the beaten track: **Desolation Sound**, mile190E: bleak, treeless, shunned by humans? "Our residence here was truly forlorn; an aweful silence pervaded the gloomy forests, whilst animated nature seemed to have deserted the neighboring country."

Vancouver really got it wrong when he named this place Desolation Sound. It was rainy, and he was no doubt discouraged by the number of dead-end inlets he had explored, and his party couldn't find any fish or game. But the place is gorgeous— one of the most popular yacht cruising grounds on the West Coast. Much of the area is protected as a British Columbia Marine Park.

B.C. Ferries C-class, 457'
Queen of Cowichan, Queen of Coquitlam, Queen of Oak Bay, Queen of Surrey.

The water is warm enough for swimming. This doesn't happen often in salt water at this latitude—it's unusual north of San Francisco—but a quirk of geography makes tidal currents from

Tug Columbia *with two barges of supplies and prefab housing for North Slope oil development, 1975. At night such a barge would display red and green lights, which may be difficult to see.*

both ends of Vancouver Island meet here and create water temperatures higher than any other place on the British Columbia coast. The warmest is in Pendrell Sound, where it's sometimes 78 degrees (25.6 C)

Off the beaten path: **Jervis Inlet** (east of **mile 156E**), like many along the coast here, is like a fjord in Norway. For boaters used to waters where there are roads and houses along the shore, this deep winding canyon is their first real taste of the roadless, unsettled North. Near its head is Princess Louisa Inlet, dramatically scenic, the destination of thousands of small craft each year.

It's worth the trip. Mystery writer Erle Stanley Gardner said:

> "There is no use describing that inlet. Perhaps an atheist could view it and remain an atheist, but I doubt it.
>
> "There is a calm tranquility which stretches from the smooth surface of the reflecting water straight up into infinity. The deep calm of eternal silence is only disturbed by the muffled roar of throbbing waterfalls as they plunge down from sheer cliffs.
>
> "There is no scenery in the world that can beat it. Not that I've seen the rest of the world. I don't have to. I've seen Princess Louisa Inlet."

Did you know?

Early English explorers spoke so often of King George, who had an unusually long reign, that they came to be known to Natives as "King George men." Most early Americans on the northwest coast hailed from Boston, so Americans came to be known as "Boston Men."

Reached through narrow Malibu Rapids, the inlet is four miles long, with a marine park and dramatic waterfall at its head. (The rapids is one of those places vessels should traverse at slack water.) Vancouver passed the entrance in a small boat, but thought it only a creek. Don't expect a wilderness experience, though; in summer there will be many boats.

Look for the smokestack and mill at **Powell River**, east of **mile 185**. In 1897, Herbert Carmichael and two other men looking for a site for a paper mill explored the mainland coast from Vancouver to Desolation Sound in a small sailboat; they looked into almost every creek. When they found Powell River falls, with 50,000 horsepower waiting to be dammed and the salt water close at hand, they knew they'd struck pay dirt. The mill they built grew to be the largest paper mill in the world.

DAY EIGHT
VERY EARLY

Tips For Mariners: In Georgia Strait, if your barometer drops to 29 inches or lower with a clear sky and you notice a long swell starting from the southwest, expect bad weather in three hours.

Watch at night for vessels displaying three white lights in a vertical line. These are tugs with tows—barges, log rafts, and so forth—more than 600 feet behind them. Watch out if you cross behind the tug. Some very large barges or very long rafts may be marked by the dimmest of lights, and be traveling quite fast, able to trample the unwary mariner who strays into their path. Look carefully at the tug and barge in the photo on opposite page. The barge would be almost invisible on a dark night. Every few years it seems there is an accident involving a barge and a boater who crossed behind a tug at night, without realising what it was towing.

This part of British Columbia is known as the Sunshine Coast, and is very popular with yachts-men.

Howe Sound is the next bay to the north of Vancou-ver. On occasion, Princess vessels may loop through here, if their Seymour Narrows schedule allows.

On the east side of the sound is one of the most expen-sive waterfront neighborhoods in Canada.

On the left is Bowen Island, and Snug Cove, a particu-larly popular spot for excursions and picnicers who would board the vessels of the Union Steamboat Company in downtown Vancouver. Today many Vancouver residents have second homes here.

Dawn Princess in Howe Sound, B.C.

There are many, many inlets on the northwest coast. Vancouver and his men had to explore each one.

If your ship happens to loop though Howe Sound, notice how the landscape changes from the south to the north sides. The shores on the sound's north side are much more lonely, with fewer settlements. The steep mountains and long arms of the sound cut the road; auto travelers must ferry across the sound to continue north. This is your first taste of what most of the north coast is like: dramatic steep, forested shores, where man is only a visitor.

"***Dawn Princess*, Howe Sound, Sound, B.C. September 6, 1997:** Up early this morning from my hotel for a long walk in Stanley Park with the sun coming up in the mountains and all the waiting ships in the bay lit up with that low slanting light. Short bus ride to aqua taxi jaunt across to Granville Island, a bustling farmer's and craft market on a narrow channel just across from downtown. The afternoon in Gastown - exploring the old warehouse neighborhood converted into galleries, artist's studios, shops and eateries. The elegant *Dawn Princess* at four, like a ghost from the 1920's, tugging gently at her lines, as if eager to carry us north. Tugs bring in a log ship right beneath my private balcony. I'm a boat buff and the close up look at the action was impressive.

"Glorious sunny evening as we slide under Lion's Gate Bridge and out and around the corner into this peaceful sound. The many who had been on the upper decks with me drifted away, to their cabins, to dinner, to the view decks below. But a handful of us linger, to marvel at nature's changing canvas before us - the purple black shape of the islands, the reddish yellow sky and water, and a lone yacht slipping in to anchor before the night envelopes us all."

After you approach **Vancouver Harbor**, look at the distant shore to the west. This stretch is part of the **Gulf Islands** (Canadian), which together with the **San Juan Islands** (American) to the south, form an extremely intricate and sheltered archipelago, containing rural villages, hidden beaches, quiet anchorages—all the elements of great small-boat cruising. The passages between the islands are subject to swift tides, and prudent mariners should heed the admonition from Sailing Directions that "no attempt should be made to pass through against the tidal stream."

The store at Olga, Orcas Island, WA. The American San Juan and Canadian Gulf Islands offer a wide variety of truly excellent camping and boating opportunities.

I didn't, one black fall night, in a 70-footer. Foolish me:

"**October 17, 1982, Dodd Narrows, B.C.** Went through against a big ebb in the black. Close one! Plus we were towing a gill-netter with engine problems. Fortunately I shortened the

The $2.5 Million Herring Set

For a period in the late 1980s, the market for herring was so hot that Japanese buyers were known to fly out to the fishing sites with briefcases full of cash handcuffed to their wrists.

Canadian fisherman Don Dawson hit the jackpot in 1987, with one 970-ton set in Barkley Sound, on the west coast of Vancouver Island, worth $2.5 million. Several other vessels helped

transport the catch. When Dawson's boat, the *Snow Cloud,* arrived at the Ocean Fisheries plant in Vancouver, plant officials had a case of champagne waiting.

VANCOUVER

Away, away - Dawn Princess *slides towards Lions Gate Bridge and the open waters of Georgia Strait beyond.*

Joe's Log

You may get a glimpse of totem poles in Stanley Park, on the right after passing under Lion's Gate Bridge.

tow line before we started through. If I'd known it would be so bad I'd never have started, but once we were in, there was nothing but try and get through, swerving violently back and forth in the current. The guy we were towing had to steer his boat to stay off the rocks. After we got through I called him on the radio.

" 'Oh,' he says, 'That wasn't too bad—except I bit my cigar in half..' "

Your voyage ends amidst the bustle of commercial traffic in one of the Northwest's busiest harbors. But imagine how it was in 1792, when British explorer George Vancouver came seeking the Northwest Passage, that legendary passage back to the Atlantic Ocean. Between here and Skagway, Alaska, 900 miles north, lay many inlets like this; each had to be explored mile by mile. Most of the exploration was done by rowing and sailing in small launches lest they miss a narrow entrance that might lead to the Northwest Passage. These were frustrating trips:

"The inlet now took a N.W. by W. direction, without any contraction in its width, until about five o'clock in the evening, when all our hopes vanished, by finding it terminate, as others had done, in swampy lowland producing a few maples and pines, in latitude 50 6', 236 33'."

—Captain George Vancouver, *A Voyage of Discovery.*

Over the next three summers, the boat parties' hopes of gaining the fame of being the first to find that elusive passage will vanish in many such dead end inlets.

I hope your trip has been all that you hoped it would be. For myself, this book and map have been an opportunity for me to share the experiences myself and others have had along these myriad waterways. Thank you for letting me be your companion!

*First snow, my
Point Baker
cabin, 1974.*

Author's Note

Your graceful Princess ship is a great way to see the Inside Passage and the northwest coast. Amidst the enjoyment of traveling in such craft, it is easy to forget that for many thousands of fishermen, mariners, and their families, the Inside Passage is the highway between their homes and their places of work. In spring and fall especially, when the weather has turned against the traveler, the highway can be rough indeed for these small craft. In 1974, for instance, we caught our last fish near mile 1,000 on October 9, in a mean 40 knot breeze, and it took us three days of difficult traveling in our 32 footer to get back to our cabin at Point Baker. From my journal, the night we arrived:

"Point Baker, 10 P.M., October 12, 1974. Ran three days to get here, most through ugly weather. Hardly saw another boat or house; spent both nights in lonely and wild spots. Today ran through Rocky Pass, with the last of the light and a few ducks and geese trading back and forth, and finally across Sumner Strait, to tie once again to our float in a black and empty cove.

"Everything was as we had left it (we'd been away six weeks) except the skiff had sunk. We bailed it out and rowed ashore. Our dog went off to sniff around his old haunts, and we cleaned and lit the kerosene lamps, built a fire in the wood stove, and found the rum.

"Outside the wind began again, working at a loose shingle like a dog at a bone, and our lights shone out on the wild and unfriendly night. We'd made our winter money, and our lives seemed filled up in a way they never did in the south."

Things to Do in Vancouver

Plan time on your trip to explore Vancouver, a particularly liveable and exciting city. A vibrant mixture of races, a dramatic waterfront setting, and a dynamic arts and business community combine to make Vancouver a memorable port of call. Many of the sights are easily accessible from where your ship docks.

If you do nothing else, take a walk through spectacular Stanley Park.

Within walking or short taxi distance is much of the city core with almost unlimited shopping and dining. There is also a subway/elevated rail system called the Skytrain which makes getting around fairly simple.

A few blocks east of Canada Place, where your ship may tie up, is Gastown, where the city was first settled, and today an eclectic neighborhood of old warehouses made into restaurants, artist's lofts, condos, and all manner of shops. Do you have a feeling of déjá vu as you walk around here? You may have seen a movie filmed here: Gastown is popular with cinema producers.

Chinatown is a few more blocks to the south (consider a taxi) and its size reflects Vancouver's popularity with Asians. This is the real thing: if you don't read Chinese, make sure your menu has English as well. With the waters of Georgia Strait and the North Pacific close at hand, many restaurants feature live tanks from which diners may select their meal.

Water buses wait at the Granville Island dock for downtown bound travelers.

Visitors and Vancouverites alike are indeed fortunate that its founders set aside the 1,000 or so acres that today is Stanley Park. It features restaurants, a zoo, the ubiquitous totems, but most of all a stunning waterfront setting right next to down-

There are a number of excellent art galleries in the Gastown area of downtown Vancouver.

town. A popular walk leads through the park to a dramatic overlook at Lion's Gate Bridge, where all manner of marine traffic can be seen in the tide that pours in and out of Burrard Inlet.

Take the foot ferry to Granville Island on False Creek. Granville Island is a combination of a farmer's and craftsmen's market, with restaurants.

Within walking distance west of Granville Island is the Vancouver Maritime Museum, whose showpiece exhibit is the brave little steamer *St. Roche.* When the Canadian government decided to send the ship and her crew of Canadian Northwest Mounted Policemen from Vancouver to Newfoundland via the Northwest Passage, that is, through the arctic ice, it was to be a voyage that made history. They steamed for seven weeks, got frozen into the ice for nine months, and then set out again once the ice freed them. Their long-awaited freedom was short-lived; the ice locked them in again after just three weeks, this time for 10 months!

If you have time, consider a flight to Victoria - float planes fly regularly from downtown. The capital of British Columbia, Victoria seems more like a bit of England than fast paced glitzy Vancouver.

The Museum of Anthropology

In the early 1900s, collectors made it their business to preserve the hauntingly beautiful, almost mysterious artwork of the coastal tribes of British Columbia. Much of what they found or purchased is housed today in a specially built hall in the Museum of Anthropology at the University of British Columbia. If you have any interest in Northwest Indian art, this is a must stop; their collection rivals any in the world.

Hood Bay, AK

A Northern Journal

Port Chilkoot, AK

Point Baker, AK

S.S. Prince George at Skagway

Acknowledgments

I am indebted to a number of unusually talented people, without whom this book would have been far less than what it is.

In particular to my designer, Martha Brouwer, of Waterfront Press, for her skill and grace in taking a sheaf of text, maps and drawings and fashioning them page by page into art.

To artists John Horton, Rie Muñoz, Marvin Oliver, and Nancy Stonington for their very special talents and for allowing me to use examples of their fine work.

To my old pen pals, John and Peggy Hanson, for their ideas, and valuable suggestions.

To John J. O'Ryan, for allowing me to quote freely from his unusual book, *The Maggie Murphy.*

To Glenn Hartmann, for his excellent editing and valuable ideas.

To John Pappenheimer, of Waterfront Press, for his continual support, excitement, and direction.

To Colin Veitch, Karine Armstrong, Dean Brown, Lisa Syme, Commodore John King, Captain Grahame Burton, Captain Bernie Warner, Neil Bennett, and many others of Princess Cruises for their help, vision and support.

To my family, for encouraging me through a long project.

To many friends and shipmates, in all manner of craft, in many a breezy cove and strait, for sharing so many stories of the coast.

And finally to old Mickey Hansen, passed away but not forgotten, for his kindness in taking a greenhorn kid under his wing aboard the old *Sydney,* in 1965, showing him the way of a ship and the true magic of The North.

Bibliography

Allen, Arthur, *A Whaler & Trader in the Arctic*. Anchorage: Alaska Northwest Books,1978.

Anderson, Barry, *Lifeline to the Yukon*. Seattle: Superior Publishing, 1983.

Armstrong, Robert H. *A Guide to the Birds of Alaska*, Seattle: Alaska Northwest Books, 1991.

Blanchet, M. Wylie. *The Curve of Time*, North Vancouver: Whitecap Books Ltd., 1990.

Bohn, Dave. *Glacier Bay: The Land and the Silence*. New York: Ballantine Books, 1967.

Bolotin, Norm. *Klondike Lost*. Anchorage: Alaska Northwest Publishing, 1980.

Caldwell, Francis, *Land of the Ocean Mists*, Seattle: Alaska Northwest Books, 1986.

Canadian Hydrographic Service: *British Columbia Pilot, Vol I & II* . Ottawa, 1965, 1969.

Craven, Margaret. *I Heard the Owl Call My Name*. New York: Doubleday Books, 1972

Eppenbach, Sarah. *Alaska's Southeast*. Seattle: Pacific Search Press, 1990.

Farwell, Captain R.F. *Captain Farwell's Hansen Handbook*. Seattle: L&H Printing, 1951.

Gibbs, Jim. *Disaster Log of Ships*. Seattle: Superior Publishing, 1971.

Goetzmann, William & Sloan, Kay, *Looking Far North, The Harriman Expedition to Alaska*, 1899, Princeton: Princeton Univ. Press, 1982.

Graham, Donald. *Lights of the Inside Passage*. Madeira Park: Harbour Publishing, 1986.

Hill, Beth. *Upcoast Summers*. Ganges: Horsdal & Schubart, 1985.

Hoyt, Erich. *Orca: the Whale Named Killer*. Buffalo: Firefly Press, 1990.

Huntington, Sydney, *Shadows on the Koyukuk*, Seattle: Alaska Northwesst Books, 1993.

Iglauer, Edith. *Fishing With John*. New York: Farrar, Straus & Giroux, 1988.

Jackson, W.H. *Handloggers*. Anchorage: Alaska Northwest Publishing, 1974.

Jacobsen, Johan Adrian. *Alaskan Voyage 1881-1883*. Chicago: University of Chicago Press, 1977.

Janson, Lone, *The Copper Spike*, Anchorage: Alaska Northwest Books, 1973.

Jonaitis, Aldona, editor. *Chiefly Feasts*. Seattle: University of Washington Press, 1991.

Jonaitis, Aldona. *From the Land of the Totem Poles*. Seattle: University of Washington Press, 1988.

Kent, Rockwell, *Wilderness*, New Haven: Leete's Island Books, 1975.

Larssen, A.K., and Sig Jaeger. *The ABC's of Fo'c's'le Living.* Seattle: Madrona Publishers, 1976.

MacDonald, George, *Chiefs of the Land and Sky*, Vancouver: UBC Press, 1993.

Macfie, Matthew. *Vancouver Island and British Columbia.* London: 1865.

Mckeown, Martha. *The Trail Led North: Mont Hawthorne's Story.* Portland, Oregon: Binfords & Mort, 1960.

Moore, Terris, *Mt. McKinley, The Pioneer Climbs,* Seattle: The Mountaineers, 1981.

Muir, John. *Travels in Alaska.* Boston: Houghton, Mifflin Co., 1915.

Murie, Margaret, *Two in the Far North,* Seattle: Alaska Northwest Books, 1975.

Murie, Olaus, *Journeys to the Far North*, Palo Alto: The Wilderness Society ,1973.

Newell, Gordon and Joe Williamson. *Pacific Tugboats.* Seattle: Superior Publishing, 1957.

Nicholson, George. *Vancouver Island's West Coast.* Victoria: Moriss Printing, 1965.

Ritter, Harry. *Alaska's History.* Bothel: Alaska Northwest Books, 1993.

Rushton, Gerald. *Echoes of the Whistle.* Vancouver: Douglas & McIntyre, 1980.

Ryan, John J. *The Maggie Murphy.* New York: W.W. Norton & Co., 1951.

Sherwonit, Bill, *To The Top of Denali*, Seattle: Alaska Northweat Books, 1997.

U. S. Dept. of Commerce. *United States Coastal Pilot, Vol 8 & 9.* Washington, D.C. 1969.

Upton, Joe, *Alaska Blues.* Anchorage: Alaska Northwest Publishing, 1977.

Upton, Joe, *The Coastal Companion*, Bainbridge Island, WA: Coastal Publishing, 1995

Upton, Joe, *Journeys Through the Inside Passage.* Bothel: Alaska Northwest Books, 1992.

Vancouver, George. *A Voyage of Discovery to the North Pacific Ocean and Round the World,* London, 1798.

Walbran, Captain John T. *British Columbia Coast Names.* Ottawa: Government Printing Bureau, 1909.

White, Howard, editor. *Raincoast Chronicles: Forgotten Villages of the B.C. Coast.* Madeira Park: Harbour Publishing, 1987.

Index

**British Columbia and Yukon Territory
place names:**

Other

Joe and Mary Lou Upton

Traveling northwest waters since 1965 in small craft and large, Joe Upton gained intimate knowledge of the coast from Puget Sound almost to the Arctic Circle.

In the 1970s Upton lived and fished out of a tiny island community in the roadless wilderness of Southeast Alaska. His first book, *Alaska Blues*, based on those years, was hailed as "One of those books you want to proclaim a classic" by the *Seattle Post Intelligencer*.

In 1995, Upton established Coastal Publishing to produce illustrated maps and guidebooks for Alaska cruise travelers.

Upton lives with his wife, Mary Lou and two children, on an island in Puget Sound, and spends much of his summers traveling and fishing along the northwest coast.